GET A JOB

D0776371

Get a Job

Labor Markets, Economic Opportunity, and Crime

Robert D. Crutchfield

NEW YORK UNIVERSITY PRESS
New York and London

NEW YORK UNIVERSITY PRESS
New York and London
www.nyupress.org

References to Internet websites (URLs) were accurate at the time of writing.
Neither the author nor New York University Press is responsible for URLs that
may have expired or changed since the manuscript was prepared.

LIBRARY OF CONGRESS CATALOGING-IN-PUBLICATION DATA
Crutchfield, Robert D.
Get a job : labor markets, economic opportunity, and crime / Robert D. Crutchfield.
pages cm. — (New perspectives in crime, deviance, and law series)
Includes bibliographical references and index.
ISBN 978-0-8147-1707-3 (hardback)
ISBN 978-0-8147-1708-0 (paper)
1. Discrimination in employment—United States. 2. Race relations—Economic aspects. 3.
Crime—Economic aspects—United States. I. Title.
HD4903.5.U58C78 2014
331.5—dc23
2013046960

New York University Press books are printed on acid-free paper,
and their binding materials are chosen for strength and durability.
We strive to use environmentally responsible suppliers and materials
to the greatest extent possible in publishing our books.

Manufactured in the United States of America
10 9 8 7 6 5 4 3 2 1

Also available as an ebook

To Danielle, Rashida and Brandon

CONTENTS

ACKNOWLEDGMENTS

For some time now I have received good-natured jabs from colleagues at the American Society of Criminology's annual meetings about this long-running, long-promised project. Their good-natured critique was right on target. Several things have contributed to the timing, not the least of which is my working style; there were also a couple of side trips into administration, in my home department and the University of Washington's Graduate School, which probably added a bit of delay too. More importantly at this point, the project's long-running development means that I owe debts of gratitude to many more people than I otherwise might have.

Every author, in thanking others, expresses appreciation for their contributions while saying that the faults and weaknesses of the book are theirs alone. That is especially the case here. As I acknowledge in the first chapter, I decided, at times, to move beyond the data and try to use my work experiences in juvenile probation and adult parole, and the experience of growing up in Pittsburgh's Hill District, to add insights to what I and others have observed via our research. That means that this book is especially susceptible to those faults that are the author's own. I have greatly benefited from the comments, critiques, and insights of others, including their words of caution. I have endeavored to answer the critiques and make as full use of their insights as I knew how. And I have taken their cautions seriously, even when I have elected to plunge ahead.

I would like to acknowledge and thank the National Institute of Justice for supporting my research (grant number 2000-IJ-CX0026), the National Consortium on Violence Research for both financial and collegial support, and in recent years members of the Racial Democracy, Crime and Justice Network, for feedback and encouragement. Thank you to Randy Olsen and the staff of the Center for Human Resources Research at The Ohio State University for access to National Longitudinal Surveys of Youth (NLSY) data sets and for assistance that made the nearly impossible possible, and the US Bureau of Labor Statistics for giving me permission to use those data. I want to acknowledge and thank John Warren of the Bureau of Police of the City of Pittsburgh, and Shanna Christie of the Seattle Police Department, for assistance in obtaining maps and data.

I owe much thanks to my colleagues in the Department of Sociology at the University of Washington, which has been my academic home for more than thirty years. I am a better sociologist as a result of living, studying, teaching, and working in the rich environment provided by the department and university. I had the good fortune of beginning this book while I was a visiting fellow at the Institute of Criminology at Cambridge University, and was able to continue that work during a fellowship at the Rockefeller Study Center at Bellagio, Italy. I was inspired by colleagues I met at both places and I can think of no better places to learn, think, and write. I want to thank members of the Deviance and Social Control Seminar at the University of Washington, who have heard far more about labor stratification and crime than probably any of them cared to hear; nevertheless, those colleagues have with grace and generosity helped me immensely to advance this project. I want to especially thank my colleagues Albert Black, George Bridges, Herb Costner, Jeff Fagan, Jerald Herting, Laurie Krivo, Ross Matsueda, Jody Miller, Ruth Peterson, Becky Pettit, Rick Rosenfeld, Stew Tolnay, and Joe Weis for comments, suggestions, discussions, and collaborations that helped this to be a better project. And of course I must thank anonymous reviewers who improved my work with suggestions and critical comments, and for making me look at things in different ways.

I want to say a very special thank you to a group of past and current University of Washington sociology graduate students, without whom—literally—this book could not have been completed. Tim Wadsworth worked with me early on and became my primary colleague in advancing significant portions of this project, and then went on to contribute significantly on his own to the literature that is the backbone of this book. Heather Gronniger was invaluable in the construction of data files, and she spent countless hours analyzing NLSY data. Kristin Bates took the lead in analyzing the data and making sense of our results in a study of young women, labor stratification, and crime. It is her insights that I have been able to depend on here. Kevin Drakulich was not only helpful in sorting out some of the conceptualization but he generously said, when I asked how I might best display results from some analyses of interaction effects, "It's probably easier for me to go ahead and create the figures for you than to teach you how to do them." I've now gone back to him on repeated occasions and asked for different forms of those figures. I don't doubt that he now wishes he had showed me how to construct them. I will always be appreciative of his contribution. April Fernandes gave me both editorial and conceptual suggestions on early chapters, but probably her most important contribution was making me laugh, especially when I was trying to make progress on this manuscript while serving as department chair. As this project neared the finish line, I was suddenly confronted with the need to create figures and maps in a form that would work for NYU Press. I was stymied, but Tim Thomas came to my rescue and did quick and fantastic work. Suzanna Ramirez read, commented on, and corrected chapters, and helped with citations. Then she found useful data for me. Then she helped me to think through the international implications of the labor stratification and crime thesis. I appreciate all of those contributions. But Suzanna may never fully appreciate how important her questions, comments, encouragement, and very direct way of saying things were, during a period when I was struggling to move this project forward. I hope someday to be able to repay the debt that I owe to Suzanna.

Thank you, John Hagan. When I told John about the manuscript that I was working on, and every time that I have seen him since, he has been encouraging. He introduced me to Ilene Kalish at New York University Press, and when I wondered if I really had anything to say that was worth publishing in a book, he assured me that I did. Everyone thanks their editor, and I want to thank Ilene. To say she was patient is a gross understatement. To say she was encouraging cannot begin to capture how she helped me to move along when I was stuck. When I was concerned about being too personal in the book, Ilene encouraged me to take chances and to not be concerned about proper academic etiquette. When I did what a lot of us do—retreat into writing about data and coefficients—Ilene leaned on me to write more accessibly, but she leaned in a very gentle but firm way. The form of this book took a shape slightly different from many academic books, not because Ilene allowed me to do that, but because she encouraged me to do that. I would also like to thank Caelyn Cobb at NYU Press, who has that wonderful combination of patience and persistence that I needed to get things finished.

My colleague, my wife Susan, not only coauthored one of the important papers that this book is built on; her ideas were central in the early development of the labor stratification and crime thesis. She's read and commented on more of this manuscript than either of us wants to remember and her support, encouragement, and editorial eye were critical to its completion. I want to thank the boys who long ago were on my juvenile court probation caseload—those parolees and probationers I supervised, but from whom I learned so much, when I was a parole agent for the Pennsylvania Board of Probation and Parole, as well as the dedicated people I worked with in Erie and Sharon Pennsylvania, and the colleagues, staff, and judges who were at the Mercer County Pennsylvania Juvenile Court when I worked there. It will be obvious to any who read on that these people were central to the development of my thinking about how work and labor markets are connected to crime. Finally, I want to thank the men and women, and boys and girls of The Hill District and Homewood neighborhoods in Pittsburgh, and of the Central District and Rainier Valley in Seattle. Their struggles, their perseverance, their stumbles, and their resilience are where this book comes from.

1

Modern *Misérables*

Labor Market Influences on Crime

I heard the news first in a phone call from my mother. My youngest brother, Robby, and two of his friends had killed a man during a holdup. Robby was a fugitive, wanted for armed robbery and murder. The police were hunting him, and his crime had given the cops license to kill. The distance I'd put between my brother's world and mine suddenly collapsed. The two thousand miles between Laramie, Wyoming, and Pittsburgh, Pennsylvania, my years of willed ignorance, of flight and hiding, had not changed a simple truth: I could never run fast enough or far enough. Robby was inside me. Wherever he was, running for his life, he carried part of me with him.[1]

John Edgar Wideman's book *Brothers and Keepers* is the tale of two brothers; the younger Robby's early life and incarceration in a Pennsylvania prison, convicted of felony murder and sentenced to life. The other, John himself, now a Brown University professor, was on the faculty of the University of Wyoming when he wrote the above passage. *Brothers and Keepers* is also a tale of their Homewoods; one of Pittsburgh's black ghettos, where the Wideman brothers came of age. John's Homewood of working-class neighborhoods was peopled by blue-collar families.

Most of the parents and some of the children had immigrated from the South. But a dramatic change occurred by the time Robby came of age. Ten years after John, Robby's Homewood was an edgier, faster place with a street life that was not always the most virtuous. The social fabric of the community had changed, as had its culture. By the time Robby became an adolescent, Homewood's streets were a lure to the dark side for many black boys and young men, including the youngest of the Wideman brothers. And while Robby sat imprisoned in Pennsylvania's Western State Penitentiary, Homewood changed yet again when the steel mills, which had employed thousands of her residents, closed.[2] Most of those mills were later demolished, along with the dreams and the basis of a good economic life for working-class Pittsburgh families. Many of those families were immigrants from the South, to what Nicholas Leman and others called the Promised Land.[3] As the twentieth century ended, the once Promised Land of Homewood would produce many more stories of crime and suffering.

The objective of this book is an exploration of how labor market experiences influence crime. Both the violent and property violations of individuals and variations in rates of these crimes are affected by the economy and people's relationship to it. Work is central to who we are, the well-being of our families, and it determines where and how well we live. Whether they are black or white, Latino or Asian, Native American or immigrant, the chances of a person becoming involved in crime is related directly to the employment and opportunities available to them, or indirectly through the characteristics of the places where they live and spend time. As a sociologist for more than thirty years I have become convinced that the stratification of labor—how people become slotted into good jobs and not-so-good jobs—is a substantial contributor to where they live, the lifestyle they lead, and their criminality. And this understanding is consistent with the folk knowledge I learned from coworkers and in the streets when I worked first as a juvenile probation officer and later as a parole agent for the State of Pennsylvania. Here the effect of labor stratification on young men and women, children, and communities, including those like Homewood, will be the focus.

The notion that people become slotted into positions is certainly at odds with the conceptions of the United States that many Americans hold dear, but even though it is inconsistent with our national self-image, it is the reality for most. To be clear, I do not argue that we are positioned into specific occupations, but rather that tiers exist. Those born into a particular tier have a good chance of remaining there. Although systems of stratification that perpetuate such patterns are not the focus of this book, I will touch on how employment opportunities, resulting crime, and criminal justice system exposure help to maintain the status quo for many.

The Economy and Criminals?

The hero of Victor Hugo's *Les Misérables*, Jean Valjean, was sent to prison for stealing bread to feed his sister's starving children; a noble act of larceny because of his motive. This imagery lies at the root of popular expectations that when economic times are tough some will turn to crime in order satisfy needs. Of course some people likely do commit crimes because of need, but then others among us, who are less noble than Jean Valjean, turn to villainy simply for wants that will not be satisfied by work and saving. It is intuitively appealing to attribute criminal actions to material motives—and so many of us expect that unemployment will lead to crime, and that the economically less fortunate will do more of it. We extend this conception of the poor when we presume that the stresses of their lives, and the brutal conditions that some of them experience, lead them to engage in violence.

The general public easily, and with little question, accepts the idea that crime can be attributed to a poor economy. But recurring anomalies suggest that this may not, or at least not always, be true. For example, during the Great Depression of the 1930s the rates of some crimes declined, even though unemployment rates exceeded twenty-five percent for extended periods. Thirty years later, during the 1960s, along with sustained economic expansion the US experienced large increases in both property and violent crime rates. Considering the link between economy and crime more globally, it is no secret among criminologists that comparative poverty rates are not highly correlated with crime rates within western industrialized nations. And while some of the poorest nations of the word have high crime rates, many poor countries have relatively low rates. At the same time, even among industrialized nations, it is difficult to explain their relative rankings based on their

Figure 1.1. US Homicide Rate, 1900–2002: Rate per 100,000 Population
*Includes 9/11 terrorism deaths
Source: National Center for Health Statistics, Vital Statistics

economies. The US continues to have astoundingly high rates of homicide, even though it has one of the world's most productive economies and its people enjoy a comparatively high per capita income.

Consider the trends in homicide during the twentieth century (Figure 1.1). Murder is probably the best—but by no means perfectly—measured crime during this period. Logically we would not expect the decline that occurred in the 1930s or the increases of the 60s, but more deaths from homicide makes some sense during the economic displacement of the 80s and early 90s. And now that the US has experienced the deepest recession since the Great Depression, it is not clear that homicide has increased appreciably, at least not across the board.

While the image of a desperate yet heroic Jean Valjean may capture the romantic imaginations of readers of Hugo's novel and the patrons of the Broadway musical, we should recognize that a more accurate stereotype may be the teenager who mugs a schoolmate to steal his expensive athletic shoes. Notice that here I include this image too as a stereotype. Both the hero of *Les Misérables* and the thief of a pair of Air Jordans present too limited pictures to convey how economic forces affect crime. There are, to be sure, those who come to crime in desperation because legitimate opportunities are closed off to them. Criminologists have long recognized this motivation. There are also delinquents who can reconcile or rationalize mugging a schoolmate because, "Why should he have those shoes if I can't?" And of course, the neutralizing power of this self-posed question is even more compelling for someone with sufficient might to force his will. These images and their explanations, though, are also too limited to help us understand the link between the economy and employment and crime.

The last half of the twentieth century, the United States witnessed major economic shifts that included the deindustrialization of traditional manufacturing cities and regions, and a reversal of some demographic flows. Many migrants departed places that a generation earlier had attracted those looking for work. Jobs, and not surprisingly the people that follow them, moved out. Chicago and Detroit, Pittsburgh and Cleveland, Youngstown and Gary all experienced the loss of substantial portions of the industries that had given them their identities. Rather than rebuild, retool, and modernize in these industrial capitals, corporations elected to open new manufacturing plants elsewhere. First they moved operations to Sunbelt states with cheaper labor costs, and ultimately many producers moved some or all of their manufacturing operations out of the US in search of even lower-cost labor. We all now recognize the latter portion of this trend as the process of globalization that is perhaps the most significant force in the current world economy. Companies and workers everywhere are now linked together in ways that affect life everywhere.

Included among the products of globalization are changing crime rates. In some places the community changes that result from globalization might reduce the incidence of crime by bringing increased prosperity, but at times the opposite occurs. William Julius Wilson's account of what happens in desperately poor American urban neighborhoods when jobs are lost as a result of deindustrialization includes increases in crime.[4] Emil Durkheim and Frederick Tonnies wrote of the disruptions to social life that accompanied early European industrialization. It is not hard to imagine that the disrupting influences that accompanied the shift from agrarian to industrial economies in nineteenth-century France and Germany may now change societies and increase crime in those nations where multinational companies site facilities and jobs today. Industrialization and urbanization fractured cultural and normative systems of nineteenth-century agrarian societies. The reduction of social control that resulted from normative disruption allowed deviance in general, including crime, to increase. Conversely, there will be newfound prosperity in some formerly destitute communities when global economic forces cause companies to bring in new jobs. This may cause crime rates to drop. The addition of industrial jobs to formally nonindustrial areas will have both crime-producing and crime-reducing influences.

Two different processes are at work as a result of globalization. First, the loss of jobs from industrial economies has dire consequences in First World cities; second, the changes that accompany the arrival of modern industrial concerns profoundly affect social life in those places where jobs move to. Here I will focus on the former, but on occasion I will attempt to comment a bit on the latter as well.

"Buddy Can You Spare a Dime?" or "Give Me Your Wallet!"

The changes that happened in American cities in the last half of the twentieth century as a result of deindustrialization were different than those experienced by people during the Great Depression. While the latter saw some declines in crime, the former saw increases, especially of violent crime rates. In actuality during the Depression some crime rates fell—notably homicide, which not only did not increase (note Figure 1.1) but appears to have declined—but other rates increased (e.g., burglary).[5] It is the case, however, that crime rates during the Depression were not what we would simply predict using the popular conceptions about the relationship between the economic well-being of the populace and crime. I suspect that crime did not increase more because there was pervasive, widespread unemployment, which affected many groups and segments of society. We should take care not to romanticize this period. Life was hard. Families struggled to function economically, and people suffered. But when so many were out of work it is possible that the relative deprivation felt by Depression-era families may have been mitigated. There was a sense of widespread struggle and people needing to pull together to support one another. One gets a sense of the approach to life of Depression-era families and workers when reading excerpts from the manuscripts of the Federal Writers' Project, 1936–1940. This program enlisted writers to interview and describe "real people." The quotes below are taken from that effort.

> I've knowed people though that's been willin' to work and somehow couldn't get along. I know a woman that had saved and bought her own house, and took care of her sick mother too. Her husband got out of a job and she was out down to one day's work a week. Her mother died and she didn't have money to bury her with. That was one Friday night back in the summer. Up to late Saturday they didn't know whether they was goin' to be able to bury her or not. Some of the neighbors went around and took up a collection to pay the grave diggers and buy the lot. Then this woman made arrangements with the undertaker and they got her mother buried Sunday mornin'. I heard the other day she was losin' her place and I expect she has held it long as she can.
>
> A collection come hard back then because so many people wasn't gettin' full time. I've been glad that Jim's got to work so steady. Up to now we haven't had to draw any rocking chair money. That's what they call the unemployment money, you know. Of course nobody don't know in these times when they'll be laid off. Jim'll work as long as he can get work though.[6]

Here, neighbors themselves on hard times come to the aid of a family in particular distress. Work is clearly a scarce and valued commodity.

> The next morning I was at the mill gates an hour before bell time. There I found all of my fellow workers and I joined in their conversation. Each asked the other what they had been doing during the lay off and what were they going to do with their first pay? There were predictions, laughingly made that Fat's saloon would do a rushing business on pay night. But under all this gay jesting everyone of us knew that when the order was finished in a few months, we would again be laid off, to a tramp the streets while we collected our unemployment compensation checks and

then back on relief we would have to go until the mill started running full time again. We had gone through this routine many times in the past ten years and each one of us knew that he would go through it many times in the future. But that knowledge could not dim our spirits today because we knew that while the mill operated we would be able to eat what we wanted, we could dress our families and have a dollar left so that when meeting our fellow workers in Fat's saloon on Saturday night each one of us could stand up to the bar and pay for a round of beers.[7]

The boom and bust cycle described here persisted for most workers from 1929 until the start of World War II. Others' comments put the blame on everything from crooked politicians to automation to the bosses, but a fairly common theme running through these narratives is that of working people struggling together.

Clearly there were those during the Depression whose suffering was less and still others who thrived, but in general there was a collective notion that Americans, as well as the populations of many industrialized nations, were suffering together. There was a broadly felt collective despair. While this period did not produce especially high crime rates, there were political movements to unseat the leaders of government and industry. The Communist Party in America experienced its greatest period of popularity. There was conflict during the Depression, and working people expressed their displeasure with the way the country and the economy were going.

The 1960s economic boom time was very different. Though the economy was strong, crime increased, as did political activism and conflict. That crime "boomed" along with the economy has been characterized as a paradox. Our traditional theories and explanations would have made predictions to the contrary. It is likely that a number of social forces contributed to this seemingly anomalous pattern. Two are likely very important: the baby boom, and the substantial social changes that that took place in the US and in other western democracies after World War II.

In the 1960s large numbers of postwar baby boomers entered schools, hung out on street corners, and learned to drive. We overwhelmed institutions. New schools had to be built; radio stations and the entertainment industry more broadly came to cater to us, we changed popular music, and entered the crime-prone teenaged years. It should not be surprising that crime and delinquency increased. We were the largest group of people of the most crime-prone ages, fourteen to seventeen, that western nations had experienced.[8] It was natural that crime would increase, but also the institutions that control adolescent behavior— schools, churches, community centers, and communities themselves— were overwhelmed by the onslaught. There were just so many of us. Other factors contributed to the 1960s crime boom that accompanied its economic boom, but more on that in a bit.

To explain post-World War II crime trends, sociologists Lawrence Cohen and Marcus Felson advanced their routine activities perspective, which explains how normal patterns of daily behavior that brings people who are motivated to commit crimes together with potential victims in the absence of guardians increases criminality.[9] Cohen and Felson were explicitly concerned with the paradox of growing crime with increasing plenty. The conclusion they drew from their analyses was that changes in routine activities, in particular social changes that increasingly moved social life away from home and into the public sphere, brought motivated criminals and potential victims together in the absence of effective guardians. Other postwar lifestyle changes contributed to crime growth. The presence of more cars, which facilitate crime, are also themselves targets for crime. The growth in possession of portable electronic devices (easy to steal) and more dual career couples (no one at home to protect against burglary) contributed to increased postwar crime rates. Perhaps the most important lesson that we can learn from Cohen and Felson's study is to beware of single-item or issue explanations (e.g., "the economy") of crime that are popular with the media and are too often sought by too many politicians. The economy is but one, albeit important, factor that contributes to fluctuations in crime. Our focus here is with the linkage between the economy, specifically labor markets, and crime. That linkage is one part of a very complex story.

In contrast to the Depression era, job losses at the end of the twentieth century seem to have led to very different feelings among those pushed to the margins of the labor market. Crime rates grew in the 1960s and 70s, but then leveled off and began dropping by the 1990s. Economic hard times at the end of the twentieth century did not spark considerable political social movement mobilization. In fact, these issues did not appreciably spark debate in national political campaigns. Not until a mortgage crisis, gasoline prices rising above $4.00 a gallon, and the Great Recession began during the protracted 2008 presidential race did candidates calling for social change get traction with the electorate.

The shift from a manufacturing to a service economy (some say to an information economy) has affected not just blue-collar workers, but those working in ancillary businesses and in corporate offices as well. In many neighborhoods that have been hard-hit by the shifting economy there is both despair and anger, and despair and anger can be powerful criminogenic forces. This is especially so since the worst of the job losses have been concentrated in select inner-city neighborhoods. These places exist within big cities where entire industries have downsized, and in small towns where one or two plants may have been the major employers or even the only large-scale source of jobs. What is different from the Great Depression is that the despair is more focused and less widely distributed throughout the population. In fact, the deepening disadvantage for some has continued while others rode waves of a booming economy and growing income inequality. The uneven negative consequences to communities of economic change have been effectively described by Wilson in his book *The Truly Disadvantaged*.[10] Blue-collar workers who lost low-skilled but well-paying jobs had less capacity to roll with economic changes. Some of them could find jobs, but not like their old jobs with General Motors or US Steel. Frequently their new jobs did not come with twenty-dollar an hour paychecks, benefits, or the security that came with union contracts. Their new jobs are less likely to be what politicians have come to call "family wage jobs."

Wilson initially called communities where the poor were concentrated and isolated from the social and economic life of the city "underclass neighborhoods." This label denotes their fundamental difference from the broader poor who are economically distressed but not isolated and concentrated in geographic areas, not as removed from contact and interaction with nonpoor others.[11] The residents of underclass neighborhoods were hit hardest when jobs began to disappear in large numbers in the mid-1970s. When the poor are not isolated, they interact with people who might be conduits to employment opportunities; the neighbor brings back to the block news that his firm might be hiring a few people to work on a loading dock or in a stockroom, for example. Nonunderclass poor children attend school not just with other poor children, and though their parents may be out of work, they regularly see others going to and arriving home from a day of labor. Children whose neighbors have work can imagine a better life because they see families who have such lives. In underclass neighborhoods children see less modeling of lives to hope for. They are less likely to interact with children substantially better off than themselves, and their parents are less likely to receive that timely tip about employment opportunities.

Already at the economic margins, the communities and the people occupying underclass neighborhoods have few reserve resources to combat dramatic drops in the employment rates. Many who live there worked in low-level service sector jobs, and when blue-collar workers were laid off from manufacturing companies they began competing with these low-skilled service sector employees for work. So underclass neighborhoods experienced the double whammy of lost manufacturing jobs and heightened competition for lower-paying service sector jobs. Wilson described a number of social problems as consequences of "when work disappears"—and one of the most important and most devastating for community is crime.

This approach to making sense of the patterns of association between economic factors and crime in the twentieth century will, to some, come across as too ad hoc. Perhaps it is. I will return to this issue later, after exploring the important role that work plays in the social lives of people and their communities, to try for a more systematic explanation of these patterns.

In the first decades of the twenty-first century the global economy is suffering through what many are calling the Great Recession. Plants have been shuttered, jobs lost, homes foreclosed, and government revenues are down. The latter means that there are fewer services for the effected, and states are letting people out of prisons to save money. This would appear to be prime time for an increase in crime, which explains why most criminologists I know have been asked by media representatives, family members, and their jogging partners, "How much has crime increased?" This question too, I'll take up later when turning toward that less ad hoc attempt to explain the patterns of the twentieth century.

And Then There's Race

The changes brought about by the deindustrialization of which Wilson writes should be seen in the historical context of other social forces shaping American social and economic life. In addition to baby boomers entering adolescence, another feature of 1960s American social life that likely contributed to more crimes was disappointment. Like the Widemans, many black families joined the Great Migration to find their Promised Land, to find jobs, and to find better futures for their children. By the mid- and late 1960s, their children were frustrated by that unfulfilled promise and the basic failure of the American promise to them. Two things occurred: political mobilization linked to the civil rights movement, and crime. And, as a consequence of both, crime control in the guise of law-and-order politics came to be an emphasis for both the federal and state government.[12] The legacy of this shift in crime control policy has had very real ramifications for African American communities from the beginning, but they are especially pronounced in recent decades.[13] Law and order is also an increasingly determinative force in Latino communities. The importance of the massive increase in the imprisonment of Americans will be discussed in a later chapter, but for now we should recognize that these changes have been linked to the growth of the black population in cities and the civil rights movement, and, like these social changes, it is very important to the link between the economy and crime.

In the late 1950s and 1960s African Americans in the North and West watched with interest the events that were taking place in Selma, Birmingham, and Nashville. They cared deeply about what was happening to their brothers and sisters in Georgia, Mississippi, and Florida. And when the movement came north, they joined in the effort. Not long after the northern front of the civil rights movement was opened, voices like those of Malcolm X, Stokely Carmichael, and Huey Newton called to young people left out of the economic boom and frustrated by the failure of the North to deliver on the promises of the Great Migration to the Promised Land to rise up. Others, like Robby Wideman and his friends, and later like some of the boys and young men on my probation and parole caseloads, chose neither church-led civil rights activity nor calls to organized resistance. Although frequently invoking the rhetoric of revolution, they turned to crime.[14]

Labor market disadvantage cannot be reduced just to racial inequality. There is evidence that labor market marginality is criminogenic in both majority and minority populations. But because racial and ethnic antipathies have historically disadvantaged some in access to labor markets, especially for preferred jobs, these factors can aggravate the effects of joblessness, unemployment, and underemployment on criminality.

Americans seem to hate talking about race, but few factors have been more important in American history than our conflicts and differences between racial and ethnic groups, and this has certainly been true when we consider either crime or employment. As is the case in many other nations as well, one cannot really appreciate the dynamics of recent economic changes on social life without considering racial and ethnic conflicts. European nations increasingly find that ethnic differences complicate their economic, social, and political lives at home as well as in former colonies. In those countries where corporations are setting up factories or contracting with local manufacturers there are issues of who benefits, who is exploited, and who controls decision making when industry arrives. These were issues during America's Industrial Revolution, they remained important issues when African Americans moved out of the South in great numbers to compete for jobs in the North and when Asians were exploited in the building of nineteenth-century railroads, and they remain contentious issues now that jobs have been disappearing in some places. At the heart of contemporary arguments about immigration are questions about ethnicity and who works for whom.

We cannot seriously consider the changes in the Homewood section of Pittsburgh between the adolescent years of John Wideman and those of Robby without recognizing that it was and continues to be a black community, profoundly affected by migration from the South in the postwar years, the hopes of the civil rights era, and the loss of jobs that accompanied the decline of the steel industry in the 1970s and 80s.

In some places, early twentieth-century industries drew workers from among Eastern and Southern European immigrant groups. In Pittsburgh Czechs, Germans, Croats, and Italians worked the steel mills. In Chicago Greeks, Italians, and Poles found jobs in the stock-yards. There was competition and at times conflict between immigrant groups, and with native white workers. With the First World War the first streams of what became the Great Migration—the massive movement of the black population out of the rural South to urban areas in the North, South, and later the West—began. And with this new group of workers a new level of conflict over who got to work which jobs ensued.

The Great Migration was propelled by the collapse of "big cotton" in the South, the region's ongoing oppressive race relations, and the attraction of jobs and the promise of a better life up North. This massive people flow continued into the 1960s and introduced dark faces to northern cities to an extent previously unseen. Large black communities were established in New York's Harlem, Chicago's South Side, Cleveland's Hough, Pittsburgh's Homewood and Hill District, and in most other big or industrial cities of the North, Midwest, and West. Like immigrants before them, these beach heads, largely ethnically homogenous communities, provided new arrivals with housing and a socially welcoming place to begin their new, very different, lives. What was different for these particular communities—black communities—compared to the ethnic neighborhoods populated by Italians, Irish, Poles, and Croats was that they, like African American communities in Detroit, Philadelphia, Washington, and later Los Angeles and San Francisco, were and for the most part remain racially segregated.[15] They were not just beach heads for new arrivals. They did not get to follow the pattern of white ethnics, moving in succeeding generations out of their ghettos as their economic circumstance improved. As sociologists Douglas Massey and Nancy Denton have described in their book *American Apartheid*, the African American urban experience has been one of being restricted to and concentrated in tightly controlled sections of cities like no other group.[16] Where the restrictive, segregating bonds were loosened the pattern has been a movement by a few, usually by integrating neighborhoods adjoining the ghetto, which then usually rapidly resegregate.[17] To be sure, at the turn of the twenty-first century there are African Americans who have successfully colonized areas that remain and are likely to remain predominantly white, but they are relatively few. Racial residential segregation has lessened a bit in America, but for the most part its cities are today nearly as segregated as they were before the beginning of the modern civil rights movement.

Even though African American workers were able to build economically and socially more secure lives for themselves and their families with the move north, they still faced marginalization in the labor market. Some companies refused to hire them. Others restricted them from desirable positions, and until rather late in the century they were denied membership in some industrial unions, and still today have difficulty achieving membership in some craft unions.[18] Consequently, when low-skilled, blue-collar jobs began to disappear from American cities and the last hired was the first fired, this disproportionately fell upon blacks. As a result, a higher proportion of African American laborers have had to find jobs in the lower sectors of the American labor market, the secondary sector, where they have been paid less and have had fewer benefits than their brethren who were fortunate enough to land blue-collar, primary sector manufacturing jobs.

In African American communities today, the population faces the combination of a higher likelihood of individual workers being laid off from manufacturing jobs, workers being bumped from low-sector jobs by displaced manufacturing employees, and the concentration of social problems because of racial residential segregation.[19] To some extent Latino populations in the US suffer from lesser versions of these same processes. What this means is that criminogenic forces that result from the shifting labor market have caused even more crime in black and brown neighborhoods than they might in the residential districts populated predominately by whites.[20]

European countries are experiencing two different migration patterns that include some similar racial and ethnic dynamics, although of course they have very different racial histories than do nations of the Americas. Western European nations that held colonies as a result of the age of conquest increasingly have new black and brown citizens electing to seek opportunity in the colonizing nation. Britain, France, the Netherlands, and others extend citizenship or at least easier immigration to those born in their former colonies. As a result, more people have freely migrated in recent decades. In the United Kingdom the need for workers brought on by World War II fueled immigration from the West Indies just as the hunger for workers in the United States drew blacks to Detroit and Cleveland. In Cardiff Wales, Tiger Bay became the largest black settlement in Europe and continues as the longest continuing black community in the European Union, when Jamaicans moved there to work in ship building. Today Tiger Bay is subsumed in the Butte Town section of Cardiff, and while it is not as segregated as the South Side of Chicago, it is set apart from the remainder of the city. London, Paris, Amsterdam, and Rome all have blacker and browner populations as a result of their nations' colonial histories.

The other force "darkening" Europe is the movement of cheap labor in the form of guest workers. In Germany, large numbers of guest workers have come from Turkey; in Italy from Africa. Economic strains resulting from reunification have been exacerbated by anti–guest worker sentiments that have boiled up in Germany. In Berlin there is a Turkish enclave where the dominant language is Turkish, which troubles some Germans. There exists a tension between this community and the larger community, with Turks complaining that they cannot really ever become German and Germans complaining that the Turks do not want to really become German. Germany is not the only European state where there are substantial anti-immigrant sentiments.[21]

One can reasonably expect that to the extent that these countries lose manufacturing as a result of globalization, they may experience the resulting problems seen in the US. To the extent that racial and ethnic stratification focuses the negative consequences onto ethnic populations, which are increasingly people of color, they may reproduce troubling patterns that are similar to those in the US. French riots in Parisian suburbs in 2005 were a response to the government's attempt to roll back some long-standing job protections for younger workers. Minorities who have long existed on the economic margins seized this opportunity to object to being kept at arm's length from the French dream. Spain has experienced riotous attacks on Latin American immigrants because natives perceive them as spawning gang activity. Interestingly, it is reported that one of the major gangs is called the Latin Kings, the same name as one of Chicago's long-standing gangs.

America's job losses began early because some of its industries, notably steel and automobile manufacturing, did not reinvest, upgrade, and remain competitive with their counterparts in Europe and Japan. It remains to be seen if Europe and Japan can avoid the substantial loss of manufacturing that continues to occur in the US, and by doing so avoid the social problems faced by the latter. Deindustrialization has happened in some European cities. Dublin, long before the economic miracle that characterized that city since Ireland's initial entry into the EU (dubbed the Celtic Tiger because of its booming economy before the Great Recession), was desperately bad off after Ford and other man-ufactures shuttered plants there just as they had in the States.

The challenges of limited employment are not restricted to the industrial nations of the so-called north. Since South Africa's libera-tion their own precarious social and economic postapartheid reality has been complicated by the influx of immigrants from poorer sub-Saharan nations. Even with its problems, South Africa remains the major eco-nomic force in Africa, and as have workers in the Americas and Europe, Africans from throughout the sub-Saharan region have sought better lives in the mines and farms of their prosperous neighbor nation. The democratic government of South Africa already had a daunting task to deliver on the promise of improved social and economic well-being that was the hope of liberation. That task has become more difficult with the influx of these immigrants. Unlike the movement of many workers to European industrial countries, many of South Africa's immigrants are not legal residents.[22] They do provoke some of the same nativist and ethnic resentments that are seen elsewhere.

What South African geographers call "the apartheid city" has changed in ways that allow native/immigrant tensions to be observed. Historically the apartheid city was white within the city limits with an Asian (Indian) section on the periphery and black townships lying on the outside of the city limits. Transport from black townships and Asian districts to the city was difficult, especially from the former, but workers could, with considerable effort, get to service jobs in white residential districts and to the places of somewhat more substantial jobs, if they were lucky to have one. In spite of the demise of the apartheid regime and its pass and residential laws, unsurprisingly, the legacy of the apart-heid city remains. Today, though, a new place has been added. Black townships have swelled because of desperately poor work seekers from other nations. Sometimes it is outside of—and in some instances away from—the long-standing black townships, where squatters' camps seg-regate their residents. There is resentment among some portion of the black South African population of these interlopers because they are seen as competitors and a drain on already strained social services (of course, the same objections argued by anti-immigrant activists in the US and Europe). This resentment was behind anti-immigrant, most of whom were Zimbabwean, riots that rocked South Africa in 2008.

In South Africa it is not the loss of jobs that is causing social distress, but ongoing unemployment and importantly the stratification of labor, the hierarchical arrangements that decide who gets which jobs and who is preferred in the labor market, that is the source of social problems. It remains to be seen how labor markets will be ethnically stratified in developing nations where manufacturing is moving to and what consequences will occur as a result.

Gender

Persistent problems in disadvantaged communities are family disruption and uneven marriage markets, too frequently leaving women to support children alone with modest incomes. We cannot seriously consider the consequences of labor stratification's effect on crime without looking at women's work. First, even though traditionally sociologists evaluated the class standing of families by focusing on the education and occupation of the male head of household, this practice became (if it was not always) very problematic in the second half of the twentieth century. For decades now most adult women, even those with small children, have worked outside of the home.[23] Families have increasingly depended on two breadwinners to have a shot at or to maintain middle-class lifestyles, and in the case of families existing in depressed cities and counties, to keep their household heads above water. Second, many women begin working when they leave school and expect to continue if and when they have a family. While we may not know as much about their expectations and frustrations as we do about young men, it is likely that we have to take both into account in order to fully appreciate the effects of labor stratification on social life and crime. Third, a growing number of women are the heads of their households.[24]

These changes are further complicated by the historic disadvantage that women have faced in the labor market. Women's work frequently has had the characteristics of the secondary sector. They have not been paid as well, even when doing equivalent work. They have frequently not had access to as many benefits as their male counterparts, employers too often assuming that they'll be covered by their husbands' health care, and we all know about the glass ceilings that have inhibited the likelihood of women's promotions—the promotions that help to solidify bonds to work.

And then there are children. Employers have used them as excuses to not promote women. For families, children are (usually) both a positive and a negative: A negative because they are expensive, and a positive because of the utility that wanted children bring when they are planned. When they are not planned or not wanted, they add to the economic and social burdens of struggling families. And, when the mother is very young, children can seriously limit her future options for education and work. But for our purposes, children are something else as well. They are an important source of bonding.

Labor market experience may well not predict female criminality. I think that we do not have as many good answers about how work will affect potential criminality among women as we do among men, but this question needs to be taken seriously. Perhaps by doing so, we can begin to at least build conceptual models for considering the question. It is safe to assume that policies and practices that support women and families, pay inequality patterns, and welfare reform will have important influences on the well-being of children and communities.

Further, when we think about women of color, many of the difficulties of living in distressed communities are exacerbated. For African American women, the fact that so many young African American men are now in prison or have a prison record, and that so many struggle to find quality, stable employment, makes family life an especially economical and child rearing struggle. And today, the proportion of African American births to single women is increasing again after a period of decline.[25]

Latino women have some of these same challenges, but perhaps less so. The Latino male imprisonment rate is lower than that of African Americans, and a smaller proportion of children are born to single parents. But they have other problems: both men and women frequently working in very low-wage, unstable jobs, sometimes seasonally; issues with the Immigration and Customs Enforcement agents and their practices if they are undocumented; and perhaps increasingly, profiling by employers and law enforcement even if they are documented.

What about Crime?

Imagine my surprise when I began studying the relationship between work and crime and I found out that criminologists have not found unemployment to be an especially good predictor of crime. After all, more than a few years earlier, when I worked as a parole agent in Pennsylvania, we "knew" that the best way (though by no means foolproof) of keeping our clients (agency speak for parolees) from returning to prison was to get them a job. But now I realize that systematic analyses have sometimes found that unemployment significantly predicts crime, but other analyses find the opposite. Surely, however, there must be something to the linkage between work and criminality.

When initially writing about the effects on neighborhoods of joblessness, Wilson included among the consequences increases in crime. Likewise, Massey and Denton included increased crime among the negative results of racial residential segregation. Neither Wilson nor Massey and Denton specified or speculated about the specific mechanisms by which crime would be increased. This is not a criticism of either work. They, like others before, reasonably assert that economic and social distresses are criminogenic forces.

Subsequently, in work with criminologist Robert Sampson, Wilson has written about how a decline in social capital in destitute communities makes them less capable of protecting themselves from crime.[26] This argument builds on Sampson's earlier, and since extended, work on social disorganization theory that explains the macro variation in crime rates across neighborhoods.[27] My arguments, which are central to this project, are very compatible with modern social disorganization theory.

Others have offered accounts that begin to shed light on how employment changes have influenced communities and their crime rates. Especially illuminating are a group of urban ethnographies that studied Philadelphia, New York, and Chicago neighborhoods. Sociologist Elijah Anderson's study of black street life in Philadelphia focuses on the consequences to local culture when people are poor and have very limited employment opportunities. The cultural pattern that emerges among a portion of the population—the code of the street—supports criminal lifestyles and the use of violence in some instances. Anthropologist Mercer Sullivan's *Getting Paid* is a study of how young men in three Brooklyn communities adapt to their employment realities. The areas have different unemployment rates, workers across the three neighborhoods have opportunities for different kinds of jobs, and consequently the reactions of young people, including their criminal activity, varies. Sociologist Mary Pattillo-McCoy's *Black Picket Fences* focuses on an African American middle-class neighborhood in Chicago. The economic circumstances of the residents she studied are not as desperate as those considered by Anderson or some in Sullivan's study, and the neighborhood is not as distressed as those which Wilson has focused on. It is very important to note that Pattillo-McCoy's study site differs from white middle-class communities in two very important ways. First, it borders disadvantaged, underclass neighborhoods; and second, the fiscal life of residents is considerably more precarious than that of the white middle class. These differences are a consequence of the continuing racial residential segregation of US cities.[28] As a result, the community and its residents are exposed to and experience more crime than their white middle-class counterparts.[29]

These studies begin to paint a picture of how, under the strain of job losses, community crime patterns are affected. When combined with quantitative research about work and crime that has been published in the past fifteen years, we begin to flesh out mechanisms by which the economy affects criminality.[30] We must remember, though, that the scholarship specifically on unemployment and crime is quite mixed; as described above, at times we find that it increases crime, other studies find that it actually leads to a decline in some types of crime, and still others find that employment rates seem to have no effect on crime.[31]

An additional complication is presented by criminologists Terrence Thornberry and R. L. Christenson, and John Hagan.[32] They argue that one of the problems with much of the extant literature is that it assumes that unemployment causes crime. Both analyses show that we need to consider the reciprocal effects of criminal behavior on employment as well. Those who end up with a criminal record as a result of their criminality are considerably less successful on the job market. A growing literature amplifies this point. Devah Pager has found in experimental audit studies that both white and African Americans with criminal records do less well in their job search than others of their race who do not have a record.[33] Interestingly, she also found that African Americans without a felony conviction are considerably less employable than whites with a record.

Parolees on my Pennsylvania caseload in the early 1970s sometimes lied about their status to get jobs. This presented a dilemma for both of us. If they were found out, bosses could fire them because they'd lied on their job application. This happened to several men that I worked with. On at least one occasion, I am convinced that a parolee's new crime and return to prison could be linked directly to job loss after he was fired for lying about his past conviction. Men who'd lied to secure a job presented me with a dilemma because I was obligated to verify their employment and check up on their attendance and work. Generally, I tried not to out them if I knew that they'd lied. This required a bit of creative parole supervisions. Fortunately for me, and I think for them and their job prospects, I wasn't as closely monitored as they were. I made the choice that their continued gainful employment was more important than the forms I was required to submit. That's how convinced I, and other parole agents, were that work matters.

Furthermore, we know that it is not just whether people have work that matters to their lives and their involvement in crime, but the type of work they do and their relationship to the labor market. If we think back to the earlier description of Hugo's Jean Valjean's desperate crime, we must acknowledge that this link is not always as simple as "need leads to crime." In light of what we now know, we should recognize that simplistic notions about the relationship between unemployment and crime have limited utility, yet the connection between work and crime is of substantial criminological importance. In the chapters to come I will trace out how the economy, through employment, affects individual criminality and collective crime rates.

Why Do They Do It?

At the heart of nearly all criminological inquiries is the simple question, "Why do they do it?" Of course if we knew that, many of us criminologists might join the leagues of the jobless, but perhaps it is worth beginning by thinking about criminal motivation. We might say that there are three basic crime types: pecuniary crimes, entrepreneurial crimes, and expressive crimes. By pecuniary I mean those violations that are for immediate material gain. Classically these are various forms of larceny. One might include robbery here, but because of the interpersonal violence that is inherently a part of this form of acquisition I think it better, like law enforcement and most criminologists, to think of it as a crime of violence, much of which is expressive crime, but not all of it. Included among pecuniary crimes are the larcenies of both the lower and upper classes. It is important for our purposes that we distinguish these two categories, because the economy and individuals' relationship to it is likely to propel motives for criminal behavior differently based on one's social position.

By entrepreneurial crime I mean that subset of pecuniary crimes where individuals engage in businesslike criminal practices for financial gain: drug dealers, organized criminals, those involved with certain corporate crimes. These types of crimes should be distinguished from the other pecuniary crimes because, while they may be motivated by the same forces, these entrepreneurial crimes are more likely to lead to real financial gain. This makes them especially attractive to criminals from disadvantaged circumstances and the greedy of the more prosperous classes. This is not a new idea; the compelling case for this distinction was made long ago.[34] The average burglar or petty thief really cannot make a living at it, and even when comparatively successful, they hardly obtain measurable financial success. By contrast, a select few drug dealers and organized criminals can make a living with these pursuits. Here too, though, we should be careful not to fall into popular stereotypes. Low-level drug sellers do not do very well. A study of drug markets reported that low-level—especially entry-level—street dealers actually make less than minimum wage when the highs and lows of selling are averaged and the cost of buying product from their wholesaler—their overhead—is considered.[35] The contrary is the stereotype that disadvantaged street youth too frequently buy into. They think that working in drug markets is an easy way to do better than working a "slave job"— their description of the low-level, unglamorous options usually available to them at places like McDonald's. In his autobiographical account of growing up, sometimes on the wrong side of the law, Nathan McCall, now a *Washington Post* reporter, recounts how the reality of being a drug dealer was much different from the mythology.

> I quickly discovered that dealing wasn't so easy as it seemed. Selling reefer was a round-the-clock hustle that required more time and energy than I wanted to invest. Unloading a single O.Z. (ounce) sometimes took up to an hour . . .
>
> . . . I finally had to admit that I lacked the discipline to be a good dealer. Dealing drugs is harder than any job I've had, then or since. To this day, I laugh when I hear folks say drug dealers are lazy people who don't want to work. There's no job more demanding than dealing drugs. It's the only thing I've really tried hard to do, and failed at.[36]

In a story about a Seattle nonprofit that tries to prepare offenders to compete on the job market, a *Seattle Times* reporter quoted a source who said,

> Many of the jobs start at minimum wage, but [he]—who's completed an apprenticeship and is looking for a job in construction—figures it's more than he was making when he was selling dope once you factor in all the bad days and the time behind bars. "When you really add it up, hustling is harder than a regular job and it's less than minimum wage," he said. "The only thing is, it's faster."[37]

Research findings affirm the validity of these accounts. Economist Peter Reuter and his colleagues, studying drug dealing in Washington, DC, found that two-thirds of those selling on the street did so while they held jobs in the legitimate economy and that few netted more than minimum wage from this side business.[38] Economist Steven Levitt and sociologist Sudhir Venkatesh, studying in an undisclosed city, report that although gangs make more money from drug sales than from alternative forms of income, the premium is cancelled by risk, both legal and illegal, and overhead. They too conclude that individual street level dealers make roughly minimum wage.[39]

Even though the reality of drug income for most is far less than popular mythology suggests, I include dealing among entrepreneurial crime because for the few who work their way up past the lower rungs of the distribution ladders, it is possible to make a living at it—at least until rivals or the police take you out. And even if it usually does not lead to financial success, the hope that it will motivates many entry-level dealers.

Organized crime is the classic alternative route to "the good life" for people from disadvantaged backgrounds. By classic I do not mean that many people take this route, but that organized crime has been described by commentators as an alternative ladder to the standard paths for upward mobility.[40] As is the case with both employment in legitimate business or in illegal drug markets, one can start low and work their way up over time to positions that bring increased financial rewards.

Other examples of entrepreneurial crimes are acts by corporations that bolster the financial gain of upper-level management and the corporation itself. I might have included stockholders in the last category in the past, but corporate scandals in recent years involving accounting fraud actually had the effect of defrauding stockholders. Any real discussion of the economy, employment, and crime has to acknowledge these types of crimes. As we saw with the savings and loan scandals and then with the accounting fraud scandals (Enron, Tyco, Arthur Anderson, etc.), and most recently and vividly the Ponzi schemes on Wall Street, these crimes negatively affect the economy via their effects on pricing—for example, the price of energy in the case of Enron—and by their negative influence on stock markets, the damage done to employees and retirees, and perhaps most clearly on workers.

Expressive crimes, many of which are violent crimes, are the "cleanest" category. Here we simply include the standard set of crimes counted by the FBI and most police departments: murder, assault, rape, and robbery. These are crimes of interpersonal violence whether committed against strangers, acquaintances, or intimates. But they also include various forms of vandalism, including a lot of graffiti-painting or "tagging." For our consideration of questions of how employment affects crime and criminality, expressive crimes may be the most interesting. People typically (with the exception of robbery) do not engage in these crimes for financial gain, but the literature is clear that the occurrences of these crimes are related to economic patterns. The question is, why?

Answers to this question tend to be of two types. Corresponding to popular fears of the poor are cultural and subcultural notions which assert that among the disadvantaged are those who have developed values and beliefs that allow or even encourage them to violently victimize others. The second type of answer focuses on the social structural circumstances of individuals and their communities that create violence, or allow aggression to be less checked than in the wider society. There are too few writers who effectively bridge these two types of answers to the question of how economic factors, including jobs, cause violent crimes.

Fundamentally, we must recognize that research has long shown that the material motivations for crime are not strong predictors.[41] Many offenders themselves, as well as the police, the media, and some criminologists, choose to explain the link between poverty, unemployment, and income by saying that people do it because they want or they need. The empirical research literature, however, finds weak and inconsistent links between economic factors and property crimes, both pecuniary and entrepreneurial. To be sure, there are those who enjoy the material fruits of their criminality, but it is unlikely that needs or wants alone can explain crime. Some other force, in addition to needs and desires, is required in order to cause most people to commit crimes.

In this volume the focus will be on violent crimes and the pecuniary crimes of the lower classes, violations frequently referred to as common or street crimes. To a limited extent I will touch on lower-end entrepreneurial crimes as well. Why leave out the balance of entrepreneurial crimes and the pecuniary and even violent crimes of the upper classes? These crimes, after all, are considerably more damaging to both economy and society. There are several reasons for the choice, not least of which is my interest in getting a better understanding of street crimes. First, the options for the disadvantaged in society are far more restricted than for those from more preferred circumstance. The latter may more freely choose from sets of options that include criminality, and while the disadvantaged too are making choices, their choices are more constrained and their decisions are made with restricted freedom. Thus the motivations for the former are likely to be a bit different from the latter. One can distinguish them by the proportion of greed in their motivation. I would assert that much more of the relatively wealthier criminal's actions are propelled by greed than of the relatively poorer. The poor person is more likely to be influenced by anger, hopelessness, and the utter despair of those around them. They may not be contemporary Jean Valjeans, but they are considerably closer to Hugo's hero than the corporate executive raiders and reckless gamblers, who likely enjoyed seeing *Les Miz* on Broadway from opera-pit seats. The second reason for making this choice is that street crimes, perhaps misguidedly, propel so much of our public policy and discussions. And finally, it is simply because including the other crime types is too much for one volume and for one research agenda.

The Coming Chapters

To make sense of how the jobs and the labor market influence crime rates of social collectives—nations, cities, neighborhoods—we need to begin by considering the observed patterns and distributions of crime and how social scientists have tried to explain those patterns. In the next chapter I will describe in more detail what we know about the connection between work and crime and begin an expanded explanation of this connection. In Chapter 3 I will focus on the findings of recent work that has attempted to develop a more complete understanding of how labor markets and individuals' participation in the work force influence criminality. Chapter 4 focuses on delinquents, in particular that large group of "criminals" who are not yet of working age but whose behavior nevertheless is influenced by the economy. Chapter 5 will focus on community ecology and crime, and address questions of how the work and school experiences of residents are conditioned by the characteristics of the neighborhoods and local labor markets in which they live. In chapters 6 and 7 I will expand these ideas, which have been primarily developed and tested using urban US data, to rural areas and other nations. In chapter 8 I'll draw some conclusions, speculate on policies that might mitigate the problems described, and consider new directions for research.

Revisiting Homewood

The Homewood of the 1950s, where John Wideman, now a very successful professor and writer, grew up was a community with sections that were somewhat better off economically than most of Pittsburgh's other black neighborhoods in The Hill District and on the North Side. Certainly Homewood also had its blighted, struggling sections. By the time Robby Wideman was a teenager, the considerable social changes that occurred in the 1960s were being felt on Homewood's streets. John describes Robby as growing up with a taste for the fast life of those streets and a desire to make a quick buck. One can easily guess that the higher crime rate that hit Homewood, as well as other communities in urban America in the 60s, was in part a consequence of frustrations felt by the children of Great Migration movers. This second generation learned during their youth that the promise of the northern Promised Land exceeded the reality. Robby was a part of that generation that wanted more than the life the steel mills promised.

Then in the mid-1970s, Pittsburgh's mills began to disappear. In the 1980s some of them were dismantled and sold for scrap metal. Local politicians made stirring speeches about how Pittsburgh and its people would ride out the economic storm together. By the turn of twenty-first century government leaders were proclaiming that the city of Pittsburgh had come back. There were new service sector and corporate jobs, but the mills were gone. Mill workers who could leave had pursued work elsewhere; those that could not move were left in despair, discarded by the steel industry and apparently forgotten by those politicians who'd promised that they would ride out the storm together. Homewood, once the vibrant community of John Wideman's youth, now had sections that are best described as underclass. There was less hope in Robby's Homewood of the 1960s than in John's of a decade earlier. There is even less hope there now.

An Up-Front Confession

Much of this volume is taken from work that I have been doing over the past two decades and the work of others that I have read along the way. But some of the perspectives and interpretations that I will offer come from no peer-reviewed journal, university press, or conference presentation. Some of it will not come from my data analyses or systematic observations that I have made as a sociologist. My interests in these topics began with debates between sociologists over the comparative importance of poverty and income inequality as factors that could predict violent crime. It was exposures that I had prior to being trained as a sociologist that led me to seize on dual labor market theory's framework for understanding the creation and persistence of social inequality. Those same exposures helped me to develop what I later came to call the labor stratification and crime thesis to try to explain how labor force experiences affect criminality. The two significant exposures were growing up in Pittsburgh's inner city, and working for three years in probation and parole.

I spent my adolescence in Pittsburgh's Hill District at a time when big steel was the city's identity and the source of a better life for working men and their families. The mills went through boom and bust times, layoffs, and strikes, but in Pittsburgh and in the small cities and towns of Western Pennsylvania people believed that over the long haul sweating in those dark, hot, dangerous, dirty mills would take care of you and yours. Even so, there was crime in The Hill, a virtually all-black inner-city enclave just above Pittsburgh's central business district.

Robby Wideman, who I believe is just a few years younger than me, came of age a few miles away in another such enclave. I did not know the Widemans, but one of Robby's "rap partners" (those convicted with him), Cecil, was for a brief time in my Boy Scout troop when he was probably eleven years old. Robby's frustrations that we can read about in *Brothers and Keepers* were the frustrations of my classmates and neighbors. The hopes of the Promised Land were held by members of our family's church and by the adults living around us. Nearly all, including my parents, had come from the South. I had left Pittsburgh by the time so many frustrations and hopes were crushed by deindustrialization, but my sociological view has been profoundly affected by my hometown.

I did not plan to be a juvenile probation officer (PO) when I graduated from college, but like many career turns, that one just happened. I spent one year working in a rural county in northwestern Pennsylvania. Within the county were two small adjoining cities that had grown up around steel mills. Some of the kids on my first caseload were from the gritty sections of those towns, others from mostly poor rural areas. A year after starting that job I moved to Erie, Pennsylvania, where I worked for two years as a parole agent for the Pennsylvania Board of Probation and Parole. I learned a lot from our clients, my coworkers, the streets of Erie, and from visits to prisons and jails and treatment facilities (including a couple of training stints). One of the important things I learned early on is considered a no-brainer for all POs: that a parolee with a job is far more likely to stay out of jail.

As I considered the debate over poverty versus income inequality and found myself being drawn toward dual labor market theory as an explanatory tool for how both economic conditions are products of labor market arrangements and how they are linked to crime, I found that my Pittsburgh and parole officer experiences were increasingly influential in my thinking. As I began writing this book I envisioned an academic manuscript that would bring together my research and that of others in a rather traditional scholarly treatment. But as I have continued writing, it has gotten increasingly personal. By that I mean that there have been times that our methods or the data that have been available to me will not allow me to draw particular inferences or conclusions, but I am confident that the perspective of the kid from The Hill who became a PO may add a bit to my analyses of the economy and labor market's effects on crime.

I do not doubt that some of my colleagues will read this and in places find that these personal interpretations go beyond what the data tell us. At times they may feel that we do not yet know something or that there isn't research that supports a particular position. I have accepted the probability of such comments. I am convinced that by adding personal perspectives, we may enrich our debates and advance our understanding. John Edgar Wideman realized that no matter where his brother was, Robby carried a part of John with him. I have come to recognize that the people of The Hill carry with them a bit of all of us who left— and so I choose to enrich this account with theirs.

2

"Get a Job"

The Connection between Work and Crime

My first encounter with Walter was in his mother-in-law's living room.[1] Walter was not too long out of prison after serving a few years for a robbery conviction. A skinny, sullen young man who looked even younger than his early twenty-something years, Walter was transferred to my caseload from that of another agent. I had been told that he was not a real problem but that he was having a difficult time finding a job, and so much of that first meeting focused on his job search—or perhaps I should say his lack of a job search. Working was not something Walter was terribly interested in, but both his recent bride and her mother, sitting and staring at me from across the room, were more acutely aware that he needed to find a job than he was. I suspect that they were as interested in keeping him from being returned to jail for a parole violation, for failing to follow job search instructions (from his previous supervising agent and now reiterated by me), as they were in any income that he might generate. Walter compliantly nodded affirmatively when I told him that he had to find a job and that beginning the next morning he would have to spend every morning walking the streets of Erie, Pennsylvania knocking on doors and submitting applications. Each day he was to drop off, at the front desk of the parole board's district office, a list of the places that he'd applied to that day. Why the emphasis on Walter finding a job? Because even though I had been a parole agent for just a year and was essentially the same age as Walter, I recognized that he would not remain out of jail if he did not find work. Either we would lock him up for a parole violation, or he'd commit a new crime.

The robbery that sent Walter to prison was a violent crime, but like most robberies it had a pecuniary quality to its motivation and was, to be painfully honest, even more stupid than most criminal acts. Walter had no more interest in work before going to the joint than he had once paroled. It all started one night when he was sitting in a bar drinking with a buddy. They wondered how they could keep the good times rolling when their money ran out. Instead of cashing a check (or, had it been today, going to an ATM) like most of us might, they followed an old man out of the bar, mugged him just down the street, and then returned to the same bar to continue drinking. The victim returned to the bar to seek help and call the police and saw his assailants (who apparently did not notice him), which of course led to their easy capture and conviction. No Jean Valjean these crooks. While their crime was motivated by money, how they came to criminal behavior is a more complex tale than the hero of Les Misérables quest to feed starving relatives.

I cannot remember a single training session that told me, a novice parole agent, of the importance of parolees having a job. But it was certainly part of the lore and my informal education in the office. If Walter did not start working, the lifestyle that got him busted once would likely get him busted again. So, what might the research on employment and crime look like today, should parole officers elect to consider it?

What they would find is that much of the past research has focused on individuals' current or recent income, poverty status, or unemployment. More recent scholarship, however, has included more concern with how people or groups come to be in a particular circumstance— why they are poor, for example. When we speak of the economy and crime it is important to recognize that the way that the economy touches the lives of most people is through their relationship to the labor market. They are poor because they do not have a job, or because if they are employed their job pays too little, or because they are members of a group that has been historically marginalized from the mainstream of the labor market. They live in slums or on the streets because their irregular employment allows them to afford only very low rents if any at all, and they have little or no hope of ever becoming a home owner. They live in a city, state, or nation characterized by high income inequality because the industrial composition where they live tends to consist of options for elite, high-income occupations and low-paid jobs for those who serve the former. I would guess that Walter invested little or no energy pondering most of these issues, but he, like the rest of us, was affected by his relationship to the legitimate economy, and in his case it was his lack of employment, his lack of connection to the labor market, and his minimal desire to find a job that was central to his lifestyle and criminal involvement. To understand how the economy affects criminality we have to focus on work, because ultimately crime requires an act by an individual, and individuals' points of contact with the economy are their jobs or, in the case of juveniles, their parents' jobs.

The explanation of how work influences crime that I will advance here compliments some of the major arguments that have appeared in sociological criminology in recent years, and will contrast with some long-standing theoretical explanations. Regarding the latter, the current position, which I refer to as the labor stratification and crime thesis, focuses considerably more on the social and economic structure than do traditional subculture of poverty arguments.[2] Edward Banfield especially, and to a lesser extent Charles Murray, who treats some aspects of social structure seriously in his analyses, give a passing nod to those structural forces, but they essentially center their arguments on the cultural values that individuals (or groups) have internalized which drives their and their progeny's criminality. These positions are very different than that espoused by Elijah Anderson, who links the emergence of "a code of the street" to the long-term social and economic disadvantage of segments of the populations.[3] Because Anderson's explanation centers on the lack of jobs that are available to many residents of disadvantaged inner-city neighborhoods, the labor stratification and crime thesis is very compatible with his position.

The labor stratification and crime thesis is also very compatible with positions taken by William Julius Wilson, who ascribed the emergence of an urban underclass at the end of the twentieth century to job losses resulting from deindustrialization, by Douglas Massey and Nancy Denton, and Ruth Peterson and Lauren Krivo, who emphasize the role of racial residential segregation in causing and maintaining economic disadvantage and crime.[4] Much like Mercer Sullivan, who in *Getting Paid* traces both life chances and crime to the legitimate and illegitimate opportunities that are available differentially to young people, I argue that the kind of work that people have access to is conditioned by where they live, and their work and that of those who live around them helps to determine their participation in crime.[5] And, just as sociologists Mary Pattillo-McCoy and Karen Parker treat space, especially the particular characteristics of neighborhoods and sections of cities that matter as central to their analyses, I too will emphasize the importance of geography.[6] Central to the labor stratification and crime thesis is how employment and disadvantage in the context of disadvantaged places affects crime and crime rates.

What the labor stratification and crime thesis is *not* is a full-throated endorsement of materialist explanations of crime such as that proffered by Robert Merton in his classic "Social Structure and Anomie," where he argued that much crime occurred because of reactions to blocked opportunity, in an effort to improve material wants and needs.[7] Yes, I acknowledge that at times people engage in crime because of such wants and needs—but alone, this is too limited of an explanation.

That said, we should begin by acknowledging that just how the economy, and certainly employment, influences crime is not as straightforward as common sense suggest. In both the case of explaining individual criminal behavior and variations in crime rates, it looks increasingly more complex than one would at first expect.

Unemployment, the Economy, and Crime

Until recently criminologists focused their study on how unemployment was related to criminality, but, as I have said, that correlation is inconsistent; some scholars find a positive relationship,[8] while some find that unemployment levels increase some crimes but not others.[9] For instance, Steven Raphael and Rudolf Winter-Ember report that the decline in property crime that was observed in the 1990s was largely due to falling unemployment rates. Others report negative relationships for some types of crimes,[10] while others find inconsistent or no association.[11] John Worral concluded, after considering a wide range of factors that should be taken into account when examining the association between unemployment and crime, that the effects of unemployment are "slow moving," its force being felt over extended time.[12] When this is taken into account, he concludes that unemployment rates do increase crime rates. One thing that we can be sure of is that researchers have not consistently found the simple relationship between unemployment and crime (the former increasing the latter) that the public expects, but the weight of the evidence does suggest that unemployment produces some additional crime. Recognizing these patterns—or more accurately, the limited pattern—recent work has more broadly examined the connection between the economy and crime, in particular moving beyond the question of whether people have jobs or not. One strand of this research considers the types of jobs that people hold and the characteristics of their employment. This focus has been timely because as the economies of the US and other traditional manufacturing nations have changed, political conversations have increasingly been about the kinds of jobs that are available to workers. The popular political call for more "family-wage jobs" has paralleled the emergence of the publication of research on the stratification of labor and its effects on crime. Both the politicians (sometimes) and the researchers now recognize the importance of not just a job, but a high-quality job.

Another important research strand has used other economic indicators to get a handle on how crime is related to the economy. For example, economists Philip Cook and Gary Zarkin examined business cycles and found that particular types of crimes responded differently to economic changes. Burglary and robbery increased when things were down, but auto theft increased with better times.[13] They also found that violent crime (with the exception of robbery) was unresponsive to changes in business cycles. Richard Rosenfeld and Robert Fornango reported that consumer confidence is a more reliable predictor of changes in criminal behavior than unemployment rates.[14] As consumers become more confident, they contribute to a more robust economy, which leads to decreases in robbery and property crimes. Rosenfeld and Fornango believe that high consumer confidence explains an important part of the "great crime decline" that we witnessed during the 1990s.

These and other studies have increasingly pointed us toward development of a more complex understanding of how economic forces are related to crime rates and criminality. This is especially so for violent crime. Does the economy or work matter for homicide, assault, and rape? I think so, and in the coming pages I'll try to make that case.

The Stratification of Labor

Part of what makes the Walters of the world behave the way they do and causes the Robby Widemans to be frustrated by their circumstance is a combination of what's inside of them—goals, aspirations, drives, and beliefs, but also what their communities are like—along with the nature of and amount of opportunities available, educational options, role models, and network connections to jobs. In turn, these options and opportunities are affected by the local labor market, the nation's labor market, and increasingly in recent decades, global forces. These economic and social forces come together to determine the options that are available to young people, and they help to determine how they will react to those options, including work options and criminal options.

The labor stratification and crime thesis emphasizes that all jobs are not created equal and that there is not open competition for jobs. Building on dual labor market theory, which was developed to explain why some groups, notably but not exclusively marginalized minorities, are persistently poor, disadvantaged in competing for jobs, and in the economy more broadly, the labor stratification thesis leads us to study how joblessness, unemployment, and job quality together influence crime and criminality.

Central to dual labor market theory arguments is an oversimplified distinction between primary and secondary sector jobs.[15] Primary sector jobs are characterized by relatively higher pay (family-wage jobs), good-benefits, and a measure of job security, where employees have a reasonable expectation of future employment and perhaps even promotion. Often workers in such jobs begin in low, entry-level positions and with time and seniority their pay, benefits, and perhaps most importantly their job security, increases. Included in this category are a wide range of occupations from the classic professions of law and medicine to the blue-collar industrial jobs that many twentieth-century American families built middle-class lifestyles on. In the Homewood that John Edgar Wideman grew up in, many men held primary sector jobs in Pittsburgh's steel industry.

In the case of professions, income, security, and benefits are a function of training and credentials. In the case of many blue-collar workers, the characteristics of their jobs were a consequence of the labor movement and the combination of the health of their employing industry and the negotiating power of their union. Between the poles of the classic professions and unskilled, blue-collar unionized work the other primary sector jobs are arrayed, based on the extent to which positive benefits accrue because of characteristics of the job and those of individuals occupying them, and the characteristics of the industry and the social organization of workers and work. With deindustrialization, it is the loss of primary sector jobs that has hurt people, families, and communities. In many instances, when primary sector jobs disappear there is increased competition for secondary sector jobs.

Primary sector jobs are the right stuff for building a middle class, and for conforming lifestyles. They are the jobs that we value sufficiently to get to work regularly and on time. They are the positions that we value enough that they influence and structure our days and habits, and we build our lifestyles around them. As a consequence they are less conducive to crime. People who have to be at work on a job that they value are less likely to lead a life of carefree late nights in bars, on street corners, and in marginal company engaging in questionable behavior. In addition to the immediate consequences of such behaviors—exhaustion, hangovers, jail, injury—the loss of a valued job because one cannot regularly perform up to par, or is too often tardy, or a no-show, adds additional cost to more reprobate lifestyles. People with primary sector jobs have fewer motivations for involvement in low-end pecuniary and entrepreneurial crime, and are less likely to lead lifestyles conducive to the chance occurrences that typify much violent criminal behavior. It was to one of these jobs that I hoped my parolee, Walter, would find his way, but I fully expected him to instead end up in the secondary sector, if he found a job at all.

Such secondary sector jobs are low-paying, with few or even no benefits. Secondary sector workers' jobs have less security and employment is frequently unstable, and therefore occupants of these jobs are more likely to be in and out of work. The workplace is structured so that there are very limited opportunities for advancement. One does not easily build a promising career in a secondary sector occupation. Examples of these jobs are unskilled and nonunionized construction workers, many of whom are picked-up for day work; unbonded security guards; most gardeners; those hired temporarily to unload trucks; piecemeal workers; low-end restaurant jobs (not professional waiters in swanky upscale eateries); and frequently retail workers, especially those in some "big box" stores. The prototypical secondary sector job may well be employment in a fast-food restaurant—thus the title "McJobs" that has been used popularly to denote low-end employment.[16]

While primary sector jobs give one a good income, a prospective career, and something additional to lose, there is little to lose should one be fired from a secondary sector position. In other words, McJob holders are liberated from having to worry so much about being able to perform well or even up to par. When the fed-up boss fires them for being late or too often a no-show, little is lost. As a result these people have motivations, because of sparse wages, to dabble in larceny and to seize opportunities to moonlight as a street corner drug dealer. Also, without the constraints of a job worth losing, they can more freely lead a "street" lifestyle that increases their chances of becoming involved in violence.[17] Steven, a parolee living in a rural Pennsylvania county, had a McJob prior to prison. He and his buddies supplemented their meager incomes with the proceeds from burglaries. It wasn't so much that they needed more money, but a feeling of nothing to lose, of "Why not" or "What the hell?"

It is important to emphasize that instability is a characteristic of secondary sector jobs. Perhaps one of the reasons that unemployment has been inconsistently found to be related to crime is that it is too limited a concept. People who tend to be employed in secondary sector jobs frequently cycle in and out of work. Whether a person is classified as a secondary sector worker or unemployed according to the decennial US census or the monthly Current Population Survey (CPS) is more a function of the current work circumstance of a respondent when they fill out the questionnaire or are interviewed by a census employee.[18] In earlier work I found utility in a study of Seattle neighborhoods in not distinguishing between secondary sector workers and the unemployed, and in that analysis the two variables were combined.[19] The labor stratification and crime perspective argues that it is this instability of employment (secondary sector work, unemployment, and being completely out of the labor market), or labor market marginality, combined with the lack of desirability (value) of secondary sector jobs, that is criminogenic.

The traditional unemployment rate statistic is too narrow in the other direction as well (in addition to failing to count secondary sector workers who cycle in and out of work), because this frequently used and reported statistic represents the number of people currently out of work and searching for work.[20] Three important groups of people are left unaccounted for in the widely publicized unemployment rate used in research: those who are working part-time but desire full-time employment; discouraged workers (people who have given up on the legal labor market and are no longer looking for gainful employment, such as Walter until I cracked down on him, though the effect didn't last); and those who, when employed, work at jobs that are below the radar of the state bureaucracy. Examples of this last group are the large number of men in many cities who are day workers. These men gather at understood places in the hope of being hired to work for a few hours, almost always off the books. Today, home improvement stores such as Home Depot and Lowes Home Improvement Stores frequently draw these workers. Both the men hoping to be hired and potential employers know where prospective workers gather. Typically a jobber, the person hiring, will drive up in a pickup truck and say that he needs five guys. Either the first five into the truck or the five that he selects from the crowd will work that day for low wages, no benefits, and without the protection of systems such as workmen's compensation and unemployment insurance.

Elliot Liebow's classic study *Talley's Corner* tells the story of day laborers in Washington, DC in the early 1960s.[21] Talley and his buddies worked irregularly in this system and in other secondary sector jobs. The day worker system continues to function in many cities. In Seattle along Second Avenue, African American, Latino, and white men gather near the Millionaire Club in the hope of finding a day's work. The Millionaire Club is an assistance program for unemployed or homeless people.[22] In upscale Santa Barbara, California, mostly Mexican men gather within a few blocks of the scenic beaches for the same purpose. These men in Santa Barbara, Seattle's "millionaires," and Talley and company are marginalized workers, but many of them do not appear in most of our statistics, not even those reported in recent studies that have sought to broaden our conceptualization of the relationship between work and crime. Day workers frequently do not appear because they are difficult for survey workers to find (many are homeless, very mobile, or of questionable immigration status); as mentioned above, employers do not pay into government systems for them; and many, when they work, are paid off the books, in cash. As a result, even these broadening studies are inherently conservative and thus may underestimate the effect of labor marginality on crime and crime rates.

A word about illegal labor markets and the underground or shadow economy in general is in order. The later includes the former, but they are not synonymous. The underground economy includes all sorts of off-the-books work, including the employment queues described above; the large number of black, Latina, Asian, and white women who clean houses or, to use their vernacular, who do "days work"; and jitney drivers in Pittsburgh's black communities (for a vivid portrayal see August Wilson's *Jitney*).[23] Also in the off-the-books economy are those who labor as entrepreneurs (e.g., back-ally mechanics, beauticians and barbers who do hair in their homes) and hustlers (e.g., pimps, prostitutes, fences, and bookmakers).[24] Criminologist Jeffrey Fagan and economist Richard Freeman, reviewing a large number of both quantitative and qualitative studies, concluded that many young criminals "double up" by earning money in both the legitimate and illegitimate economies.[25] Fagan and Freeman argue that these options should not be seen as either-or, but rather as a continuum used by some to gain income. Indeed, a number of petty burglars on my adult parole caseload did just that. They worked low-wage, sometimes temporary jobs, and when opportunities to steal or fence something came along, they took advantage of it. My parolee Steven, whom I introduced earlier, and his buddies did just this. People move farther along this continuum toward the illegal end where wages are lower, jobs are less stable, and employment is less promising—where the local labor market is more stratified.

The following example helps to explain how I believe that the stratification of labor works at the individual level to increase the probability that nonpecuniary crime may occur. Consider the options on a 1975 weekday night of two young Pittsburgh men.[26] The first is an entry-level, unionized steel mill worker. He has been told that when he accrues six months of seniority that he can "put in" to be moved from the labor crew (sweeping, cleaning, and doing some of the most undesirable tasks in the mill) to an apprenticeship for one of the semiskilled or even skilled positions that pay better and have better working conditions. The union, long ago, negotiated a good medical plan and generous salaries, even for those in entry-level jobs. Workers in the mill are members of the United Steel Workers of America, a union that historically had been successful at protecting the jobs and benefits of its members.

The second young man is employed by a fast-food franchise. As is typical of these employers there are few benefits, the pay is low, and there is little or no expectation on the part of this or any other employee of advancement within the company. If he stays around for a while and is lucky, he may someday become an assistant manager, which pays marginally better than he currently makes working the counter (though even as assistant manager and even perhaps someday as manager, he will spend a considerable amount of time at that counter or over the fryer).

Both men are approached in the late evening by out-of-work friends to go out with the boys and have a few drinks. Our steelworker, as much as he would like to join his friends, considers and declines because he *must* be on time for his day turn shift, and he cannot arrive hung over.[27] His job, with its present and potential future benefits, has given him a stake in conformity that leads him to a decision to not accept the invitation—not because he differs from his friends on values or beliefs, but because his job has value.

The second young man considers the opportunity to socialize with friends and in the context of his McJob. He accepts. If he is late for work or even fails to show, what does he lose? If fired he can simply go to the fast-food franchise across the street and get a job of equally dubious quality. Obviously the characteristics of the second person's employment do not provide the same stake in conformity that the first young man's job does.

When the boys go out for the evening, there may be no intention to engage in crime. But when they are in a tavern, or a pool hall, or on a street corner having consumed alcohol, two of the routine elements for the increased probability of crime occurring are present.[28] This group of young males, the most likely group to engage in and to be victimized by crime, includes both the motivated actors and the potential victims of crime. They may assault, even kill one another; they may mug or be mugged by others. Recall how the night of partying Walter and his drinking buddy began ended: in prison sentences.

For a contemporary version of this example I would not use a steel-worker. To illustrate how the American labor market has changed I, living in Seattle, would illustrate it using a Boeing worker, or a tech worker at Microsoft or for one of the biogenetics firms that every city, in every state is trying to attract. But it is critical to recognize that these jobs, unlike the low-skilled jobs that were available in abundance dur-ing the heyday of the industrial era, require considerably more human capital and frequently cultural capital than did those industrial jobs. So, workers in primary sector jobs are, on even more dimensions, socially further away from their age contemporaries working, or not even work-ing at all, on the margins of the labor force.

The example highlights three things about the labor stratification and crime thesis. First, it is in the company of others who are also mar-ginalized from the labor market that unstable work or joblessness is most criminogenic. Being out of work or employed in the secondary sector alone can be correlated with crime, but this context of the com-pany of others so situated appears to amplify the effect.[29] Second, the young men in this scenario did not set out for an evening of criminal-ity or, to borrow a pejorative concept from the 1990s, "wilding."[30] They instead have lifestyles that are conducive to becoming more involved in crime as both perpetrators and victims. They also may elect to engage in pecuniary crime when among their friends, but with this example I want to emphasize the spontaneity of crime that can occur as a result of lifestyles that are in part determined by labor stratification. Third, these are not two young men from separate cultures or subcultures. Their val-ues are roughly the same; what differentiates them is only their occupa-tional circumstance.

In the example above of two youthful workers, I alluded to the routine activities perspective developed by Lawrence Cohen and Marcus Felson. This perspective was first developed to illustrate why some segments of the population were more likely to be the victims of crime. Crime and victimization are more likely with the confluence of motivated actors, potential victims, and an absence of competent guardians. The motivated actors do not necessarily *need* to have set out to commit crimes; their motivation may stem from a situation that presents an opportunity previously uncontemplated. The guardians do not *need* to be the police; they may be anyone, including members of the general public, who may be perceived to be able to act against the furtherance of the crime. Regularly passing pedestrians or even watchful neighbors are at times very effective guardians. A classic example of the use of this perspective is the explanation of why taxi cab drivers have a high probability of victimization. Their job (they are the potential victim, with proceeds from earlier fares) demands that they pick up people who are unknown to them (some potentially motivated to commit crimes), who then direct them to drive to a place designated by the passenger (easily a place without guardians). In our example young men, going out for an evening of fun, may go to bars or pubs if they are old enough, or if under the legal drinking age (and if they cannot find a bartender willing to not card them or one who will not look closely at a fake ID) are likely to drink in hidden, out-of-the-way places. Either in the case of bars or in these hidden drinking spots, the confluence of motivated actors, potential victims, and a lack of guardians are more likely to be present. Again, lifestyle patterns that make this confluence more likely will occur when you have a critical mass of marginalized workers not bonded to work, with no good job to lose.

The importance of the critical mass of unemployed, secondary sector, underemployed, and discouraged workers that needs to be present to form the "situation of company" that is conducive to crime should be emphasized.[31] The reason that deindustrialization has hurt some communities so much more than others is because the jobs that are lost from a city, state, or nation and the negative consequences that accompany these losses are neither randomly nor evenly distributed. They are concentrated among already disadvantaged segments of the population and they are geographically visited upon particular, usually already weakened, communities. Remember that dual labor market theory, upon which this thesis is based, was initially developed to help to explain the continuing, not infrequently multigenerational disadvantage of particular segments of the population. Effected groups are certainly not limited to stigmatized minorities, but in many western nations such groups disproportionably bear the weight of racially and ethnically inequitably structured labor markets.

Because labor in the US has been and continues to be stratified by race and ethnicity, labor marginality is a state concentrated among minority populations. For example, African Americans have historically been overly employed in secondary sector jobs. With deindustrialization the competition for these heretofore unwanted jobs increased. Consequently, some African Americans lost primary sector industry jobs, increasing the competition for their neighbors' low-paying unattractive (or at least less attractive) jobs. Deindustrialization rippled through black communities.[32] Those displaced workers could compete more successfully for the remaining secondary sector jobs, so those who had filled jobs at the margins were frequently pushed out of the labor market. Also, because the US remains a highly residentially segregated society, the combination of dislocation from both primary and secondary sector jobs has been geographically concentrated in African American and to some extent, Latino communities.

Similar patterns have been observed in other western nations that have visible minorities. In the UK, France, the Netherlands, Germany, and elsewhere labor markets are ethnically stratified. Those nations, too, have experienced industrial squeezes as a result of deindustrialization and globalization. Some believe that the social unrest that has occurred in some nations of Western Europe is a consequence of such changes, and the continued labor market marginalization of ethnic minorities. Perhaps crime, too, in addition to unrest, is or may soon be a result.

I should say a bit about the processes associated with labor stratification when power and privilege is reserved for a minority group—South Africa, before and during apartheid, being the prototypical example. There a downtrodden black majority and two stigmatized, very minimally more privileged minorities—Coloureds (people of mixed race parentage) and Asians—were lorded over by minority whites who maintained, by the threat of and frequent use of force, economic and political power, a stratified system of labor that concentrated disadvantage socially and geographically even more efficiently than in the countries of the northern and western hemispheres. As a result, there too the concentration of disadvantaged persons is critically important in the genesis of criminality.

One is struck when traveling in postapartheid South Africa by the widespread belief that crime has become a major social problem.

Bumper stickers and graffiti call for reestablishment of the death penalty for murders and rapists. In Johannesburg there is great fear of car-
jacking, and nearly everyone you speak with has a story of a relative,
friend, acquaintance, or "someone that a friend of mine knows" who
has been the victim of a horrific crime.[33] These stories and the feelings
that they are linked to are told in the cities and townships, the small
towns, and in the rural areas. I asked villagers and the patrons of a she-
been (the unlicensed, under apartheid, pubs in townships and tribal
areas that continue to operate under questionable legal status) if the
fear of crime and the get-tough-on-criminals attitudes I saw articulated on walls and cars differed by race. After exclaiming surprise at my
question, they strongly said "no" and insisted that these feelings were
widespread among whites, Coloureds, and blacks. They attributed the
perceived increase in crime to the more relaxed enforcement resulting
from the shift from social control practices of the Nationalists Party
(the party of apartheid) to those of the criminal justice system established by the African National Congress (the party of Mandela).[34] They
also cited poverty and "all *those* people" who have come to South Africa
from other countries as criminogenic forces. So, while common citizens of the new South Africa do not attribute the crime directly to the
racialized politics of the past, the practices of the old regime continue
to reverberate through the people's perception of government. The sha-
been patrons anxiously await change, but even though they don't often
use the language of contemporary sociologists, they nevertheless recognize that the legacy of poverty and unequal access to quality education and the labor market that were central to the system of apartheid
contribute to contemporary problems. And while most people do not
know if new policies and migrants from other countries have in fact
led to real increases in violent crimes, the anecdotal evidence certainly
indicates that the people perceive this to be so.

The Stratification of Labor and Crime

The Homewood section of Pittsburgh, the childhood home of John and
Robby Wideman, was a place that some among the relatively few pros-
perous African Americans moved to in the decades after World War II.[35]
Homewood, which had black residents as early as the mid-nineteenth

century, was one of several alternatives to the older center of Pittsburgh's black community, The Hill District, which sits just above the downtown central business and commercial district (quite literally just up the hill; "uptown," as some have referred to it). The Hill, as it is popularly known, was organized like the typical northern African American community and included sections for all of the black social classes. Among those who came of age on The Hill were playwright August Wilson, legal scholar Derrick Bell, jazz guitarist George Benson, and your far less eminent author. The Lower Hill, much of which was wiped away by America's first rounds of urban renewal in the 1950s, was densely populated by very poor people. As one ascended the hill one also ascended the class strata of the community—with the exception of the federal housing projects, which ran along two-thirds of the northern edge of the community—until reaching Schenley Heights, home of the city's few 1950s and 60s–era black professionals. In the postwar years, the bounds of residential segregation were not removed but they weakened, allowing some African Americans to find homes outside of The Hill, Homewood, and the North Side, another established black community. Among the places that they moved to were suburbs that bordered Homewood.

Even before the collapse of big steel, these communities had the problems of inner-city neighborhoods including poverty, crime, family disruptions, and drugs. I was stunned as a young parole agent, a couple of years out of school, when I went to Penn State to attend a federally funded training program. There I met several probation officers from Allegheny County, where Pittsburgh is located. One of them went through her caseload, asking: "Do you know _____ or _____ or _____?" A distressing number of those she was supervising on probation were from my high school.

Although Homewood, The Hill, and neighborhoods like them in Pittsburgh and in other American industrial cities were places of hope early on, the decline of blue-collar jobs has been catastrophic for many individual residents, for families, and for those communities as a whole. Homewood now has broad stretches that are best described as underclass neighborhoods (or alternatively, for those that think that concept is too pejorative, they are populated by the ghetto poor). Like the state of Pennsylvania in which it is located, Pittsburgh and its poorest neighborhoods lost population in the 1980s and 90s. Presumably some, if not most, of that loss is a result of people moving to find more promising job opportunities in other parts of the country. Those left behind have prospects that are inferior to those of the middle- and working-class people who lived there in the post-World War II period. The economic decline stretches to those suburbs that border Homewood, which were places of relative prosperity for post-Great Migration movers. Wilkinsburg and Penn Hills, black middle-class communities in the 1960s, now have problems of unemployment, crime, and drugs that were historically associated with inner-city neighborhoods. The Hill and Homewood have suffered as a result of job losses and at the same time they have high crime rates, and they were places where the crack cocaine epidemic of the late 1980s and early 90s resulted in considerable damage to the social and economic lives of residents and businesses.

What happened during recent decades is that jobs in the steel industry and those in ancillary industries have dried up. Also, jobs in service establishments near the mills, which depended on steelworkers as customers, have closed or reduced their number of employees. Fast-food restaurants, coffee shops, and bars frequently clustered across or just down the streets from mill entrances. Places that afforded a cup of coffee and a sandwich at the beginning of a shift, and a shot and "an Iron" (Iron City beer, a long-time Pittsburgh favorite) at the end, lost their clientele to deindustrialization; many of these places have now folded too. In recent decades there has been what sociologists Arne Kalleberg calls a "polarization in job quality." He writes:

> This polarization is not new, but the duality between the primary and secondary labor markets has increased along with the disappearance of relatively low-skill, traditional, middle-class jobs with good pay and benefits, job stability, and steady promotions. The decline of the middle class has reversed the predictions of the theory of embourgeoisement, which predicted that the working class would be integrated into the middle class. Due to their greater reliance on increasingly uncertain jobs, the American middle class; has come to resemble the classic proletariat.[36] In particular, "subordinate primary labor market" jobs are among those most threatened by corporate restructuring and downsizing, and no longer enjoy the institutional protections once provided by unions.[37]

There has been a net decline in the number of employed people in the working-class sections of Pittsburgh, just as there has in Chicago, Detroit, Cleveland, and other industrial cities of the East and Midwest. Good blue-collar (primary sector) jobs have been replaced by secondary sector jobs, when they have been replaced at all. Industrial workers who could not leave the area are far more likely to be employed in the service sector today if they have work at all. This means that the large number of people formerly employed in available service sector jobs now must compete with laid-off steelworkers and those now coming of labor market age who might have sought mill jobs in earlier decades. The end result is a shift of employment distribution in working-class communities from a higher proportion of blue-collar jobs to a largely service sector—and this is especially so in black neighborhoods. They also have comparatively higher proportions of adults who are unemployed or discouraged workers. To be sure, the end of the twentieth century and the first decade of the twenty-first have witnessed growth in corporate and corporate service jobs in Pittsburgh, but these positions are not available to the traditional, displaced, low-skilled Pittsburgh workforce.

Table 2.1 presents labor force characteristics for The Hill, Homewood, Pittsburgh, and the state of Pennsylvania. Readers should remember that the entire state of Pennsylvania has been hard-hit by deindustrialization. An important consequence has been the departure of many of those who could move to find work elsewhere, so the denominator in all of these percentages have had some of the most vital, competitive people removed. The City of Pittsburgh is substantially worse off than the rest of the state in terms of the number of people employed. It is only with the percentage of secondary sector workers that the city is slightly better off (a smaller percentage of employed persons in secondary sector jobs) than the state (column 4), and this is likely a product of its decreased number of jobs (columns 1 through 3) rather than because there are a large number of industrial jobs.

But it is Homewood and The Hill that I really want to focus on. There, general unemployment rates are twice the city's high rate. And while the state and the city have large percentages of adult men who are not working, the more than 60 percent of Homewood and Hill District men who are not in the labor force can only be called stunning. This

Table 2.1. Year 2000 Labor Force Characteristics for Pennsylvania, Pittsburgh, and Select Neighborhoods

	Percent 16+ Civilians Unemployed	Percent 16+ Male Civilians Unemployed	Percent 16+ Male Civilians Not Working	% 16+ Employed Civilians Secondary Sector Jobs
Homewood	18.7	21.4	60.7	38.2
Hill District	18.1	20.3	60.2	30.4
Pittsburgh	10.1	10.3	43.4	22.3
Pennsylvania	5.7	5.7	34.8	24.5

Definition of secondary sector jobs (following Peterson and Krivo. 2010.):
Employed in six occupations with lowest mean incomes (health care support, food preparation and serving-related occupations, building and grounds cleaning and maintenance, personal care and service, farming, fishing annd forestry, and transportation and material moving).
Census tracts:
Homewood: 1301, 1302, 1303, 1304, 1207
Homewood North, Homewood South, Homewood West
Hill Districts: 501, 506, 305, 510, 511, 509
Middle Hill, Upper Hill, Crawford-Roberts, Terrace Village, and Bedford Dwellings
Source: U.S. Census

table illustrates how concentrated the effects of deindustrialization have been on these two already fragile communities.

What has happened is a concentration in Homewood, and communities like it, of people marginal to the labor market. This concentration has made Homewood socially look more like the older, earlier center of Black Pittsburgh, The Hill District. They are communities of high poverty and despair. There are few of the services that one expects to find in urban residential communities. There are abandoned houses and apartment buildings, and weeds infest empty lots that used to be housing sites. For example, in The Hill District there has not been a substantial supermarket since the 1968 riots that shook this and many other cities in the wake of the assassination of Martin Luther King Jr.[38] Residents, many of whom do not have cars, have to travel miles to do basic grocery shopping. Their only community alternatives are small, comparatively poorly stocked corner grocery stores.

Imagine the implications for young people of these communities. The prospects for the future of a middle- or high-school aged child are reasonably dampened by seeing the experience of parents and other adults, and especially from watching the kinds of jobs that those who are just a bit older than they are get—or far too often, do not get. Our question is: What are the crime consequences for people and communities of these patterns?

Map 2.1 shows the distribution of adults who are out of work in Pittsburgh census tracts. The tracts that comprise Homewood and The Hill District are noted.[39] If we define adult joblessness above sixty percent as "hyperjoblessness," we see that except for these two neighborhoods, only a sprinkling of others falls into this category. One of those areas, the North Side, is historically much like The Hill and Homewood. During the 1960s teenagers from these three neighborhoods viewed each other as rivals and sometimes clashed in ways that contemporary media and police would call gang conflicts (though it is not at all clear that there were actual gangs active in the sense that gangs have been a part of some cities' social landscape, such as in Chicago and Los Angeles). Recently the North Side has been "urban renewed," and segments of it, where new stadiums have been erected and the Andy Warhol (a Pittsburgh native) Museum has opened, along with

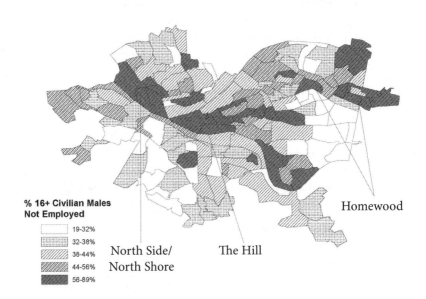

% 16+ Civilian Males
Not Employed

    19-32%
    32-38%
    38-44%
    44-56%
    56-89%

North Side/
North Shore

The Hill

Homewood

Map 2.1. Employment in Pittsburgh Neighborhoods

restaurants and bars that cater to the patrons of these attractions, has been dubbed "the North Shore." I can't help but wonder what longtime residents of Manchester and other North Side neighborhoods think about this reinvention.

Homewood, The Hill, and the North Side, the three predominantly black neighborhoods within the city, include census tracts that are characterized by hyperjoblessness. Pittsburgh's postdeindustrialization despair, which has been felt throughout most of the city, is concentrated into these three communities.

Communities and Crime

In recent years sociologists and criminologists have come back to addressing the importance of social context in their explanations of crime patterns. Modern criminology's roots are in Clifford Shaw and Henry McKay's and their Chicago School colleagues' efforts to explain why some areas of cities had high rates of crime and delinquency even though the populations and ethnic groups that occupied those spaces changed over time.[40] During much of the last half of the twentieth century, criminologists did not put much stock in social disorganization theory, the perspective developed by Chicago School sociologists to explain distributions of urban crime. Contemporary variants of disorganization theory though have found new life among criminologists. There has long been a gap between social scientists who argued on the one side for social disorganization theory or other social structure explanations for crime, and those that advanced primarily social cultural explanations. New variants of disorganization theory do a good job of bridging this gap. They have emphasized how variations in social structure and community organization lead both to crime and to belief systems (a hallmark of social culture), which then also helps to generate, or at least perpetuate, high levels of social problems (including crime). For example, in their effort to explain persistently high African American violence rates, Robert Sampson and William Julius Wilson state:

> The basic thesis is that macro-social patterns of residential inequality give rise to the social isolation and ecological concentration of the truly

disadvantaged, which in turn leads to structural barriers and cultural adaptation that undermine social organization and hence the control of crime. The thesis is grounded in what is actually an old idea in criminology that has been overlooked in the race and crime debate—the importance of communities.[41]

They go on to explain how joblessness contributes indirectly to violence because of its damming influence on marriage rates and family formation, which in turn contributes to community disorganization and high levels of violence. As I have written above, I believe that joblessness and labor market marginality, both consequences of the stratification of labor, are important determinants of criminality and crime rates because of how they affect the day-to-day lifestyles of individuals, but also because of the way these forces change communities.

In a study of 1980 neighborhood violent crime rates in Seattle, I found that residents' employment was as important, perhaps even more important, than either poverty or income inequality.[42] After all, the collective disadvantage of communities—poverty, low incomes, welfare dependence, disrupted families—are in large measure there because residents are jobless or have very low-end employment. In that analysis I used census tract data to simulate neighborhoods.[43] Seattle census tracts that had relatively large proportions of adults who were classified as being in marginal work had higher rates of violent crime such as murders, aggravated assaults, forcible rapes, and robberies. The proportion of marginal workers was defined as the percent of the census tract adult population that was either unemployed or who were workers in secondary sector jobs.[44] Marginal work significantly predicted violent crime rates after taking into account the percent of the population that was nonwhite, families living in poverty, and income inequality.[45] I did not conclude that my results mean that poverty and income inequality were spurious, but rather that labor stratification is an important reason that those low-income neighborhoods exists. After all, the incomes of the people in a neighborhood, their poverty level or their wealth, is a function of their work and positions in the labor market. And the level of income inequality that characterizes a city or sets of neighborhoods is a consequence of the overall stratification of the local labor market. I do not believe that the relationships between crime and income indicators, poverty and income inequality, are spurious because they, in conjunction with the stratification of labor, lead to or exacerbate inequalities and create higher levels of violent crime. These are important structural inequities that can lead to the kinds of neighborhoods that Anderson describes, where cultural patterns and codes of the streets emerge as a consequence of long-term collective disadvantage.[46]

With colleagues, I replicated the earlier Seattle study of neighborhood violent crime using 1990 data.[47] In that study we also compared the results in Seattle with parallel analyses of neighborhood labor market participation and crime (specifically homicide) in Cleveland, Ohio and Washington, DC. These three cities provide useful contrast on several dimensions: they represent different types of local labor markets, they are in different regions of the US, and they have very different crime patterns.

The difference in local labor markets is quite important. How individuals or groups of people within a city fare when they search for work depends on the kinds of jobs that are available. In the early 1970s, my parole agent colleagues in Erie Pennsylvania could find jobs for some of the men on our caseloads at the iron foundries that existed near the lake. Those employers, located there because of the cheap transportation of raw materials along the Great Lakes, liked our guys because we were built-in enforcers, increasing attendance at jobs that were painfully hot in summer and cold in winter (open-shed foundries with wind blowing off of the frozen lake front), dirty, and dangerous. Those foundries are gone now, casualties of deindustrialization. I wonder where, if at all, unskilled parolees might find work in Erie's local labor market today.

Earlier I commented that the Homewood section of Pittsburgh had lost population when jobs disappeared. Those who fled the downturn in jobs were, as politicians sometimes say, "voting with their feet" for locations with more prosperous economies. The cities that suffered most during the initial phases of deindustrialization were the same cities that attracted workers from the southern and midwestern hinterlands earlier in the century. Those cities attracted workers then and lost them later, because of the employment opportunities that were there and have now declined. Old-style, heavy industry attracted unskilled workers who could get wages that they had never dared to dream of. This was a function of the characteristics of the local labor market, which are a direct result of the nature of industries located in the cities of what we now call the Rust Belt. The same processes later drew software engineers to Silicon Valley, farm workers to California and Florida, and theme park workers to Orlando.

Seattle, Cleveland, and Washington represent very different types of local labor markets. Seattle, with Boeing Aircraft, Microsoft and other software producers, biotechnology, and shipping, has what might be considered a twenty-first-century economy. Cleveland, like Erie Pennsylvania, is a Great Lakes port city that took advantage of its location for easy shipping from Minnesota and Wisconsin iron ore mines to become a major steel producer. Like cities similar to it, a host of other industries developed in Cleveland because big steel was there. Washington's industry is government. There are, to be sure, many other business there, but the city was founded as the seat of the federal government and the defining characteristic of the local labor market is the government jobs that employ locals and attract related businesses.

Regarding two other notable differences between the three cities, Cleveland is in the industrial Midwest, Seattle is emblematic of the West in a number of ways, and Washington is, as the nation's capital, a place unto itself. Selected as the capital because it was in the South (the land had belonged to Virginia), its character is both southern and at the same time eastern. Cleveland's crime rate at the time of that analysis was high by national standards. Seattle has a relatively low violent crime rates, but high-recorded property crime. Washington is a high-crime city with especially high rates of homicide and rape.

Our analyses of these three cities differed from my earlier paper in several notable ways. Here the dependent variable was neighborhood homicide rates rather than violent crime rates. These analyses added measures of education (census tract high-school dropout rates), and they used data from the 1990 census of the population and tract crime statistics from each city's police department. The earlier study of 1980 violent crime in Seattle was comparatively early in the manufacturing decline in the US, so by comparison the 1990 data give us a picture after this decline was well along. We included an indicator of neighborhood educational levels in these analyses because by this time my thinking about the labor stratification and crime thesis had progressed to include more serious consideration of how patterns of employment might affect juvenile involvement in crime. In that part of the story education is a key component, so it was included in the study of these three cities.

I should note the reason for using homicide rates here. Criminologists have long recognized that different patterns of crime, police practices, and data collection procedures can make using crimes reported to police as a dependent variable problematic. Police exercise discretion in how they categorize, classify, and count crime events. One of the factors that influence this discretion is the local police culture. Since this is an analysis comparing three cities and focusing on census tract variation within those cities, we felt it best to restrict the study to a crime where less discretion is likely used (there's frequently a body to be accounted for) and one of the most accurately counted violent crimes, homicide.[48]

Essentially, the results of the earlier study of Seattle were replicated in the later time period. The same pattern of results was found. The distribution of labor in 1990 Seattle helped to explain where homicides occurred in the city. The labor stratification and crime thesis also helped to explain the homicide patterns in Cleveland, though not as well as in Seattle. Our posthoc speculation was that the results may have been weakened by the existence of large areas of inner-city Cleveland that were virtually uninhabited, presumably in part because of deindustrialization, and the loss of jobs and consequent depopulation.[49] In such places the number of residents who form the denominator to calculate a crime rate is unusually small, but these areas also have relatively large numbers of crimes, probably committed by residents at times, but more frequently than in most neighborhoods of cities by others taking advantage of the deteriorated depopulated state of the area. Our analysis found that in Cleveland, as in Seattle, places where relatively more marginal workers—secondary sector employees and the unemployed—lived had higher homicide rates than other places.

The labor stratification thesis did not successfully explain the distribution of homicide in Washington, DC. There are several possible reasons why. Homicide is significantly predicted by the percentage of the population that is black in Cleveland and Seattle, just as it is in analyses of violent crimes in other cities. Washington's black population is so large and it is so residentially segregated that other social variables are simply overwhelmed in the analyses.[50] Substantively, though, there are two other possible explanations. First, in both Seattle and Cleveland, the high-school dropout rates are normally distributed, with the average number of dropouts in the latter's tracts significantly higher than in the former's. But in Washington, the distribution is bimodal. Most Washington neighborhoods have very high dropout rates, but there are a small number of tracts with extremely low rates, and in these neighborhoods the level of education is inordinately high. This distribution captures the substantial inequality that characterizes the social structure of the US capital city. I have suggested that in terms of racial inequality, Washington, DC may be more like the apartheid cities of South Africa than like most other cities of the western industrialized world.[51] It has substantial social and economic inequalities that are very tied to racial residential segregation patterns. But since nearly all American cities have been and many continue to be characterized by hyperracial residential segregation, isn't it unfair to call Washington an "apartheid city?" The reason I use this characterization is because the American national capital carries exceptional scars and contradictions. The level of inequality is palpable there. In the figurative shadow of monuments and memorials along the National Mall, there are communities with infant mortality rates not appreciably better than in the Third World; there is hunger and homelessness, and schools that do not work. The voters and officials of the city only marginally control their own affairs. The Congress has the final say over much of Washington's governance, yet her citizens only have a nonvoting representative in the House of Representatives. Washington has and has long had a sizable black middle class, but their existence in their communities and enclaves does not counter the level of distress that people living in disadvantaged neighborhoods in the District experience.

This leads to the second potential substantive explanation for why the labor stratification thesis may not help to explain homicide in Washington. Washington may show the limit of the thesis. It may be that this perspective is useful in helping us to understand violent crime under certain social conditions, but that a city may pass beyond a threshold where the thesis has less utility. In Washington, the high level of persistent racial and class inequality may simply make labor market marginality moot because so many have so little hope and neighborhoods have been so very distressed for multiple generations.

Maps 2.2, 2.3, and 2.4 provide yet another update of the association between violent crime in Seattle neighborhoods and employment.[52] Employment data have been taken from the 2000 US census and violent crime statistics are from the Seattle Police Department's "Crimes Reported to the Police." Map 2.2 indicates the distribution in neighborhoods (census tracts) of the percentage of the population that was not working and the average annual violent crime rate is indicated by the size of the black ball in each tract. One can see that, just as was the case for 1980 and 1990, levels of violence are highest where more people are out of work. Those earlier analyses did not study people who were out of work or jobless, but rather what I called labor market marginality, the combination of unemployment and secondary sector employment. In Map 2.2 I have elected to display the total number of people who are out of work, because this is consistent with Wilson's analyses in *The Truly Disadvantaged* that focused not on the quality of jobs, but rather the simpler question of employment.[53] Map 2.3 is the same as Map 2.2, but here the joblessness of men is displayed. The patterns are the same, but they are starker. Violent crimes occur more often in those neighborhoods where large proportions of the men who live there are out of work. Map 2.4 is more comparable to the earlier studies of Seattle. Here is the percentage of men who are not in primary sector jobs; that is, they are in secondary sector occupations, they are officially unemployed, or they are simply jobless. Consistent with the notion that we must consider not only employment, but the quality of employment, we see again that those places where men are not in primary sector jobs—good jobs—violent crime is highest.

Maps 2.5 (Cleveland) and Map 2.6 (Washington, DC) are the same as Seattle's Map 2.4.[54] The neighborhood distribution of men not in primary sector jobs and violent annual violent crime rates are displayed. In 2000 Cleveland had considerably more communities with extremely high levels of labor market marginality than Seattle, but like the latter, the places where those Cleveland men live have high levels of violence. Some of the low employment—high-crime tracts in the section of east central Cleveland near but not on Lake Erie—constitutes the Hough neighborhood. Hough is the heart of black Cleveland. An upscale community in the early twentieth century, it became predominantly black and very poor in the years after the Great Depression. As large numbers of Great Migration movers arrived in Cleveland they moved into Hough and went to work in the city's mills and on its docks. In the mid-1960s Hough was ravaged by riots, and now the good jobs that earlier generations of Hough residents had are largely gone and there is a lot violent crime there.

Map 2.2. Employment
and Violent Crime in
Seattle: Percent Civilians
Not Employed in Census
Tracts

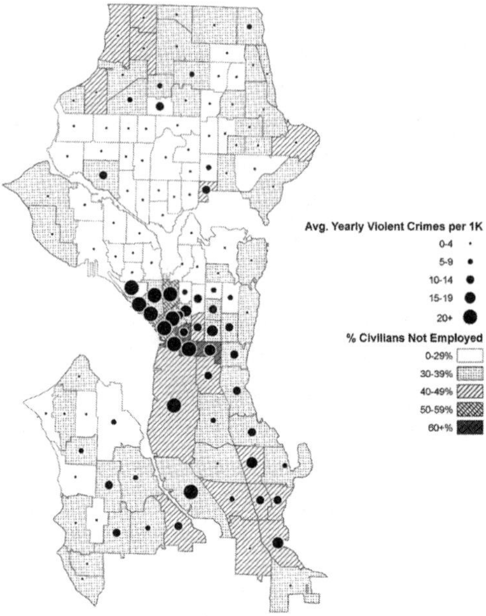

Map 2.3. Employment
and Violent Crime in
Seattle: Percent Civilian
Males Not Employed in
Census Tracts

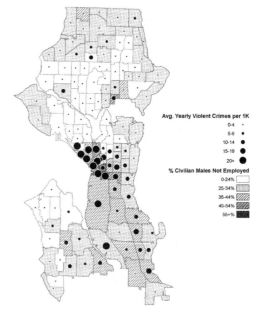

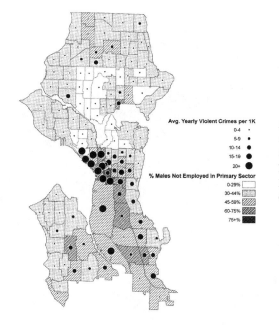

Map 2.4. Employment
and Violent Crime in
Seattle: Percent Males
Not Employed in
Primary Sector Jobs in
Census Tracts

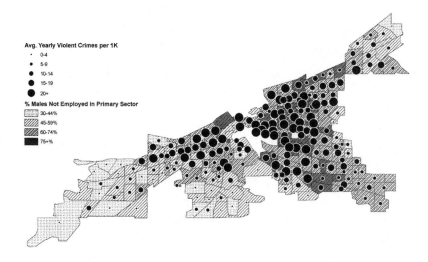

Map 2.5. Employment and Violent Crime in Cleveland: Percent Males Not Employed in
Primary Sector Jobs in Census Tracts

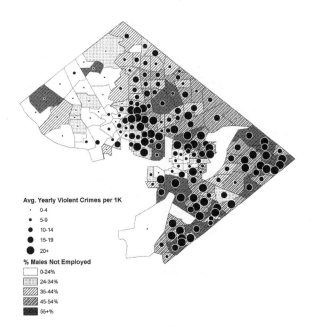

Map 2.6.
Employment and
Violent Crime in
Washington, DC:
Percent Males
Not Employed in
Primary Sector
Jobs in Census
Tracts

Washington (Map 2.6) clearly displays that the city has variation in the percentage of adult men who are not in primary sector jobs. In 2000 very high percentages of men were marginal to the DC labor market in neighborhoods in Southeast and Southwest Washington, and a not insignificant number of communities in Northeast and Northwest also had very high levels.[55] By contrast much of Northwest, which includes Georgetown, Foggy Bottom, and the stretch of Connecticut Avenue that houses Embassy Row, had very low rates of labor market marginalization. While there is correspondence between these neighborhood employment patterns and violence as there was in Seattle and Cleveland, Washington is different because much of its land area had large numbers of marginalized people living in it, like Cleveland, but it also had large expanses of neighborhoods with few or no marginal workers. Washington, more than the other two cities, is characterized by more substantial inequality across its neighborhoods. As was the case in earlier analyses of Washington, the percentage of blacks that lived in the neighborhood was still the important predictor of violence. Maps 2.7

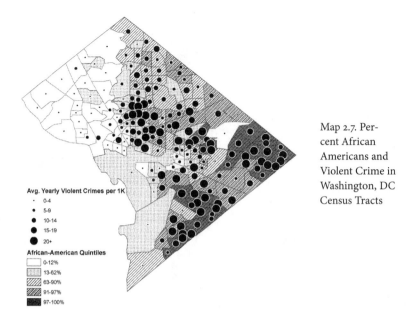

Map 2.7. Percent African Americans and Violent Crime in Washington, DC Census Tracts

and 2.8 show the percentages of residents in each Washington census tract who defined themselves as African Americans at the time of the 2000 census. Map 2.7 also includes indication of neighborhood violence rates, and Map 2.8 shows the level of male labor market marginality—men not in primary sector jobs—and the percentage of the population that was African American in those communities. Two things can be garnered from these latter two maps. First, it becomes clear why once the percentage of black residents is included in violence models that no other variable has a chance to be significant; and second, the high degree of correspondence between "black tracks" and high-employment marginality census tracts illustrates the degree to which Washington's socioeconomic inequality is cut very tightly along racial lines. The same pattern exists for the distribution of poverty and the proportion of adults who do not have at least a high-school education. Maps 2.7 and 2.8 present a clear picture of an American apartheid city. The capital of the United States of America is divided by race, by social class, and by violent crime victimization.

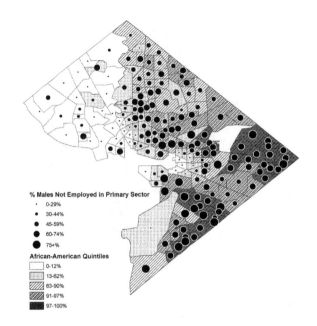

Map 2.8. Percent African Americans and Employment in Washington, DC: Percent of Males Not Employed in Primary Sector Jobs in Census Tracts

% Males Not Employed In Primary Sector
· 0-29%
• 30-44%
● 45-59%
● 60-74%
● 75+%

African-American Quintiles
0-12%
13-62%
63-90%
91-97%
97-100%

Broken Promises

Something that Washington, Cleveland, and Seattle have in common is that like Pittsburgh, Detroit, Chicago, and other eastern and midwestern cities, they were the Promised Land for strivers: African American migrants hoping for upward economic mobility, seeking jobs that would produce a better life for individuals and families. Cleveland, Washington, and Seattle differ, however, because of their varied industrial histories.

Cleveland is a classic Great Migration city. Like neighboring cities throughout the Midwest, it drew workers to its industries. Not only African Americans from the rural South, but also southern and Midwestern whites and Eastern and Southern European immigrants, were drawn to Cleveland and the hard work of the mills, plants, and docks. Even today, the city remains ethnically very heterogeneous. Cleveland residents could count on good, low-skilled jobs until the mid-1970s, when the processes of globalization and deindustrialization began moving jobs away from it and other industrial centers in the Rust Belt. Even before the resulting job losses Cleveland had rough neighborhoods with high crime rates, but it was not typically among the dubious national leaders in either violence or property violations.

Washington, which I uncomplimentarily refer to as an American apartheid city—not to disparage the citizens of the District, but America's ongoing race relations and the way that DC is managed by Congress makes it a not unfitting description—was early on a beacon to African Americans. It was founded to be the nation's capital, and its major industry remains government. Washington was one of the cities that freed slaves flocked to after the Civil War, even though earlier in its history there had been a substantial slave market there. Although labor there too was stratified, during the nearly one hundred years between emancipation and the modern civil rights movement, DC was known among African Americans as a place of opportunity. Thus the appeal to strivers, those looking to work hard as they devoted themselves to bettering their lives and those of their families. Earlier in the twentieth century than in most cities, a black middle class emerged in Washington. When the federal government began to consider African Americans for jobs that were not just the lowest end menial occupations (in the 1950s and 60s), more possibilities opened up. But in the 1960s crime also began to surge in Washington. By the turn of the twenty-first century, the District suffered from having among the nation's highest rates of homicide and rape.

Seattle is the Johnny-come-lately of these urban areas. It is a young city, founded in the middle of the nineteenth century but not even beginning to come of age until the Alaskan Gold Rush of the 1890s (and some would say not until after the 1962 World's Fair). Among Seattle's first big, successful businesses was timber, and also those that outfitted prospectors on the way to the gold fields and fleeced the few who actually returned with it. It was World War II that made Seattle a significant industrial city. Boeing Aircraft and the shipyards drew workers from other parts of the country. Although there was a very small African American population before that time, those who came to work in the war industries, and servicemen who discovered both Seattle and neighboring Tacoma when stationed there, produced substantial growth in the black community. Also, historically with relatively large Chinese, Japanese, and Filipino populations, Seattle's ethnic composition is different than most eastern and midwestern cities. Today the aerospace, hi-tech, and biotechnology industries compliment older concerns still working in manufacturing and in the bustling port. Seattle's crime patterns are not unlike that of other cities, but rates are comparatively low.

The strivers who came to these cities, as well as other places offering job opportunities, included the parents of John and Robby Wideman and the men and women who populated The Hill District of my youth. They found work that at the time seemed to fulfill the promise of better lives, but among their children were the fortunate—John Edgar Wideman, August Wilson, and many more, including myself—as well as those who choose less legitimate paths, such as Robby Wideman and Walter of my parole caseload, and many of my high-school classmates, some of whom sought work in Pittsburgh's steel mill based economy only to have hopes and dreams dashed with deindustrialization and the city's economic collapse. Among my high-school friends are those who could leave the city for better opportunities and others whose lives have been a continual struggle to find decent work, and still others who got strung out on heroin or crack, or turned to entrepreneurial crimes in the drugs or sex markets. The labor market marginalization that faced many immediately after deindustrialization and continues today is an important part of the story of what motivates those who choose a criminal path—Robby and Walter, and for those whose lives of economic marginalization makes crime conducive lifestyles more likely even if they never consciously decide to become criminals.

American cities attracted workers from other places—sections of the US, from Europe and Asia—because of the promise of good work. In varying degrees these promises have been both kept and broken over time, and the promises have been kept differently by race and ethnicity.

In this chapter I have described how employment influences lifestyle and how crime becomes more or less likely when a person is marginal to the labor force and living in close proximity with others who are also out of work, or who toil at less than promising jobs. In the next chapter I will dig a bit deeper into how urban patterns make a difference for individuals whose lives are lived and negotiated within the labor market.

3

Why Do They Do It?

The Potential for Criminality

Many people ask, "Why do they do it?" They are not inquiring about neighborhood rates of violence, but rather they want to know why an individual engages in crime. Why did Robby Wideman and his friends decide to shake down a fence, leading to his murder? Why did Walter mug an old man? After all, I didn't have neighborhoods on my parole caseload. I had individual clients, because individuals commit crimes. It is important to note that our understanding must take seriously the social ecology of crime, and it is clear that many politicians' and members of the general publics' reactions to crimes, as well as criminal justice solutions, do not adequately consider the social context in which perpetrators live, work, and violate the law. But it is also important to link that ecology to individual actions. When does the unemployment rate matter? How does the economy affect behavior? How do national and local labor markets affect individual actions? How specifically can we connect Robby's and Walter's behaviors to their social circumstances? Obviously the causes of their behavior are not solely a matter of their social circumstance or the labor market; the individual actor certainly matters too. Sociologically we are trying to understand why some individuals, in the context of their social environments, commit crimes. After all, most people, even among those from the most downtrodden places, do not engage in full-scale criminality.

I have described how holders of secondary sector jobs will tend to have lower stakes in conformity than primary sector jobholders. In the example of two young Pittsburgh men, I contrasted their respective feelings and attachments toward the places where they are working and their commitment to their jobs. Before going on, I need to more carefully examine how individuals link to their workplaces and why we might presume that primary sector and secondary sector workers differ in how these linkages are made and perpetuated, what this potentially means for criminality, and the evidence for these connections.

First, I should be careful to note that it is reasonable to expect that chronically unemployed and discouraged workers have even fewer stakes in conformity on average than even secondary sector workers. I do not know that we can make this same distinction for all unemployed people, since, as was pointed out earlier, secondary sector workers tend to move in and out of the ranks of the employed far more frequently than primary sector workers and even among those in some primary sector jobs, there are spells of unemployment.[1] Adults who are among the long-time unemployed or who have given up on the legitimate labor market are substantially different than people who find periodic work in the secondary sector or those who have been "RIFed" (fired due to a reduction in force) from what they thought were high-quality positions.[2] Consequently, I can reasonably assert that the chronically jobless will have positive motivations for crime (both pecuniary and entrepreneurial violations), and with their lower stakes in conformity, lifestyles that on average may be as conducive to criminality (including violent crime) as secondary sector workers and the inconsistently employed.

As I described earlier, primary sector jobs are characterized by better pay, stability, good benefits, and opportunities for promotion or advancement. According to Michael Piore, primary sector workers are also more likely to develop and maintain important social contacts with coworkers and in occupationally based associations, organizations, or networks.[3] Lawyers join bar associations, physicians routinely are members of local, state, and national medical associations, and most blue-collar industrial workers historically have belonged to unions.

In contrast, in the secondary sector of the labor market pay is typically low, benefits are few if any, there are little or no opportunities for advancement, and perhaps most importantly, the jobs are unstable.

These jobs are not designed for people to stay in them for long periods. Employers can easily replace workers because of the low-skill requirement and little or no training costs, and frequently do. Perhaps because of this instability, secondary sector workers' close friendships and networks tend to be developed in their neighborhoods, and close contacts are maintained with those who are where they come from.

A number of scholars have reported the results of research finding that primary sector workers do in fact tend to have higher incomes and experience less job turnover than people employed in secondary sector positions, but limited work has been published that addresses other important differences between the two sectors. I used the General Social Survey to examine some of these other differences.[4] Secondary sector workers are more likely to have been unemployed at some time during the past ten years, and to expect that their jobs might end within the next twelve months. They reported lower job satisfaction and indicated that their jobs were a less important part of their lives than did primary sector workers. Secondary sector employees spent more of their off-hours socializing with neighborhood friends, and the men were more likely to spend their evenings in taverns and bars than their primary sector counterparts. Clearly it is not just the income and job stability, both of which are very important, but other aspects of secondary sector employment that are associated with particular lifestyle patterns as well.

A criminologist reading the descriptions of these two occupation categories cannot help but think of social control theorists' assertions that people are less likely to become engaged in crime if they are bonded to important institutions and units of society: if they have something of value to lose if they participate in criminal activity.[5] For adults the workplace is such an important unit. In their life-course theory of crime and delinquency Robert Sampson and John Laub describe employment as an important social bond that inhibits criminality in young adults as they transition from the roles of children, where schools and family of origin are important units with which to bond.[6] As they move through the life course into more advanced years, jobs remain important.[7] A job is important for this bonding process, but all jobs are not created equal. A position that holds promise for the future—a primary sector job or family wage job—provides better bonding potential than work that does not.

Another important aspect of control theories is the notion of "stakes in conformity." While some control theorists literally mean by this a commitment to a dominant normative order—conventional concep-tions of what is right, wrong, and appropriate—I do not think it is nec-essary to go that far. When I say that primary sector jobs provide an important stake in conformity, I simply mean that these jobs provide something of such significant value that their occupants weigh its lost potential when deciding on behavior. At times this will mean that the person with something to lose will walk the straight and narrow. At other times they may focus on the probability of detection, or they may go to some effort to preserve the appearance of conformity. What is important for the labor stratification and crime thesis is not their com-mitment to the conventional normative order, but their recognition that it is important to protect a valued resource: their economic stake in conformity, their good job.

We must recognize that the movement into other adult patterns of life provides important stakes in conformity as well. Notably the estab-lishment of adult intimate relationships is a very important bond that inhibits criminality.[8] The capacity to have such a relationship, how-ever, is also tied to one's labor market success. William Julius Wilson noted that a major problem in underclass neighborhoods is the decline in the number of marriageable men. When men do not have jobs on which they can support a family, they are not good marriage pros-pects. The lack of jobs, when combined with the large numbers of Afri-can American men who are in prison and the relatively large number who die before their time, have caused a consequent unbalanced sex ratio and lowered marriage rates to become a major social problem in black America.[9] And dramatic increases in imprisonment in recent decades have increased divorce there, too.[10] These patterns are related to increases in poverty—especially children's poverty, the expansion of underclass neighborhoods, and, not surprisingly, to increases in crime and delinquency.

When young adults work in the secondary sector of the labor mar-ket or are completely out of work, they have both affirmative motiva-tions for engaging in crime that will satisfy material wants and needs, and they are free to engage in life styles that potentially create crime-conducive situations. In order for the latter to occur they must have, in their proximity, others who are similarly sufficiently free from stakes in conformity to pursue these lifestyles as well. This occurs in neighborhoods like The Hill and Homewood in Pittsburgh, Cleveland's Hough, and in too many of DC's neighborhoods, which have disproportionately borne the weight of deindustrialization. There will be such places throughout American cities, and possibly those of other western industrialized nations too, where historic patterns of inequality have focused and sometimes amplified the ill effects of economic change.

Susan Pitchford and I, using data from the National Longitudinal Survey of Youth (NLSY), studied how the work experiences of a sample of young adults were related to their involvement in violent and property crimes. We found that those with unstable employment were more likely to have committed both violent and property crimes. Unstable employment, measured here as the amount of time respondents were out of the labor force, is an important byproduct of segmented labor markets (or dual labor markets). Clearly those out of work would score high on this variable, but so too would many who were working part-time and those who were employed in the secondary sector. Even after taking into account standard demographic predictors like age, sex, marital status (all of which were significant predictors of crime), and race (not a significant predictor in these analyses after the others factors are taken into account), as well as measures of education (significantly negatively related to violent crime involvement, but not property crime), income, and military service, we found that the men and women in the NLSY sample engaged in more crime when they were marginally employed. Family income was unrelated to violent crime after these other factors were taken into account, but it positively predicted property crime involvement. That is, being from a low-income family did not lead to more violent crime, but perhaps more interestingly those who were better off more frequently reported that they engaged in pecuniary criminality (entrepreneurial crimes, such as drug sales, were not studied in these analyses). The NLSY oversampled people from lower income groups and African and Latino Americans, so we should be cautious in concluding that this finding means that middle-class young adults commit more property crimes, but it does suggest that income need is less a factor motivating pecuniary crime than popular conceptions suggest.[11]

A great many people believe that sending a boy off to the military will make a man of him. In fact, when testifying before a Washington State Senate Committee on behalf of the State's Juvenile Sentencing Commission, I was asked by a senator why we needed to worry so much about "all those darn treatments and rehabilitation programs, because, by God, when I went into the Marines, boot camp sure straightened me out." Never mind that studies of the correctional system boot camps that became popular policy in the last decades of the twentieth century generally find them not to be either rehabilitative or deterrents.[12] In our analysis we found that the NLSY respondents who were in the military were more likely to have committed crimes in the last year. We did not conclude that the military makes them do it, but this finding does suggest that we might want to closely examine the military and criminality before shipping wayward youth en masse to the armed forces as a crime prevention strategy. Though the pay is relatively modest, other characteristics of a job in the military—benefits, future possibilities, stability—are very much like a primary sector job. On the other hand courts, both juvenile and adult, have been known to indicate that charges might be dropped in some cases if a young man were to elect to enlist. This may be a practice of the pre–all volunteer army, but when I worked as a juvenile probation officer in Pennsylvania during the late stages of the Vietnam War, this was not infrequently the outcome of cases involving juveniles who did not have an extensive record and who were no longer in school. With the military struggling to meet recruitment goals during recent wars in Iraq and Afghanistan, this may have again been practiced in some jurisdictions.

Young women were included in the sample used in the earlier analyses, but the labor stratification approach was not fruitful in explaining their criminality. The women in the sample were, as is ordinarily the case, far less likely to have participated in either violent or property crimes. The inability of labor market participation to help us to understand the limited female criminality that was observed is not surprising, since others have reported that social psychological factors were superior to structural determinants in explanations of female criminality.[13] Not being convinced that labor markets and social structure were not an important part of the story, I, along with my colleague Kristin Bates, looked more closely at women's employment, social structural position, and some family factors.[14] Expecting that women with more obligations and stronger ties to families would be different than those without these connections, we considered these women separately. Since there were so few violent crimes among the young women who were among NLSY respondents, we focused our analyses on property offenses and drug use. The two types of violation are very different. Women with weak social ties used more drugs when they had better jobs, more job satisfaction, and when their spouse or partner (if they had one) spent more time out of work. They were less likely to use drugs when they themselves spent more time out of work. None of these factors increased drug use among women with strong family ties. So when it comes to women's drug use, we have to conclude that their labor market experience is not what we expected, except for the negative influence of an out-of-work man in the house. We elected to not make too much of these seemingly confusing findings. It is possible that what we are picking up here is more recreational drug use among better-off women (those with more education were also more likely to have used drugs).

Property crime is a little more consistent with expectations. Women with weak family ties, in short-duration jobs were slightly more likely than others to have committed property violations. Women with weak ties were also more likely to be involved if their spouse was spending more time out of work. None of these factors mattered for women with stronger family ties. It seems terribly traditional, but it appears that family ties make more difference for these young women's criminality than does their work experience—but their employment, and the work of their partners, does matter. So even if not a strong determining force, the labor market is a factor in female criminality.

Local Labor Markets

A feature of the NLSY that we took advantage of in these analyses is the "geocoding" of cases. Individual respondents in the NLSY can be linked to the county in which they reside, and census data can be included in the analyses. These linked data allowed us to consider the social and economic context of the local labor market in which these young adults were working (or not working). Now clearly, the arguments that I have offered so far are that the neighborhood social context matters. But here the county of residence is the contextual unit in the analyses. There is no way that a county can reasonably be considered a theoretically sound proxy for a neighborhood or community. But what a county reasonably does represent is the local labor market. So here the unemployment rates for counties of residence are a measure of the health of the local economy and labor market in which the respondents to the NLSY were holding or seeking gainful employment.

We found that the criminogenic effect of spending more time out of the labor market did not occur everywhere. The effect was only observable in counties that had above-average unemployment rates. Where county unemployment rates were comparatively lower, being out of work for more time does not appear to increase criminal involvement. This is an important finding. It is in the context of others who are out of work that an individual's employment circumstance matters for their criminality. This supports the contention that it is in a situation of company of others who are marginalized from the labor market that work is important. If we think back to the example of the young Pittsburgh men encouraged by their friends to go out drinking, one of them in a primary sector job the other in a McJob, we gain an appreciation of the importance of this finding. The primary sector worker employed in the steel mill was not likely to join his friends, but the secondary sector worker with the McJob appears to be no more likely than the former to become involved in violent crimes unless there are others who live around him who are similarly situated in the labor market or out of work all together. For the negative effects of marginal jobs to have their real influence, we need the presence of those friends who issued the invitation to our secondary sector worker. It is not just the individual's circumstance that matters, but the individual within the social setting.

Neighborhoods and Young Adult Crime

So the conditions of local labor markets do matter in increasing the likelihood of criminal involvement for young adults when they are marginally employed—but what about their neighborhoods? Do they matter? After all, in the example that I have been using, it was other marginally employed young men who attempted to persuade our steelworker and his neighboring McJob worker to go out on a work night. While

I didn't specify, the implication was that these tempters lived nearby. Do neighborhoods matter too? My colleagues and I used data from the NLSY97 to address this question.[15] The Center for Human Resources Research (CHRR) at the Ohio State University and the Bureau of Labor Statistics (BLS) closely guard geocodes that allow the linkage between information about each respondent and the census tract in which they live (appropriately, so to ensure the anonymity of NLSY respondents). We were allowed access to these data to examine both labor market participation and young adult crime and juvenile delinquency. In those analyses, as we and others have reported, people who were marginal to the labor market, either unemployed or in secondary sector jobs, were more likely to violate the law. The other factors effecting criminality were sex (women of course were less likely), age (crime declines with age, as we have long known), those who had been suspended from school earlier, and race/ethnicity. Surprisingly, the only neighborhood factor that was associated with criminal involvement by these respondents was racial composition, and the relationship was not as most would expect. Young adults who lived in communities where there was a larger black population were less likely to be involved in crime *after the other factors were taken into account.* So in these analyses, neighborhood employment rates do not appear to matter as a determinant of adult criminality; what is important is the individuals' work circumstance. Putting our past research together with the more recent analyses, we have to conclude that local labor markets at the county level do condition the effect of employment on adult criminal behavior, but the circumstances of their specific neighborhoods do not.

What do these results do to our example, and, more importantly, for the labor stratification and crime thesis, which emphasizes the importance of context? They require a more nuanced approach to the notions of relevant environments and peers. Perhaps this newest result is because neighborhoods, measured here as census tracts, are too limited when considering the situation of company that influences young adult men and women. For instance, in inner-city Seattle there is a restaurant and bar named The Point. Its clientele is not drawn exclusively from the African American community, but one is subject to see great diversity from that community there. Black political officials, businessmen and women, and professionals rub shoulders with laborers, the jobless, and a few more thugs than the ownership of the establishment would frankly prefer. But, another dimension of the diversity is that The Point draws its patrons not just from the census tract where it is located, or even just from nearby tracts, but rather from throughout the central portion of Seattle, the south end of the city, and its southern suburbs. The same is true in Pittsburgh, where adults from the multiple neighborhoods of The Hill District congregate on Center Avenue, the main drag of the black community. Adult social life is not limited to those living immediately around them. Their territory, if you will, is more expansive; thus the null results for neighborhood/census tract effects on the relationship between adult work circumstance and aggregate employment.

The county or local labor market, on the other hand, is likely a more meaningful unit. Let's continue with the two examples used in the last paragraph. If King County's (Seattle) unemployment rate is high, or if the quality of work is low there for many workers, a marginally employed young man or woman stopping in The Point for a drink or a bite is more likely to encounter others similarly situated. Similarly, if our steel mill worker in Pittsburgh of the 1970s stopped off on Center Avenue for a social moment, he would have been likely to encounter other primary sector workers when the mills were booming, or more secondary sector or jobless workers after deindustrialization struck. A holder of a McJob in either circumstance will be influenced toward or away from crime-conducive lifestyles by the mix of people encountered in these and similar social settings. In both circumstances *the health of the local labor market influences social life*, and consequently the resulting crime of young adults.

A word about our race results are in order. Net of other social and demographic factors, family income, and work circumstance, we did not find that race was related to criminality. These results suggest that the long and repeatedly observed correlation between race and crime— African Americans committing more crime—may be explained by seriously taking employment and educational differences into account. Also, NLSY respondents living in predominantly Hispanic neighborhoods committed less crime. While this may surprise some in the general public and may disappoint politicians using immigration as a political wedge issue, it is not new news. In recent years criminologists have reported similar patterns using other data.[16] This pattern too is net of other factors including individual poverty and neighborhood disadvantage.

The Younger and the Older

In addition to the young men like those used in my example, there are two other groups that must be considered: the most crime-prone portion of every population, teenagers, and the least crime-prone, older (age thirty and up) adult men and women. When the good blue-collar jobs began disappearing from America's industrial cities the first group to feel the effects were younger workers, because the jobs that were there for earlier generations were not there for them, and because those who did have jobs in mills and plants were the last hired, and therefore the first to be fired. It was not long after deindustrialization in the US began that its effects started to reach longer-term workers, who assumed that their jobs were secure. These workers, in the past, had endured downturns in their fortunes when recessions caused cutbacks and layoffs. They also knew well that there was a cyclical nature to the heavy industries that employed them. Too, there were in their histories times of hardships resulting from prolonged strikes. They were, however, not prepared for the jobs to disappear and never return. In the song "My Hometown," Bruce Springsteen, singing of a New Jersey mill town, says,

> Now main streets whitewashed windows and vacant stores
> Seems like there ain't nobody wants to come down here no more
> They're closing down the textile mill across the railroad tracks
> Foreman says these jobs are going boys and they ain't coming back to
> Your hometown, your hometown, your hometown, your hometown.[17]

Deindustrialization brought a new and ominous future to the social life of America's industrial regions.

There is an apocryphal story, possibly an urban legend, which conveys the pattern of disbelief that existed in working men during this period. As the story goes, a group of laid-off, middle-aged steelworkers were drinking their morning coffee in a diner immediately across the street from the Monessen, Pennsylvania steel mill where they'd been employed. The conversation that morning, like it frequently did, centered on when the mill would reopen. While these men sipped their coffee and talked of getting out of debt and their plans for when they returned to work, the mill across the street literally disappeared, brought down by dynamite in smoke and dust. They had not been told; they were unaware that it had been scheduled for demolition.

Stress, mental illness, and marital and drinking problems afflicted laid-off workers in Detroit, Cleveland, Youngstown, Pittsburgh, and across the Rust Belt, but it is very unlikely that many of them turned to crime to satisfy their material needs or adopted lifestyles that substantially increased their criminality. Members of this demographic group are less likely than younger men to become involved in crime if they were not already so engaged, even with the loss of jobs, hope, and dignity.[18]

Even among men less tied to hard-working conforming lifestyles, age is a powerful rehabilitating force. A scary moment for me as a brand-new adult parole agent (after my stint as a juvenile PO) was when I walked through the district office with my supervisor, he telling each of my new coworkers, "Give me your murders." What he was asking for was the face sheets of their clients that POs carried in a binder. This was to be my initial caseload. At twenty-two, the prospect of a caseload of men who'd done time for murder was not one I relished. I had not known it, but the office's paroled murderers were older men—the group least likely to recidivate, the easiest to supervise. When my caseload was expanded to include Walter and his cohorts my job got considerably tougher. Both the older parolees as well as older laid-off steel mill or auto plant workers are much less likely to turn to crime than are younger men.

Their teenage children and younger siblings, on the other hand, are a different story. The teen years are a time when many, perhaps even most, kids engage in delinquency. Self-report studies have long found widespread law violating behavior across social classes, races, and ethnicities. Parents recognize that adolescence is a time of pulling away; when teenagers' friends and what they think, and the influence they have, supplants that of their parents. To some extent we don't really need to explain the widespread delinquency of fourteen-, fifteen-, and sixteen-year- olds.[19] But we must be concerned first with which among them are more likely to engage in serious forms of delinquency. Second, we need to concern ourselves with the behaviors that may be a harbinger of more serious crimes later in their lives. Third, and central to our focus here, what are the delinquent and criminal consequences of social conditions—in the present case work, the economy, and disadvantage?

In a study of Cleveland, Ohio's crime rates, sociologists Lauren Krivo and Ruth Peterson used arrest rates as the indicator of census tract crimes so that they could look at how age and employment were linked to different types of crimes.[20] They found, consistent with the labor stratification thesis, that young adults were more likely to have been arrested for violent acts in census tracts with higher levels of labor instability, juvenile delinquents appeared a bit less directly tied to labor market conditions, and older adults' arrest rates were influenced by joblessness but not by unemployment rates and secondary sector employment.

Regarding the question of the mechanism by which employment patterns influence teenagers'— people below the age where they are ordinarily expected to work—participation in delinquency is important. I will explore this more in the next chapter, but essentially the labor stratification and crime thesis recognizes (like control theory, which is a part of its foundation), that for school-aged children jobs are less important determinants of their lives and lifestyles than their families, schools, and peers. Criminologists Joseph Weis David Hawkins, Richard Catalano, and their colleagues argued that the societal unit that was most pivotal for the regulation of childhood behavior shifts as children age, with family being the most important for younger children and school becoming dominant in the preadolescent and earliest adolescent years, and finally the emergence of the peer group and to some extent the broader community in adolescence.[21] A great deal of research has shown that success in school and attachments to school are negatively associated with delinquent behavior.[22] Also, kids who are good students and involved in school-sponsored activities are probably going to end up with a peer group that is less delinquent than those who have poor grades and are disinterested in school.[23]

But what of kids and jobs? A great many people think that effective delinquency prevention requires after-school employment. Presumably this belief is based on the "idle hands are the devil's workshop theory of delinquency." Some criminologists find the popular focus on juvenile employment curious, since there are studies that have found that high-school aged children who work are, in general, more likely to violate the law than those who do not. These findings should at the very least give pause to those pushing jobs as the answer. The relationship between juvenile employment and crime, like that of adults, is more complex than either the popular belief in its necessity or of simplistic interpretations of observed positive correlation between work and delinquency. While this complexity will be explored more fully later, for now suffice it to say that which is widely agreed upon: school and not work is important for kids when it comes to determining their lifestyles and delinquency. And we are increasingly learning that the health of the local labor market is important for determining how children will relate to school, teachers, and education generally.

Most readers heard from their parents, or can imagine hearing them say, something like "Do well in school if you want to get ahead, have a good future, and a good life." For many, maybe even for most, this advice rings true—even for teenagers who at the surface act as if they do not hear or believe that mantra. Now imagine an out-of-work or marginally employed parent in an underclass neighborhood where few adults have jobs, and those who do are in McJobs, offering the same advice. It is then not hard to also imagine teenagers responding, or at least thinking to themselves, with tongue firmly planted in cheek, "Yeah, you mean like you did!" Young people may not know the details of their parents' employment circumstances, but they can recognize when those around them played by the rules and still their lives came up economically lacking. How, in this situation, can one reasonably expect that juveniles, most of whom can at times be a bit skeptical of parental points of view, will be as likely to invest in school as their counterparts in better-off communities? The argument is that children will, where their parents and other adults are marginal to the labor market, be less likely to do well in school or develop positive attachments to teachers and education. As a result, delinquency is more likely to happen.

This problem is compounded in inner cities that have subpar education systems. Schools there are trying to educate student bodies who are likely to come to school not ready to learn as a result of hunger, familial problems, language difficulties, and more. Some teachers and administrators in such schools make valiant efforts, but frequently with underfunded budgets they are unlikely to be capable of counteracting the pessimistic message sent to children as a result of the general distress in their communities and their parents' and adult neighbors' negative labor market experiences.

Fewer Good Jobs, Yet the Crime Declines

Deindustrialization ravaged American working towns in the last twenty-five years of the twentieth century, but crime declined. Might not this disconfirm any argument claiming that job losses and a shift away from family wage jobs promotes crime? The crime decline certainly needs to be accounted for in this argument, and there are two important points that do this. First, as was the case for understanding crime patterns during the Great Depression, here we should avoid single variable explanations of crime patterns. Other things besides deindustrialization are happening in the US, and some of these social forces repress criminality. Patterns of American employment did change, but not everyone was negatively affected. As I described above, the decline of low-skilled manufacturing affected some communities far more than others. Also, the age distribution of the population has been shifting upward, which means that a smaller proportion of the population is within the most crime-prone years (fourteen to twenty-four); the crack epidemic abated; and there has been a massive increase in imprisonment. Second, many—probably most—American communities benefited from a robust economy during the final decade of the last century and in the years prior to the Great Recession which began in earnest in 2008, and this has brought downward pressures on crime.[24] The positive economic growth benefited some, while others added to a growing underclass. Sociologist Karen Parker described the social and economic factors that caused some communities to benefit from the crime decline while others did not.[25] Together these social and economic changes have added to more substantial income and social inequality in the US. This inequality is not just economic; it also exists in the likelihood of victimization, the probability of living in crime-infested neighborhoods, and in the chances that one's children will succumb to crime and delinquency.

With other forces pressing crime down, increasing labor stratification can help us to understand the current distribution of crime across communities. Even though Pittsburgh, Cleveland, Washington, and cities like them experienced declining crime rates between the 1980s and 2000s, within them are communities that have to a lesser extent experienced the blessings of lower violence and victimization. According to Parker, the crime decline has benefited upper-, middle-, and even most working-class communities far more than it has those growing underclass neighborhoods most affected by deindustrialization and increased labor stratification. It is within such neighborhoods that nightly news broadcasts too frequently are reporting about young men, especially black and brown youngsters, being shot down even as crime in the wider city in which they live has declined.

Finally, there is a third and very important reason why neither the public nor policy makers should be complacent about the drop in crime in the face of increasing distress in the labor market. As John Worral pointed out, the effects of the labor market on crime is very likely to be delayed.[26] If the marginally employed are more likely to influence crime rates not solely for material reasons but also because of frustration, anger, unregulated lifestyles, and the long-term influence of social and economic disadvantage, the current labor market distress resulting from the Great Recession may be just beyond the horizon. The effects of labor market stratification on crime is very likely not a short-term effect, but one that takes a while to develop—and then perhaps endures.

Broken Promises

Crime and delinquency become more likely when there are more people out of work or marginally employed. Crime occurs because marginally employed adults have motivations for engaging in pecuniary crimes, and where there is a situation of company created by concentrations of marginally employed people lifestyles conducive to criminality, including violence, are more likely to develop. And delinquency increases because areas with high levels of labor instability are not conducive to supporting an "education matters" message to children, resulting in poor school performance and ultimately higher rates of delinquent involvement.

Again, the argument is that social context matters. For children and for adults, how those in the immediate vicinity—the neighborhood, as well as the broader context, the local labor market—matters. Certainly individuals have agency, and we must remember that individuals in even the most dire labor market circumstances have choices, but we must also remember the young men that Mercer Sullivan studied in Brooklyn. Their choices were circumscribed by both the job opportunities in their area and the adult networks that they had or did not have. I will explore the implications for children and the results of research on them in chapter 4.

Central to America's national rhetoric is that hard work is justly rewarded. When Americans moved from farms and villages to pursue opportunity in growing industries they did so holding firmly to that belief, and built lives on the promise that their hard work would produce a better life not only for them, but for their children. For no group was this truer than for the African Americans who moved north and west to flee Southern oppression and to find their Promised Land of jobs, opportunity, and equality. Instead they found cracks in the promise, and while many migrants did considerably better than they and their families could have in the rural south, their children soured on the incomplete delivery of the promise. My friends and I never knew the concept of Great Migration. All of us were either born in the South or were of parents who moved north in search of a better life. Even after learning that our parents and friends were a part of one of the most substantial demographic shifts in human history, most of us did not make the connection between their quest for a better life and the lives that we were living. We did not think of the Motown sound as connected to the music of our fathers, though it certainly was. So it was not angry frustration for the dream not being delivered that motivated us. We didn't appreciate the North because it was better than the South, just as the children of immigrants are not comparing their lives to those lived by their parents in the old country. Our frustration was a consequence not of disappointment in the Promised Land; our anger was a product of being excluded. Robby Wideman and his friends were not going to be satisfied by lives that were better than their parents' worlds in the rural South. Those intergenerational differences made up the emotional landscapes of many American inner cities throughout the 1960s and early 1970s.

At the start of the twenty-first century, changes in the US and world-wide economy led to broken promises for not only the people of the Great Migration, but for many working people of many races and ethnicities. Crime is but one response to those broken promises; it disrupts social life, adds high cost to local, state, and federal budgets, and makes life harder, especially for those already hurt most by deindustrialization and globalization. But we should remember that crime is a less socially changing (damaging in the minds of some) consequence than some alternatives, and it holds less real hope for the downtrodden than some of those other alternatives might.

4

"I Don't Want No Damn Slave Job!"

The Effects of Lack of Employment Opportunities

Most Americans, perhaps even most residents of Western nations, view the individual as endowed with both the capacity and the responsibility to govern their behavior and to a large extent, their destiny. As a result, non–social scientists read arguments like those presented in the preceding chapters with some skepticism. "I know they have had it tough," they say, speaking of the poor, the chronically unemployed, and other disadvantaged peoples, "but they have to take some responsibility for themselves and go out and find a job, and there is certainly no excuse for crime." This is a sentiment expressed by many voters and by politicians, but one that runs contrary to a wealth of social science evidence. Some of these same people would make some significant exceptions to the individual responsibility philosophy for children, although even that consideration is changing of late. Increasing numbers of juveniles are punished as adults for a growing array of crimes. Nevertheless, most of us believe that the young are subject to forces external to themselves that guide and sometimes compel their behavior. Parents worry that their children will be influenced by the wrong set of peers. Moral crusaders demand laws that protect the sensitive, formative years from the evil influences of movies, music videos, computer games, and the Internet. We worry and struggle about these things because we expect that these, as well as other social forces, influence the behavior and the development of children. Those with this viewpoint generally do not accept that the young adults that I have discussed so far can be understood or in part pardoned for having social forces influence them. The questions here are, does work affect juvenile behavior, and does the economy matter for them? Does it affect juvenile delinquency?

It is easier to trace a link between unemployment or marginal, unpromising employment to the criminality of young adults. After all, if they do not have responsibilities to occupy their time and a promise for the future, frustration or the lifestyles that may emerge might reasonably lead to crime. But since we ordinarily do not expect children to work in most western industrialized economies, why might fluctuations or changes in the labor market influence their behavior?

For some, the same logic that is popularly applied to young adults should work with teenagers (never mind that these ideas don't work so well for adults): "They have too much time on their hands." Then there's the junior Jean Valjean explanation: "Ghetto youth are delinquent because they cannot satisfy basic needs and wants." Or, "They need the discipline that comes from holding down a job." These, and like sentiments, are the motivations for the belief that after-school and weekend jobs are important features of successful delinquency prevention programs. The problem with this point of view is that the "idle hands" explanation for delinquency, which argues that if young people do not have productive, supervised, good things to do with their time bad behavior occurs, has not been supported by research. Filling idle time does not reduce delinquency. This should not be a surprise; delinquency takes but minutes. Much of it occurs during the course of average behavior during the average teenager's day. They break into a house on the way home from school because the homeowner left particularly attractive targets (iPods, computers, other easily carried valuables) conveniently inside a sliding glass door (notoriously easy to lift off the track and open) that is shielded from the view of neighbors or others on the street by hedges or fences. Or on the way home from midnight basketball, they find it more fun to get into mischief with friends than to go directly home. Because delinquency takes so little time and so much of it is spontaneous, it is not practical to sufficiently fill up youthful hours to an extent that it would make much of a difference. So simply getting kids jobs after school, which might be a positive experience for some kids, usually will do little to prevent delinquency by itself.

Midway through my tenure as a juvenile PO, a group of kids that I, tongue firmly in cheek, called the Hole in the Wall Gang (named after a group of desperados that frequently turned up in the westerns that I watched as a kid), were petitioned to the court that I worked in. I dubbed them this because they were anything but desperados or criminals, and frankly it was hard for me to seriously think of them as delinquents. They actually lived just across the border from the Western Pennsylvania county that employed me, in a rather remote rural area. They were placed on probation by my county judge because their crimes were committed in our county. The Hole in the Wall Gang was described in the sheriff's reports as a burglary ring. Their offenses were a series of break-ins, usually barns and other farm outbuildings. They didn't take much, and sometimes didn't take anything. After getting to know the case and the "gang," I concluded that they broke in out of boredom; like those who climb the highest mountains, they did it because they (in their case barns and not Mount Everest) were there. They were not doing well in school, and they were engaged in no school activities. They did not cause trouble at school, and in fact might have been the "nerd group" if it had been a few decades later and they'd been a little smarter. Their families were pretty stable, but poor. Like most teenagers they looked more to their friends than to their parents for guidance and influence. Had their crimes occurred in even a slightly less rural setting, it is likely that they would have been given a few months of unsupervised probation and then had their cases dismissed. Instead, we were to be stuck with each other for a year.[1] Would the members of the Hole in the Wall Gang have avoided juvenile court if they'd been employed? Obviously I cannot know that, but I'm skeptical; but as for school, that's another matter. I will return to the gang, along with others on my former caseload, in the coming pages to explore how economic forces and jobs affect juvenile delinquency.

Working Kids

What about the other motivations for after-school employment programs, such as the junior Jean Valjean theory of crime? It may not be a very good explanation for young adult crime, but perhaps it's more credible for explaining some juvenile delinquency. Conceivably, giving young people jobs so that they can pay for some of their own expenses and have money in their pockets may have positive benefits. Likewise, the discipline of finding and holding a job may provide both immediate and long-term benefits, if the lessons learned make it more likely that they will be more capable of holding good employment in the future.

But these positive benefits must be weighed against potentially harmful outcomes of this employment. If a job cuts into study or rest time, it may harm their school performance. If the job becomes more attractive than school then they may shift their focus and loyalty, and consequently their energies and efforts, away from their education. If the money they earn finances a more adult-like lifestyle—for example, a car and fast living—it may put them closer to rather than farther from delinquent behavior. As I said near the end of the last chapter, some researchers have found that young people who have jobs are more likely to be delinquent.[2] These scholars speculate that some of the reasons that I stated above may be the source of this finding. Also, they note that getting a job is more likely to put a fifteen-, sixteen-, or seventeen- year-old in close proximity to older youth, and as most parents have long recognized, having one's children too soon involved with older kids is not a good thing. We should also note that the jobs that kids are most likely to get are secondary sector McJobs, and as we have shown, many of the young adult coworkers they might encounter there may not the best influences.

A substantial body of evidence has been generated that tells us that a very important orienting institution for adolescents is the school. School is to the teenager as quality employment is to the young adult. When children do well in school and develop strong attachments to teachers and to the school itself they are less likely to engage in delinquency, and less likely to become involved in alcohol and drug abuse.[3] Schools not only provide an important legitimate institution for teenagers to bond to and thus prevent their delinquency, but they also clearly are the institution that gives them the basis for having a hopeful, positive future.

We should be careful, however, to not cast all student workers into the same box. Sociologists Rob Warren, Paul LePore, and Rob Mare found that simply examining the difference between the school performance of teenagers who work and those who do not masks important differences.[4] They asked a sample of high-school students to keep detailed diaries of their daily activities, and then they added the products of those diaries to a larger data set. They found that students who were getting good grades improved or maintained their academic performance when they worked a modest number of hours per week. Their interpretation of this finding is that good students, who already made it a habit of budgeting their time effectively and husbanding their resources for education, became even more focused and directed when they took on employment. For this group employment did not lead to poor grades or other problems, as they were already less likely to have been involved in problematic activities.

Other scholars empirically examined work and delinquency directly. Laurence Steinberg and Sanford Dornbusch specified that it was long working hours that could be associated with lower investments in school and problematic behaviors.[5] John Wright, Francis Cullen, and Nicholas Williams found that work did increase delinquency in high-school students who were already considered at risk.[6] They cautioned policy makers to not think of employment as the solution for these kids. Jerald Bachman and John Schlenberg, analyzing a national sample, concluded that the association between work and delinquency was attenuated when other factors such as children's background and educational success were taken into consideration.[7] Contrary to the earliest studies' conclusions, Matthew Ploeger, and Raymond Paternoster and his colleagues, report that the long-accepted positive relationship between working and delinquency is due to selection.[8] Those already more likely to engage in law violation were more likely to get jobs than those less involved in crime, and presumably the latter are doing better in school. Robert Apel and his colleagues found that a group of sixteen-year-olds in their first jobs were not more likely to be delinquent. In fact, contrary to earlier research, those who had engaged in delinquency or used drugs before getting their first job were less likely to be involved in these activities after beginning to work. Apel and his colleagues' study reported that work in the formal labor market, even including the McJobs that teenagers are most likely to have, did not increase delinquency, but that kids working in the informal economy, some of which is legally marginal, does produce more violations.[9] Finally, along with Margo Rankin, and Susan Pitchford, I and also Apel and his colleagues conclude that if juveniles are not positively engaged in school that they had better be working, because it is those who are neither attached to school nor to work who are most likely to get caught up in illegal behavior.[10]

Although these results should give pause to those who would primarily combat delinquency by developing jobs programs for high-school aged workers, there is both evidence and reason to believe that when employment in a neighborhood is a problem that youth crime will also be a problem. In *The Truly Disadvantaged* and *When Work Disappears*, William Julius Wilson argued that joblessness leads to destabilized communities unable to combat youthful waywardness and delinquency.[11] Elijah Anderson described the emergence of a "code of the street" that is conducive to crime and delinquency in areas with high rates of unemployment and marginal work.[12] *Getting Paid*, Mercer Sullivan's description of how poor and marginal community economies lead occasionally to legal employment (usually not very good jobs) and illegal work, clearly documents how the social structure and crime in communities affects their children.[13]

Recent empirical evidence also supports this contention and I will turn to that shortly, but first I should explore in some detail the theoretical explanation offered by the labor stratification thesis. This explanation is based, like that for young adult criminality, on the combination of labor market segmentation theory—specifically dual labor market theory, and what might be called a differential social control theory.[14] Central to the thesis, as is the case with young adults, is the importance of the social environment. When children live in households with adults who are not doing well in the labor market, and especially when these homes are also in communities where too many adults appear to be economically unsuccessful, their probability for engaging in delinquency escalates. Several scholars have argued that two important social bonds that potentially shield juveniles from delinquency and especially delinquent peers are more likely to be weakened in such settings: attachments to parents and to school.[15]

Three Important Messages

It sounds heartless, or perhaps even a bit Machiavellian, to argue that if their parents are not employed well and substantially and materially rewarded as much as children believe they should, that those same children will be less likely to attach affectionately and respectfully to those parents. Nevertheless, this is probably, even if not consciously, the case in part. The argument is not that poor children do not love their parents. To suggest such would constitute the same kind of ethnocentric balderdash foisted upon us by those who claim that poor parents undervalue their children.[16] Instead, the argument is that the parents' lack of success makes them less capable of delivering, in a convincing way, some critical messages. Here again we are not saying that poor parents cannot send these messages and send them with resounding success. The point is that their position in the economic and social structure makes this parenting task, which is hard for any parent regardless of class standing, even harder. What, then, are these messages?

There is the *Follow my path* message, which includes the themes of both "work hard" and "stay out of trouble." It is probably the case that many children think that their parents' jobs are boring, and that those are the last jobs they want to spend their lives doing; after all, how many fifteen-year-olds dream of sitting in an office as an accountant, or daydream of becoming a dentist, or even fantasize about being a college professor, for that matter? But even those of us not working in careers that high-school students find exciting and gravitate to at career fairs can day by day illustrate our ability to relatively comfortably maintain middle-class lifestyles; and our children, when not in the fits of despondency, anger, or generalized parental displeasures that frequently accompanies adolescences, recognize that their futures are enhanced by our relative economic success. When parents are frequently unemployed or constrained to low-end jobs in the secondary sector of the labor market, children may not know how much their parents are paid or what their benefits package contains, or even how much their parents worry about the instability of the work. But they do recognize that it is not a good thing. Children do not need their parents to be employed in an occupation that they find exciting, but they do want their parent to be employed in an occupation that is respected. Imagine, if you will, a fourteen-year-old responding to the "What does your dad or mom do" question by saying, "He works the fryer at _____ [fill in the name of your favorite national or local burger joint]." When parents are in these situations they are inhibited in getting across the all-important "follow my path" message.

Obviously children do not need to *literally* follow the career path of their parents, but there exists a template in each culture of how one moves from childhood to adulthood. The modeling of this path and teaching children how to navigate it is important for their successful progression to being healthy, well-functioning adults. Parents who are tightly bonded to their children are more likely to know their children's friends, to regulate who they spend time with, and to monitor their activities; this monitoring decreases delinquency.[17] I am arguing that when parents' work circumstance does not command the respect of their child the bond between the two is weakened, thereby allowing for delinquency. Let me be perfectly clear: I am not saying that working-class or poor families do not have good parent–child bonding. I am saying that the probability of this bonding is hindered when the parents are marginalized in the labor market. It is one more hurdle that these parents have to navigate.

My not-very-delinquent Hole in the Wall Gang probationers did not have bad parents; their parents simply had a hard time convincing them of the value of working harder in school. Another of my charges, Gabe, who was on probation for drug possession, just rolled his eyes when his parents lectured him about school. He said to me, "They want me to be like them; hell no."

Tim Wadsworth, using the National Survey of Families and Households, examined parents' employment and juvenile misbehavior. He theorized that parents who are marginally employed would have weaker social bonds with their children, and he found this to be the case. When the bonds were weaker the children performed less well in school and were more likely to have misbehaved in the previous year. Wadsworth's interpretation of his findings is that the affective strength of the parent–child relationship is weakened with the parents' lack of employment success.[18] And, as other control theorists have found, when the social bonds to parents are weakened children are substantially less likely to develop strong positive bonds to their teachers and school, which is of course associated with higher levels of delinquency.[19]

No doubt many parents, struggling themselves in marginal jobs, deliver the message to their children that they should work hard in school "so you don't end up like me." But this potentially important life lesson is also hard to sell when other adults in the neighborhood can neither deliver the follow my path message nor model that education

makes a difference. Anderson, describing consequences of the disappearance of manufacturing jobs, includes the diminution of positive
influences of the "old heads": adults on the block who, having lived "the
street life," would be listened to by the younger set. Anderson writes:

> But as meaningful employment becomes increasingly scarce for young
> men of the neighborhood and the expansion of the drug culture offers
> opportunities for quick money, the old head is losing prestige and
> authority. Streetwise boys are concluding that his lessons about life and
> work ethic are no longer relevant and a new role model is emerging. The
> embodiment of the street, this man is young, often a product of the street
> gang, and indifferent, at best, to the law and traditional values.[20]

Another parental message that is hurt in the face of marginal
employment is, *It is important that you work hard in school; that is the
key to success.* For a very long time this was the case for generations
of families. Academic success usually led to workplace successes. Now
things have changed dramatically in some communities, particularly
where poor and working-class families live. This may be changing in
a very fundamental way in other segments of the population as well.
Some speculate that the current generation of American parents and
children may be the first in which on average the children do not do
better than their parents.[21]

At the end of the last chapter I described what we can imagine happens when a parent who is striving but yet still out of a job, or a secondary sector worker, implores their child to work hard in school so that
they can have a better life only to be "chumped off" by ungrateful and
disrespectful offspring. When parents are not succeeding even when
they play by the rules, their lives are not a good conduit of the message
that education pays off. When such a family lives where there is concentrated poverty, joblessness, and labor market instability, the struggling
image of the parents are less likely to be mitigated by other adults in the
neighborhood. A problem in underclass neighborhoods is that children
do not see the model of people getting up, going out to work, and seeing it pay off, because too few adults are gainfully employed.[22]

In a study of the juvenile respondents of the National Longitudinal Surveys of Youth (NLSY), we found that when parents were

unemployed their children do less well in school, which in turn increases their involvement in delinquency.[23] Paul Bellair and his colleagues used the Adolescent Health data to find very similar results.[24] More recently, working with several colleagues, this finding has again been confirmed using newer data from NLSY data sets.[25]

A third important message that is clearly linked to the one just discussed is, *Education is valuable.* But this message comes with a caveat: it is more valuable for some people than for others. As indicated above, it does not work when the parents' work circumstance does not confirm it, but we have seen that when you hold parental employment constant their education is positively associated with children doing well in school, which in turn decreases their participation in delinquency.[26] The problem is that the inequalities of educational opportunities that exist in the US are not lost on adolescents.

Long ago, when my inner-city high-school track team visited the handsome campus of a suburban school for a meet, we walked around stunned not by the competition, but by the facilities. Where our friends on the football team played and practiced on a grassless, oil-covered field (the field, which was as hard as a blacktop road, was oiled once or twice a year to control the dust; it rendered Astroturf-like burns with an oil residue), the suburban school that we visited had a manicured grass field surrounded by a most pleasant stadium. Even their practice fields were superior to any we'd seen in the city. We didn't see much of the academic facilities of the school, but the locker rooms, track, and the equipment of our hosts left a lasting impression on us. Years later, when reading Jonathan Kozol's *Savage Inequalities*, the picture of that day came back to me.[27]

In little ways such as that just recounted, the images of education transferred through the popular media, and through common experience, parental messages of the value of education are undercut for portions of the population. A teenager coming of age in the slums of Detroit, Miami, or Los Angeles surely knew that the high-school images of the 1980s and 90s popular adolescent soap opera "90210" bore little resemblance to their experience. When Kozol writes of large portions of Chicago schoolchildren going through the academic year without a teacher, or having days when they are herded into the auditorium where they could be managed because that day no substitute could be

found, the message that their education does not matter is not lost on those children.

Kozol recounts the argument of those who say that money is not the answer to persistent disparity in academic outcomes between the middle and lower classes, but then comes to the heart of the counter-argument when he asks why, if money doesn't matter, will the government not transfer some of that pointless money which provides superb athletic facilities, teachers, and educational quality to inner-city schools and districts. Many children of the inner city don't have a hard time buying into the message that their parents are sending, but they do recognize how little their education is valued when they do not have a teacher, or when their books fall apart, or when there are no books at all, because they have replicated Dr. Kozol's analyses. Few Americans can imagine an elementary school where children cannot take home a spelling or math book because it has to be shared with other children—yet such schools exist. Educational inequality is easily observed and appreciated by a child who cannot take a book home when he sees the full book bags of other children.

Educational inequality is increased by a number of social forces including suburbanization, racial residential segregation, and high levels of joblessness. Each of these social forces reduces the tax base that local schools depend on to support local schools.[28] Additionally, many inner-city schools are hampered because a higher proportion of their students come to school with readiness to learn issues such as hunger or having English as a second language. Federal government programs have attempted to mitigate some of these problems, but inequalities persist. Even where it appears, from US Department of Education data, that suburban and inner-city schools are spending approximately the same amount per student, this is not actually the case.[29] The latter's budget includes considerably more money designated for programs such as ESL and school lunches.[30] These dedicated funds cannot be diverted to general education, so after this is taken into account it is clear that suburban schools are, on average, able to spend significantly more on their students' lessons in math, reading, history, and science than can inner-city schools.

In the study I cited earlier, my colleagues and I found that the effect of academically and occupationally unsuccessful parents was especially problematic among youngsters from central city neighborhoods.[31] This does not come as a surprise. It is very consistent with Wilson's ideas. Joblessness, persistent unemployment, marginal employment, and underemployment lead to social and economic disadvantage for individuals and for families. When the disadvantaged live substantially with other marginalized people in the disadvantaged communities that Wilson, Massey and Denton, and Anderson write of, the problems for disadvantaged people and families are compounded.[32] For children the occupational circumstance for their parents matter, but that marginalized employment is the root cause of disadvantage has additional consequences. So as we think of how employment and the economy affect delinquency, we have to include the indirect effects on both social and economic disadvantage.

Not a Dream Deferred, but a Dream Dashed

Getting a good education and obtaining its fruits in the form of occupational upward mobility and success has been the dream for the children of white, black, Native American, Latino, and Asian parents, of immigrant and natives alike. When Langston Hughes wrote about the "dream deferred" it was that of the black man, not yet the recipient of the American promise of openness and equality.[33] In the years since the Great Migration it has become increasingly clear to many young African Americans that the dream has not simply been deferred or put on hold, but that it will not happen. Now, as industrial nations, including the US, struggle with postindustrial economic changes, the children of white Americans increasingly find that they will not leapfrog their parents' occupational accomplishments as preceding generations have been able to. Many of those likely to be frustrated are but a few generations removed from immigrant experiences, their grandparents or great grandparents having moved from Eastern and Southern Europe. Only time will tell if more recent immigrants from Latin America and Asia will experience America as black migrants from the south have, with frustrations and blocks to upward mobility occurring within a generation or two of immigration—or if their experiences will be more like those of earlier waves of migrants to the US, of success followed by working-class stagnation that is likely for those without high-end, valued skills in postindustrial America. Sociologist Eduardo Bonilla-Silva argues that some "visible minorities" may become honorary whites as the US moves beyond a black–white binary and becomes more like Latin America in terms of racial classification.[34] Some groups today routinely defined as white (e.g., Irish and Italians) were not always thought of as a part of that "in group" by some "real Americans" when they first arrived in North America.[35] Without the low-skilled jobs that provided good work for earlier generations, the availability of quality education will be critical to new migrants as they try to find their place in the US, and education will also be critical for their job prospects and to how they are ultimately socially defined.

What happens, though, when the message that by obtaining an education a good life is not just possible but likely is not effectively communicated to the children of a community? For some, better-appearing alternatives—in youthful eyes that is—arise and become attractive. We should also consider the view that some residents of disadvantaged communities have of their job alternatives. They want "real jobs." "I don't want no damn slave job" is a refrain that teachers, counselors, and community workers hear in the inner city.[36] What makes it a "slave job?" For some it is simply working for someone else, especially if that someone else is "the man." But for many urban youth it is a job without respect, limited future, and low wages. It is a job where investing one's labor brings neither appreciable current or future payoffs (nor at least not the foreseeable future in their youthful time horizon). These are the jobs that may be seen as adequate for teenagers—in fast food, janitorial work, and the like—but they cannot give a young adult the income, future, and respect requisite for the lives that others seem to be entitled to.

In *Getting Paid*, Mercer Sullivan quotes a young man from a disadvantaged section of Brooklyn. The young man, Stan Williams, expressed his exasperation:

> STAN WILLIAMS: I tried to get some jobs, but they wasn't like real jobs. It was like sweeping out a store, like that, not a real job.
> INTERVIEWER: How much would you make?
> S.W.: Oh, about twenty dollars. They used to pay me by the week. Every day when they get ready to close up, I come by and sweep the place out.

INT.: How did you get the job?

S.W.: I just walked by and said, "Yo, can I sweep in your yard, mop or something?" I said, "Whatever you are willing to pay, I'll take it." But then the store burnt down.[37]

It is important to recognize that the desire for a "real job" or the rejection of a "slave job" is not an unwillingness to work. To the contrary, they are expressions of a desire to have work that has real value. It is a desire to have the kind of work that pays a decent salary and that one might enjoy.

When earlier generations of African Americans moved north in the Great Migration, and when Eastern and Southern Europeans arrived, and when whites moved from the hinterland to industrial centers between and after the world wars, people willingly accepted hard, dirty work that was sometimes dangerous.[38] They neither labeled employment "slave jobs," nor did they turn away from distasteful labor. So is it simply that, as some assert, that "they" are unwilling to work hard or to pay their dues? This is too simplistic.

Former field hands from Virginia, Georgia, and Alabama who went to Pittsburgh's steel mills and populated first its Hill District and later places like the Widemans' Homewood, took jobs that were dirty and were dangerous, but which gave them a living wage and the hope of a future, and they put distance between themselves and stoop labor, Klansmen, and Jim Crow oppression. Young whites who left Dust Bowl farms in the 1930s in the hope of finding the all too few opportunities during the Depression, or who chose a more urban or suburban life after they mustered out of the war, often accepted work that was not, to understate it dramatically, glamorous or even attractive. But those jobs promised substantially better opportunity than the options they left behind.

It is unreasonable to expect that Robby Wideman, coming of age in Homewood of the 1960s, would look at opportunity through the same framework as his father's generation. In *Brothers and Keepers*, John Wideman explains part of the difference in his life and his brother's, on the latter having been drawn to the fast life of the streets, a desire to make it big, and hope for the big score. Writing in the first person for the then-young Robby, Wideman conveys his brother's thoughts before the family moved back to Homewood from the Shadyside area of Pittsburgh.[39]

> Having a little bit of a taste behind me I couldn't wait to get to Homewood. In a way I got mad with Mommy and the rest of them. Seemed like they just didn't want me to have no fun. That's when I decided I'd go on about my business. Do it my way. Cause I wasn't getting no slack a home. They still expected me to be like my sister and brothers. They didn't know I thought youns was squares. Yeah. I knew I was hipper and groovier than youns ever thought of being. Streetwise, into something. Had my own territory and I was bad. I was a rebel. Wasn't following in nobody's footsteps but my own. And I was a hip cookie, you better believe it. Wasn't a hipper thing out there than your brother, Rob. I couldn't wait for them to turn me loose in Homewood.[40]

It is unreasonable to expect that the offspring of immigrant generations will be satisfied by what came to their parents. The parents, themselves the ones who take on the hardships of the journey and establish lives in the new land, do not even expect their children to be so satisfied. A major motivation for migrants is that through their efforts and sacrifice their children will do better, have more opportunities, and be able to reach for a dream that heretofore exceeded the reach of people like them. Little wonder then that the reality, so far short of the Promised Land for young black people in America's urban slums, sent some to the streets and others to nationalist movements. It was from the dissatisfied and angry sons and daughters of Great Migration movers that the Nation of Islam, the Student Non-Violent Coordinating Committee (SNCC), and the Black Panther Party drew members. Many others, like Robby Wideman, instead chose the fast life of the streets.

When informants told Elijah Anderson that "they didn't want no damn slave job," it was not, as many in the wider society assert, that they didn't want to work hard—but instead that they did not want to work hard at jobs with little future, low wages, and where they perceived, frequently very correctly, that they would receive little respect: in short, in secondary sector jobs.[41] Children coming of age where adults have no jobs or mostly secondary sector jobs are what Marxist scholars have referred to as "social dynamite." They are available to be mobilized by political leaders who offer them a rejection of the status quo, an ideology that offers them dignity and hope. Most American inner cities at the turn of the twenty-first century offered few such political visions or organizations. There were of course charismatic leaders, some of whom are politicians and more of whom are in the churches, but neither of which could deliver on the promise as expeditiously as charismatic street alternatives appeared able to do.

I've just written a lot about marginalized black communities, but I want to emphasize that the criminogenic effects of labor instability on young adults and children are not unique to African American people and neighborhoods. In fact, most of the research on the issue, while including consideration of race and ethnicity, has focused on no racial group, instead using data about large cities or various data sets that represents large portions of the American population. And, so far, all of the examples that I have mentioned from my old juvenile PO caseload were white kids. The story of African American labor market marginalization is one compelling story about the consequences of persistent labor inequality, but it is not the only story.

Labor Force Instability and Juvenile Delinquency

What, then, is the evidence that adult employment experiences influence delinquency? A number of recent studies have addressed the topic. My colleagues and I, using several data sets, have found supporting evidence of this linkage. We've found that both the parents' academic and occupational experiences help to predict how well children do in school. Even after taking into account the economic circumstance of both families and communities these parental experiences matter, and they influence juvenile delinquency.

Along with several colleagues, I examined the relationships of school experiences, mothers' employment, family circumstance, and neighborhoods as predictors of general delinquency—a combination of violent and property crime.[42] In that study the Children of the NLSY data set was used, because it has three valuable characteristics: it includes self-reports of respondents' delinquency, it contains data about both mothers and their children, and the respondents are geocoded to their census tract of residence. The Children of the NLSY data set was created when women from the original panel of NLSY respondents (who were between the ages of fourteen and twenty-one when data collection began in 1979) began having children. The staff at the Center for Human Resource Development at Ohio State University, who collect and maintain the NLS data sets, and the Bureau of Labor Statistics had the foresight to begin collecting detailed data about the children along with the longitudinal data that they gathered from the mothers. For pragmatic reasons they followed only the mothers and children and not the initial NLSY males as they became fathers and their children. This was a reasonable decision since the paternal activities of these young fathers is too frequently not knowable to researchers, and, even when it is, they are far less likely to be actively involved in their offspring's lives. This pragmatic decision does create one problem for the study of the labor stratification and delinquency thesis. Scholars of stratification usually focus on the occupation of the father rather than the mother, because traditionally the former was most central in defining the status of the family. The Children of the NLSY data only contain some information about an adult male residing with the mother, when one is present, and for many of the cases none was there. Even though the role of women as financial providers to the family (especially when they are single parents) no longer conforms to the traditional family conceptions, we are not confident that this is the best possible test of the thesis. We have this concern because of the nature of the female labor market: more "women's jobs" are considered and structured like secondary sector jobs. Nevertheless, we learned considerably from the study. A portion of our results is displayed in Figure 4.1. The figure uses standardized regression coefficients to display the relative importance of some predictors of delinquency (the table with the complete results of these analyses can be found in the appendix). Bars to the right of the y axis are associated with increased involvement in delinquency; those to the left of the y axis are associated with less self-reported misbehavior.

What is clear from Figure 4.1 is that the most important predictor of delinquency is the juveniles' attachment to school, which is very associated with how well they are doing in school according to their grades. What seems to not lead to delinquency is whether or not they were employed. Also, the presence or absence of a father or stepfather does not significantly predict if the young people in the sample engage

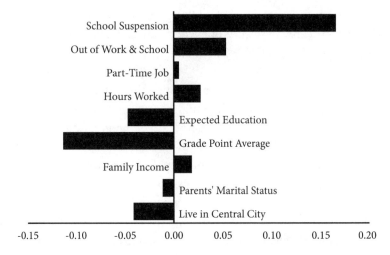

Figure 4.1. Explaining Delinquency Using School and Neighborhood Variables
The variables in this figure, with the exception of juvenile employment and father present, are statistically significant. Also included in the regression analyses were variables measuring respondents' age, sex,* race, ethnicity, mothers' education and employment, grades,* parental involvement in school, and characteristics of the census tract in which they lived. The table that Figure 4.1 is based on is included in the appendix.
*Indicates that this was a statistically significant predictor of delinquency.

in delinquent behavior. On the other hand, family poverty is linked to more delinquency.

Using the geocodes for these data, we were able to see that the racial and ethnic composition of the neighborhoods (census tracts) in which these young people lived provides an important context in which their delinquency plays out, but not in the way that many might predict. Those who live in neighborhoods with a higher proportion of Hispanic residents were less likely to become involved in delinquency. This is consistent with important research by other scholars who found that contrary to some popular stereotypes, Latino communities are less criminogenic, not more.[43] Interestingly, after taking family, educational, and employment differences into account in the analysis, the percent of census tract residents who are African American is nearly statistically significant, and that also is negatively related to delinquency involvement.

After taking other factors into account, children who worked were neither more nor less likely to engage in delinquency when compared with others. In this study we could not test the results suggested by the work of Rob Warren and his colleagues: that employment is negatively associated with delinquency for good students, work is a reasonable option to those not invested in school (and potentially positively correlated to delinquency, but not necessary causal), and employment is likely to be a detrimental influence on students who were somewhat academically marginal.[44] But the pattern of results that we found is consistent with their position because our sample contained good, bad, and marginal students.

What are not displayed in Figure 4.1 are other results of the analyses that speak more directly to the effects of variability of adult employment on youthful involvement in delinquency. While the labor stratification thesis speaks specifically to the problematic characteristics of secondary sector employment, we have not been concerned with measuring specific aspects of parental jobs such as the income and benefit packages, because we do not believe that children are knowledgeable or worry about such specifics. Rather, they have a global appreciation of their parents' work circumstance; parents are either doing well or they aren't. So we simply considered whether the parents of the children in the study were in primary or secondary sector jobs. What is critical is that their parents' education and work history were very important predictors of juveniles' school experience; parents' school and employment success indirectly influences their children's delinquency through how it influences their academic success. Parental secondary sector employment is associated with students' lower grade point averages. Grades here (school performance), as has been the case in many other studies, are strong negative predictors of juvenile delinquency.[45] Kids who don't do well in school are more likely to get in trouble, and the children of secondary sector workers get lower grades.

Paul Bellair and his colleagues have examined the consequences for children when parents are marginally employed.[46] Bellair and Vincent Roscigno found that parents' low-wage jobs and unemployment are associated with both fighting and drug use, which they attribute to negative factors in families such as reduced income and increased disruption, which harm juveniles' attachments to both family and school. Bellair and his colleagues report that marginal parental employment is related to delinquency, but this effect is mediated by school performance and attachment. They also report that the parents' work circumstance may either encourage or discourage children in the pursuit of academic success. Kids whose parents have done well occupationally, like those whose parents themselves accomplish more academically, do better in school and are less likely to engage in acts of delinquency, and this is independent of the families' income levels. Conversely, when the labor market experience of parents is more marginal, so too is their children's performance in school, and these children are more frequently participating in delinquent activity.

What each of these studies indicates is that delinquency is, in a very substantial way, a function of school experience (along with family influences). Those who get good grades are less likely to be involved in delinquency, as are those who are affectively attached to school and teachers. The importance of school performance in predicting delinquency is a more robust result than the association between juvenile employment and criminality. Of course, school success, measured by the grade point averages, is positively correlated to school attachment. As others have reported, those who do well in school like it most, and these children are less likely to involve themselves in delinquency. That said, this protective quality of good school experiences does not apply equally to all children. The effects of school on delinquency vary in some important ways, depending on community characteristics.

The results that I just described were for analyses of the full Children of the NLSY sample. Fortunately, the data can be divided into interesting subsamples: a metropolitan sample and a central city sample (not to be confused with inner cities). Central cities are the core cities of metropolitan areas—for example, the City of Pittsburgh is the core city of a much larger metropolitan area that includes many suburbs and numerous small towns. There was also a subsample of respondents who lived outside of metropolitan areas when they were interviewed. Not only are the areas from which these subsamples are drawn different; in some important respects the people who live in them are different as well, and the relationships between the social and economic factors that we studied and who they influence in terms of crime and delinquency differ as well.

Figure 4.2 displays some of the important relationships that my colleagues and I found in our analyses of the NLSY respondents living in metropolitan areas. As in Figure 4.1, the relative strength (standardized

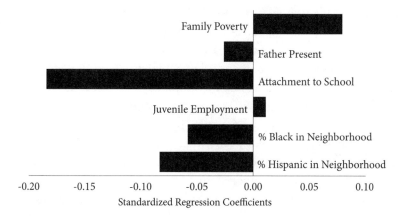

Figure 4.2. Explaining Metropolitan Area Delinquency Using School and Neighborhood Variables

The variables in this figure, with the exception of juvenile employment, are statistically significant. Also included in the regression analyses were variables measuring respondents' age, sex,* race, ethnicity, mothers' education* and employment, parents' grades, parental involvement in school, and characteristics of the census tract in which they lived. The table that Figure 4.2 is based on is included in the appendix.

*Indicates that this was a statistically significant predictor of delinquency.

regression coefficients) of factors as predictors of delinquency are displayed, with those factors associated with a greater likelihood of delinquent behavior to the right of the *y* axis, and those related to a lower probability of involvement to the left.

For the most part, these results are similar to the patterns that we found in the analysis of the full sample. School attachment, which here too is predicted by parents' work and school success, is a strong predictor of delinquency for young people living in American metropolitan areas, as is the poverty status of their families, but their employment status is not. There are two notable differences in the analyses of metropolitan, urban, young people. Here, those who had a father or stepfather present were significantly less likely to engage in delinquent behavior. So while fathers did not seem to matter in the full sample, they do in the urban sample. The association is quite modest, but it is statistically significant.

The other result that is different from our analysis of the full sample is that in examination of the metropolitan subsample, the percentage of

juveniles' residential neighborhood that is African American is significantly related to lower involvement in delinquency. This association was
close to statistical significance in the full sample, but here, like the effect
of the percentage of Hispanic residents, higher levels of black population is negatively associated with delinquency after other factors, notably school (indirectly, parents' employment and education) and family
characteristics are taken into account. To be clear, the race and ethnicity
of respondents is unrelated to their delinquency after other factors are
taken into account, but those living in predominately Latino or African
neighborhoods, holding other factors constant, are less likely to violate
the law, no matter what their race or ethnicity. These patterns suggest
that the causes of higher levels of delinquency among minority youth
are a result of the effects of disadvantage and its consequences. These
patterns are also consistent with other research that indicates that our
simplistic linking of race and crime is fundamentally flawed.[47] Crime
and delinquency appear to be more about disadvantage than about race
and ethnicity.

Labor Markets and Juvenile Pecuniary Crime

To a large extent the patterns that I have just described hold when we
study both property and violent crimes. Education directly influences
the likelihood that a child will have committed violations, and their
parents' work and educational experiences indirectly influence delinquency because they affect academic performance. Curiously, income is
not so straightforward.

Robert Merton's "Social Structure and Anomie" systematically stated
a theory of crime and deviance that is consistent with how many lay-
people believe the economy affects norm violators' behavior.[48] Merton argued that when needs and desires are not matched by legitimate
capacity to satisfy, individuals adapt; some of these adaptations produce
crime and delinquency. If you ask a person you meet at a bus stop or
on an elevator why some sections of a city have higher crime rates, they
are likely to answer that it is because the people there are poor, or that
they have high rates of unemployment, or those places are full of "bad
people" who refuse to work and therefore commit crimes. This is what
I derisively referred to as "the Jean Valjean theory of crime" earlier. I

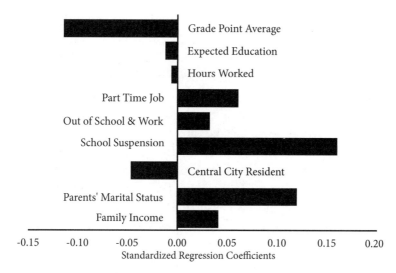

Figure 4.3. Explaining Property Delinquency
The variables in this figure, with the exception of expected education and hours worked, are statistically significant. Also included in the regression analyses were variables measuring respondents' age, sex,* race,* parents' employment, parents' education,* father's full-time employment,* and characteristics of the county in which they lived. The table that Figure 4.3 is based on is included in the appendix.
*Indicates that this was a statistically significant predictor of delinquency.

want to be clear that I am not equating Merton's theory or any version of strain theory with the Valjean theory, though the latter may be seen as a vulgarized, popular version of the former. Strain theories in general specify a more complex explanation than our lay brethren typically use in coming to their conclusions. Nevertheless, those at the bus stop and strain theorists, though they get there by less and more complex explanations, would both expect higher family incomes to suppress delinquency and that poverty, unemployment, or marginal employment would increase pecuniary crime and delinquency. This is not quite the case.

In our earlier study, my colleagues and I found that family income was positively related to participation in property delinquency.[49] Juveniles whose families had relatively higher incomes did it more, not less, frequently than did more financially challenged kids. When we take into account other factors, including academic success and parents' education and occupation, this positive relationship between family income and property or pecuniary crime still holds. "How could this be?" some might ask. Well, I sort of had the same question as a very new juvenile PO many years ago. One of my first cases was a sixteen- or seventeen-year-old middle-class, suburban white kid named Warren; his parents were together, his father was working a decent job, and his mother stayed at home to take care of my client and his sister. He repeatedly got in trouble at school and in the community, usually for petty theft and drinking. In one of my early conversations with the parents the mother literally said, "We don't know why he's like this; we've given him everything he's ever wanted." I, like I imagine many young do-gooders would have, wasn't sure if I should be stunned or if I should laugh (inside of course) at this clichéd expression of middle-class indulgence. Instead I asked myself, "How could this be?" Though just an anecdote, this story reminds us that other factors, such as the quality of parenting, are likely more important than income, the economy, or families' position in the social structure in determining how kids will behave. We should make sure that this is also remembered when we consider poor families, who also have the added burden of trying to perform high-quality parenting while struggling to survive.

To an extent these findings should not come as a surprise. Thirty years ago criminologist Charles Tittle and his colleagues published the results of a meta-analysis that found that social class was not a good predictor of juvenile delinquency.[50] Others found similar patterns.[51] These studies, like our analysis of labor market effects, use self-reports of delinquent behavior. Scholars who have contested these conclusions have countered that self-report studies focus on minor forms of delinquency, ignoring serious violations because they are too rare to measure reliably in the small samples that characterize many studies. They argue that when serious crimes are studied, usually using legal data, most often arrest data, that the economically disadvantaged are more frequent violators. In their study of the various ways that criminologists might measure delinquency Michael Hindelang and his colleagues offered a sound interpretation of these apparently contradictory research results.[52] Self-reports of delinquency, because they frequently focus on more minor violations, tap into a different domain of delinquency than police reports that focus on the more serious violations that are likely to provoke official reaction. The minor acts of delinquency are more evenly distributed among the juvenile population, while there is likely to be some form of negative relationship between serious delinquency and social class standing, albeit not a liner relationship. Also, as Farnsworth and her colleagues point out, if social class is not measured as a linear progression, but instead we consider who is living in poverty, then there does appear to be a link to delinquency.

One of the virtues of the NLSY data sets that my colleagues and I have been exploiting is that the sample sizes are sufficiently large enough to include questions about serious property and even violent crime. The initial NSLY data set (collection of which began in 1979) also oversampled lower income groups. We believe that our two findings, positive relationship between family income and property crime and a higher incidence of overall delinquency (both property and violent behavior) among children from poor families, indicates that middle-class kids engage in a substantial amount of "bad stuff" that may be only tangentially related to their privileged status, and that the poor are more likely to be involved in serious violations largely connected to their particular economic status.

Teachers of criminology know well the experience of presenting classic theories to a class only to have students raise their hands and dispute Merton or Cohen or Cloward and Ohlin because, as they say, "the biggest boozers and druggies at my high school and some of the worst graffiti writers and shoplifters were the upper-middle-class kids." We all respond to these delicious anecdotes by explaining the value of systematic observation, but even as we do, we recognize that a great deal of delinquency occurs in middle and upper class neighborhoods. To some extent some of this delinquency may be a byproduct of these kids' lives of privilege. In my classes I always enjoy the looks of disbelief and amazement on the faces of students from less privileged backgrounds when suburban, middle-class kids describe playing "mail box baseball"—driving along suburban streets after dark with a member of the group half out of the passenger side of the car, smashing roadside residential mail boxes as the car speeds pass. Or when they describe "doing donuts" on someone's lawn. These "harmless" recreational acts are not possible without a car. In fact, my juvenile probationer who was "given everything," Warren, got in trouble driving around and drinking with his buddies. Without a car, at least the violations are different. Conversely, fewer middle-class teenagers have the experience of being followed, as they try to shop in anonymity, by store security, but for kids who are stereotypically pegged as lower-class either by the location of the store or by their manner of dress, or because of their race, this is not an uncommon experience.[53]

The reason that we do not find a significant negative correlation between family income and most forms of delinquency is that minor violations occur not just in the lower-middle and working classes, but among the upper and upper-middle classes as well. Here I am using "working class" to distinguish them from the poor; the families of those classic blue-collar industrial workers discussed earlier are in this group. Teenagers from these groups as well as poor children engage in minor forms of delinquency too as they stretch their adolescent wings and are egged on by their friends. And in doing so they are not dissimilar from their more privileged age peers.[54] These behaviors should be distinguished from serious involvement in violent, property, or entrepreneurial crimes. Serious crime does occur more frequently in poor neighborhoods, and research indicates that children whose families are in poverty are somewhat more likely to participate in it.[55] We should be careful, however, not to assume that only the poor are so engaged, and not all of the crime that occurs in poorer neighborhoods is committed by the poor or even by people who live there.

Paul Jargowsky and company's paper argued that a reason that scholars do not find a social class and crime relationship is, in addition to the domain issues pointed out by Michael Hindelang and his colleagues, because we have typically searched for a linear association when instead the association is better represented by a reverse J-curve. There are higher serious crimes for the very lowest social class groups, the very poor, but no real observable linear pattern among groups more favorably situated.[56] And this fits with the results described by Margaret Farnsworth and her colleagues.[57]

Our finding is that even after taking into account measures of school success and attachment, parental education and employment, and neighborhood characteristics, family poverty predicts delinquent involvement is consistent with the reverse J-curve suggestion. It is reasonable to expect poor kids to do it more. In addition to the motivations that propel delinquents of other classes they are motivated by need, anger, and despair, and they live where there are more opportunities for serious offenses. Yes, drugs are sold in the suburbs, but the open-air markets that existed in profusion during the height of the crack epidemic tended to be in poor communities. Also, the cultural patterns that emerge when multiple generations of the residents of a community are economically and socially marginalized give rise to more serious crime and delinquency.[58]

In saying that the children of the poor are additionally motivated by need, anger, and despair, which were important parts of Albert Cohen's description of juveniles in *Delinquent Boys*, I should be careful not to paint a picture of morose, Dickens-like characters.[59] Just as the lives of middle-class suburbanites are more complex than the images presented in television's situation comedies, so too are those of the people of underclass neighborhoods. Anger and distress motivate the emergence of oppositional culture and propel some to serious crime, but there is more to life in the ghetto than that. People who live in these neighborhoods are surprised when at work or school; they become friends with middle-class people who all too frequently eventually get around to expressing their sympathy "for you having to grow up there." Life in some inner-city neighborhoods is hard, and too frequently violent and dangerous, but that is not the sum total of the lived experience of residents. They have joys, fun, and diversions as well, and sometimes juveniles there engage in delinquency for the same reason that their middle-class counterparts do; it is at times fun. And a great many— most—people who live there do not commit crimes.

What, then, can be said about labor force instability and pecuniary crime? While it does not appear that income is the reason for it, being in families where the adults did not do well in school or are not currently doing well occupationally increases juvenile participation in property crimes.[60] As is the case for violent crime, these influences on delinquency work through the school experience of adolescents. Our work, then, is not consistent with either simplistic versions of strain theory or with the fictional Jean Valjean theory. There is something about the labor force and educational experiences of parents that, independently of the family's income, turns some children off to school, and this is not a good thing for their involvement in pecuniary crime. Members of the Hole in the Wall Gang of my juvenile probation caseload were such kids. Their families, though not urban, were marginal to the labor market and hadn't done well in school. The kids themselves were not particularly attached to school. Without this mooring they elected to fill empty, boring hours by breaking into buildings.

But what about the special case of entrepreneurial crime? Is this different from pecuniary crime more generally? These crimes, as suggested above, may be more likely to be associated with living in lower-class neighborhoods because of the higher density of illegitimate opportunities there. We should remember that Richard Cloward and Lloyd Ohlin, over fifty years ago, taught us that real illegitimate opportunities would exist in greater abundance not in the poorest communities, but in those where the social structure is more organized and things are not quite so desperate.[61] These lessons have been reaffirmed by contemporary field studies.[62]

The bottom line is that poor kids and those whose parents and adult neighbors suffer labor market marginality participate in property crime for utilitarian motivations at times—but also, some portion of their delinquent behavior is, as Cohen described of gang members of the 1950s, nonutilitarian. In *Delinquency and Opportunity*, Cloward and Ohlin described what happens for adolescents who do not have access to the legitimate means of achieving the good life. They can become retreatist, dropping out of the pursuit of success and giving up goals, or they can opt for illegitimate opportunities or alternate definitions of the good life. The most available illegitimate occupations for marginalized youth are in the drug markets. A good contemporary example of the alternative objectives is described by Anderson in *Code of the Street*.[63] In the Philadelphia neighborhoods that Anderson studied, being tough and commanding respect are alternatives to the goals that are linked to the material good life pursued in the wider society.

Kids and Entrepreneurial Street Crime

It is important to recognize that entrepreneurial street crime is a subset of a larger hidden economy that exists in many inner-city neighborhoods. Sudhir Venkatesh, in his book *Off the Books: The Underground Economy of the Urban Poor*, describes a side economy of hustles, both legal and illegal, which spring up in response to marginalization from mainstream economic activity.[64] Examples of this behavior include freelance mechanics, carpenters, house cleaners, and painters, but also loan sharks, pimps, prostitutes, and drug dealers. Illegal entrepreneurial activity in these neighborhoods should be seen as springing from the same economic marginalization that produces the shady—but non-criminal—underground economy.

We should appreciate Cloward and Ohlin's invocation that just because an individual does not have access to the legitimate means of obtaining the good life, it does not mean that they can simply choose to turn to illegitimate means that will actually give them the opportunity for buying cars, houses, and the clothing that may constitute their conception of having "made it." To live like the fictional mobsters or the images portrayed in so many rap videos, young criminals would have to be very successful entrepreneurs in the most lucrative of illegal pursuits. Most have neither the skills nor the opportunity to do this, but some do. A most important necessity for adolescents who seek this route is successful, older criminals who provide skill and access to lucrative illegal opportunities.

Criminologist Jeffrey Fagan has argued that with the decline of good manufacturing jobs, the ancillary industry jobs that supported them, and declining incomes, new illicit economic opportunities have emerged because of expanded street-level drug markets.[65] As I described earlier, these options do appeal to many desperate young people, but most are likely relegated to low-level roles destined to provide economic benefits inferior to those they might obtain even from bottom end secondary sector legitimate employment. Real illegal opportunity requires the emergence of individuals or organizations that move drug marketing and other illicit enterprises beyond the atomized, helter-skelter delivery systems that exist on the street corners of some disadvantaged neighborhoods. The street market for marijuana distribution, because of the ease with which a person can enter as a seller and the relatively low-profit margin by the standard of some other drugs, is just such a market. When cocaine moved from the posh parlors, game rooms, and nightclubs of the middle and upper classes to the masses, with the development of techniques to deliver the "freebasing experience" in the form of crack, a major new opportunity was created for enterprising individuals and organizations that were unconcerned with the illegality of the trade.[66] With crack someone could step forward through glamorizing "the life" or through the effective use of terror, and attract marginalized juveniles and young adults to low, entry-level drug trade jobs. Criminologist Garth Davis described the unfortunate concurrence of the economic restructuring that accompanied deindustrialization and the emergence of crack markets.

> New York like other metropolitan areas in the mid-80s, was in the depths of a restructuring that had devastated neighborhoods both economically and socially. The effects of this destabilization were concentrated in inner cities and other historically neglected communities. In terms of employment, these areas witnessed the decimation of opportunities in the legitimate economy throughout the 70s. Jobs, particularly in manufacturing, migrated to the suburbs and other areas of the country. Nonwhite residents were excluded from a constricting labor market on a massive scale, as the loss of blue-collar and clerical jobs primarily deprived African-Americans of traditional avenues for financial sustenance and social mobility (Fagan, 1992). Increasingly, people in these communities were forced to depend on unregulated labor markets for employment and income (Kasarda, 1992). Given that drug dealing has always been a vital part of the illicit economy, it naturally followed that, as illegal endeavors became more indispensible to community life, so too did drug enterprises.
>
> These, then, were the circumstances into which crack emerged. With the intensification of poverty and social disorganization, crack became not only the most lucrative employment available in inner-city neighborhoods, but one of the few existing job opportunities period.[67]

Labor Markets and Juvenile Violent Crime

When I first began the study of labor markets and crime I think that at some level, I must have expected a version of the Jean Valjean theory to explain a link between employment and property crime. But what actually intrigued me was the possible connection between labor market patterns and violence. In earlier chapters I described the mechanisms that link labor market marginality and violent crime. A question that

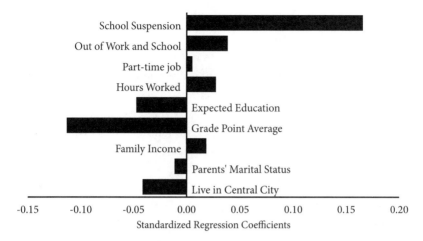

Figure 4.4. Explaining Violent Delinquency
The variables in the table, with the exception of parents' marital status and family income, are statistically significant. Also included in the regression analyses were variables measuring respondents' age,* sex,* race, parents' employment, parents' education, father's full-time employment, and characteristics of the county in which they lived. The table that Figure 4.4 is based on is included in the appendix.
*Indicates that this was a statistically significant predictor of delinquency.

remained was whether the connections that have been observed for delinquency in general and property crime could also explain how the economy is related to violent delinquency. Figure 4.4 shows results that my colleagues and I found for violent delinquency.

With violence, as is the case for other forms of delinquency, school success in the form of grade point average is one of the best predictors. Children who have good grades less frequently participate in violence. And as is the case with property crime, parents' academic and occupational success influences school success. When children see their parents' success they do better in school and are less violent. Also, contrary to popular expectations, when other factors are taken into account violence is unrelated to family income, but, interestingly, respondents who live in the central city of their metropolitan area are less likely to have engaged in violent delinquency.

Other education and employment variables' association with violence should also be noted. Juveniles who have greater expectations for education engage in less violence. This should not be surprising, as this is a measure of their stake in conformity; they are investing in their future by investing in education, and by staying out of trouble. Young people who held part-time jobs were not more likely to be involved in violence like they were with property crimes, and again the number of hours that they worked did not matter.

Two factors strongly indicate increased risk of violent delinquency: school suspension and being neither in school nor working. Young people who were neither in jobs nor school were considerably more likely to have been in trouble. This is the worst-case scenario. Far and away the best of these predictors of delinquency is school suspension (another factor associated with parental academic and employment success). Yes, young people who are getting into trouble already are the ones likely to be suspended, and it should not be surprising that they are also the ones most frequently engaging in violence. But when the importance of these two factors are taken together, should not it give pause to school administrations in the use of suspension or expulsion as a disciplinary tool?

With violence and property crime, analyses indicate that what is happening in school is very important for understanding who will become involved in delinquency. And consistent with the labor stratification and crime thesis, children whose parents are marginalized from the labor market and who themselves do not have academic success are more likely to become marginalized from school.

Implications for the Long Haul

Earlier I described—lamented—the seeming absence of politically charismatic leaders who might move disaffected young people as did Malcolm X, the founders of the Black Panther Party, and the leaders of the SDS in the 1960s. Of course, on the world and national stages there are such people (for example two of my favorites, Nelson Mandela and Desmond Tutu), but such people live a figuratively stratospheric life when viewed through the eyes of teenagers of the inner city or those mired in rural poverty. There may well be local level, grassroots charismatic leaders moving the marginalized young toward affective political involvement, but few signs point toward discernible mobilization and action. Many young people became engaged in and involved in

President Obama's run for the White House, but it is not clear to what extent this included the disaffected from the inner cities. There may be too few such charismatic, positive leaders today, but there seems to be more than an overabundance of charismatic leaders of corrupt enterprises who seized the opportunity created by the invention of crack to get the attention and adoration of some disaffected youth, and commandeer them for labor.

Three ethnographies that I have mentioned include descriptions of gangsters who effectively "manage" juveniles and young adults in the service of illegal enterprises: Ray in Philippe Bourgois's *In Search of Respect*, Lance of the Black Mobsters in Pattillo-McCoy's *Black Picket Fences*, and John Lenard, the Black Kings leader in the Robert Taylor projects that Venkatesh writes about in *American Project*.[68] Just in case the disaffected children of marginalized families and communities are too removed from the influence of such people and so-called opportunities, the popular media offers a constant flow of images calling them to the glories of the "thug life" and publishers happily jump on board with books like *Monster: The Autobiography of an L.A. Gang Member* by Sanyika Shakur aka Monster Kody Scott.[69]

Bourgois's *In Search of Respect* paints a painfully vivid description of what happens in a desperate inner-city neighborhood when a charismatic, entrepreneurial criminal is added to the mix. Bourgois, an anthropologist, lived in the New York's Spanish Harlem with his family for two years in order to study crack distribution and a crack house run by Ray, a person not likely to be defined as charismatic by the middle class but who is very much so on the streets. This setting produces crime in several ways. First there is the entrepreneurial crime of Ray and Primo, the manager of one of his crack houses, and those running the street sales. Then there are other pecuniary criminals, selling crack on the street corner with Ray's blessing, but with no real hope of ever doing much more than paying for their own habit and supplying pocket money. These same dealer-users, many of them are under the age of eighteen, also become involved in robbery, burglaries, larcenies, and other "hustles" associated with desperate junkies. Alongside them are other crackheads and junkies who do not sell drugs but participate in crime, from petty to serious, to pay for dope. Finally, depicted in Bourgois's portrait of *El Barrio* is the situation of company—the profusion of people whose potential for aggression is readily displayed—that makes violent crime more likely there. All that Bourgois observes in this neighborhood is made possible by the marginalization and isolation of so many who live there away from the world of quality legitimate work.

Another group of criminals regularly passes through the community who are important for the criminally illicit life around Ray's operation, and for the economy of *El Barrio*: purchasers who do not live there. Goods, services, and entertainment have long brought outsiders to poor and minority areas. During the Harlem Renaissance whites regularly sought out its nightspots to see black entertainers. Chinatowns from New York to San Francisco do a booming business in the tourist trade; the same is the case for the Cuban and Haitian communities of Miami, and of Mexican barrios from San Antonio to Chicago. They also come for illicit markets. They come for drugs to minority neighborhoods, and for prostitution in the same as well as in marginal white districts. They haunt Appalachia hoping to score some "shine" to take home as a souvenir or a conversation piece at their next dinner party.

In the early 1990s the Seattle Police Department ran a "reverse sting," arresting drug dealers in buy–bust operations at known open markets in the heart of the city's black community, the Central District or CD. They then replaced the dealers with undercover officers in order to arrest customers seeking to buy drugs. Of great interest—and not a big surprise to residents and merchants of the CD—the majority of those arrested customers were not from the neighborhood. They were not poor, and most were not of a racial or ethnic minority. The thwarted drug purchasers were from the University District, the predominantly white suburbs across the lake, the southern suburbs (which do have relatively large minority populations), and the rather comfortable neighborhoods on and hovering above Seattle's Lake Washington shoreline.

In the mid-1970s an African American reporter for a Pittsburgh newspaper wrote a story about two white police officers who were stabbed in The Hill District. After investigating his story, he wrote that the off-duty officers were assaulted while seeking the services of black prostitutes. The officers both survived their injuries. After the story ran, the irate wife of one of the officers called the reporter and screamed through the phone, "How dare you write that? If you could see me you'd know that my husband wouldn't be looking for no nigger." It seems that even those charged with enforcing the law go to the areas where young, poor, marginalized people struggle to make their livings in illicit market places. I and others wondered how that wife would have reacted (or not reacted) had she known that the reporter she was speaking to was a black former resident of The Hill.

In Sullivan's account of three groups of Brooklyn boys, one clearly sees varying levels of social class isolation and responses to it.[70] The African American and Latino groups live where most adults are marginal to the labor market. The adults from the neighborhoods where the white juveniles lived tended to have comparatively well-paying, blue-collar jobs. The boys from this neighborhood, which Sullivan called Hamilton Park, are mostly third- or fourth- generation white ethnics. They have some job options because their fathers and other men in the neighborhood, as well as a few local employers, provide networks of contacts to the labor market. Not far away, Sullivan recounts how boys in *La Barriada*, the Latino community, are more isolated from the broader society and how the adults are more marginal to the labor market than those in Hamilton Park. The third group, living where Sullivan called Projectville, which is predominantly black, is in very much the same situation that Wilson described when he wrote about the urban underclass or the ghetto poor as he subsequently described people living in this circumstance.[71] Each group's criminal behavior reflects the social structure of their neighborhood, the relative standing of adults to the labor market, and the labor market prospects of those juveniles.

We must be careful to distinguish the reality of the promises of entrepreneurial street crime from its reality. Teenagers facing an unpromising future of legitimate work look, with false hope, to two glorious alternatives: professional sports and organized crime, usually in drug marketing. The former is but a hopeless pipe dream to all but a scarce few. According to scholar Henry Louis Gates, the chances that a high-school student will become a player in the National Basketball Association or the NFL are substantially lower than that of becoming a physician.[72] According to the National Collegiate Athletic Association high-school basketball players have a 0.03 percent chance of playing any pro basketball, and that is likely to not be in the US playing in the NBA; high-school football players have but a 0.08 percent change of going pro.[73] Yet the myth and dreams persist. For those without athletic talent, or who recognize early that their physical skills will not take them far, the lure of big fast money in the drug trade may become alluring. Juvenile street dealers brag to their friends about the money they make. They flash roles of bills and wear gaudy gold chains. They are certain that they are on their way to becoming the next Ray (the dealer in Bourgois's *In Search of Respect*). Many times they are as mistaken as their neighbor who is convinced that he's destined to become the next Michael Jordan. The reality that most street dealers have very modest incomes (see chapter 1) does not comport with popular images of the big money drug dealer that are advanced by both popular and news media. Most local television news watchers in major urban areas are familiar with the "Live at Five" (or Six, or Eleven) remote camera footage of arrested drug dealers cuffed and being searched by hardworking police officers. Frequently, somewhere in that shot is the wad of bills and the drugs taken form the alleged dealer. This image is also seen on popular television shows and in movies, and it is also transported via the street's effective but inaccurate gossip line. The reality is that often the bills are small denominations, or a substantial portion of it is owed to the street dealer's higher-level supplier. The street dealer is most likely to be arrested when business is going well—just having made sales, including those unwittingly to narcotics agents, or a big buy. At these times they will be flush (thus the big roll), but this hides the many days and weeks when things are not going well. As I described earlier, drug dealing is a notoriously up-and-down business for the street dealer.

Readers should also note that the heyday of crack has passed. It is today less popular than it was when it arrived in many American cities in the late 1980s. In fact, there is evidence that the "crack epidemic" of the 1980s and 90s was more of a surge in media reporting than actual use.[74] It was a new way to deliver cocaine, so it changed some things on the streets where it was popular. Those who may have made a bit of money selling crack are not doing so well now. Some street observers speculate that popular beliefs about the devastating characteristics of crack addiction sowed the seeds of both the drug's popularity and its dealers' demise.

There are, to be sure, those who successfully move from being a thug to the life of street "soldier" of a criminal enterprise. And a very few of the latter ascend and actually are able to make an illegitimate living. Along the way, the lives of most, and the social life of their communities, are usually laid to waste. Nicholas Lehmann's *Promised Land* describes the hope with which early residents of Chicago's federally funded housing projects moved into new apartments.[75] Until the construction of the Robert Taylor Homes, Cabrini Green, and other developments like them, residents of Chicago's so-called Black Belt were constrained by racial residential segregation to living in overcrowded, blighted, fire-hazard tenement slums on the South Side. Observers of urban America, especially the residents of the projects, know that the hope did not last long. Venkatesh describes the relationship that developed between residents and powerful gangs because of the vacuum created in the absence of leadership and real care on the part of the city and federal housing authorities.[76] The gangs took control and made money via the drug trade, but while the upper echelons made money, the rank and file of the organization received limited financial payoffs and were subjected to the whims, sometimes violent, of their superiors. The communities first neglected and later abandoned by local and national bureaucracies are further abused by entrepreneurial gangsters.

In a world likely to frustrate aspirations for careers in the NBA or NFL, or real ascension to the truly entrepreneurial reaches of the crime world, most young people, faced with limited or even no quality job prospects, can either settle for the lower rungs of the latter or define themselves in alternative terms. This, of course, is not unlike the formulations of Cloward and Ohlin, whose version of strain theory emphasizes that not all who are denied access to the legitimate means of obtaining socially sanctioned goals have access to illegitimate alternatives that offer actual potential of culminating in the good life. These "double failures," as Cloward and Ohlin refer to them, turn to nonpecuniary sources of defining themselves. In *Delinquency and Opportunity* they described how this social circumstance gave rise to "conflict" and "retreatist" gangs, the former focusing on building macho reputations and protecting turf—the classic street gangs of the late 1950s—and the latter composed of those living life in drugged or alcohol oblivion.

Updated versions of Cloward and Ohlin's delinquents are described in rich detail by the accounts of Anderson, Bourgois, Pattillo-McCoy, and Sullivan of the neighborhoods they studied, which suffer severely from contemporary economic shifts. A few can pursue real illegal careers because the opportunities are at hand in drug trafficking or other lucrative illegal hustles, but most will experience little more opportunity to succeed in this way than they would have by conformingly pursuing school and low-level employment. Most others will develop lifestyles similar to those in Cloward and Ohlin's retreatist gangs: they spend their days in pursuit of enough money to buy a few hits of crack, a bit of heroin, or a bottle of Mad Dog 20/20.

Others, though, especially the youngest of the disaffected, will display behavior more like the conflict gangs that Cloward and Ohin wrote about. Gangs focused on reputation and protecting turf more than on illegal enterprise is the reality in most American cities. The media has fed us a steady stream of public relations for different kinds of gangs, those who are in actuality more like our traditional images of organized crime. For most gangs it is the age-old protection of territory that concerns them: some members individually engaged in the drug trade, but not as an organized crime or gang activity.

Social Context Matters

Crime for many in the most downtrodden of inner cities is a byproduct of cultural adaptations, like the street codes written about by Anderson, and produced substantially by the persistent economic marginalization of some of the inner-city communities of major cities. What is importantly different from recent cultural explanations of crime among the poor is the strong link made by contemporary scholars to the social structural conditions that beget these adaptations. Others in the past gave a fleeting nod to structural forces, but fundamentally they very much attributed individuals' impoverished circumstance to those poor people's own weaknesses. Crime and poverty were explained by a common third variable: sometimes it was the inability of "low-class" people to defer gratification, or poor maintenance of norms demanding hard work and personal accountability as a result of welfare dependence.[77] As William Ryan articulates, these explanations blame the victim for the social structural positions in which they live, within a wider society and economy whose organization perpetuates their marginalization from work and their poverty.[78]

What both the recent ethnographies and a growing body of quantitative research points out is that it is not solely within the individual that economic marginalization reaches its full potential as a criminogenic force. We have found some evidence that both individual work circumstance and family poverty contribute to criminality, but something more happens when marginalized people are in a situation of company where those around them are out of work, employed in dead-end jobs, or despair for their future because they see little hope in the experience of those around them to be make them optimistic about their economic future. In the next chapter I turn to the important contextual influences on the relationships between work, school, and crime.

"FORGET YOU!"—an in-your-face epithet dismissively aimed at an antagonizer in The Hill District of my youth—has two meanings.[79] On the surface it tells the person you say it to that they don't matter, that they are irrelevant and not worthy of consideration. But it meant more than that. Consider the first letter "F" and what stronger word than "forget" might it be substituting for in this phrase. It is similar to another replacement phrase that was used in older black communities: "Maryland Farmer," as in Lou Rawls's "you jive time Maryland Farmer,"[80] which really was seeking to put neither residents of Maryland nor agricultural workers down, but was a substitute for another phrase whose letters were "MF." For our purposes, "forget you," also has two meanings. First, it is the response of young people to those who try to pressure them into taking jobs that they define as slave jobs. The angry invocation is a consequence of feeling that to work such jobs is a put-down, a relegation to a lesser status. But second, it is what the businesses, the economy, governments, and society seems to regularly say to those consigned to the bottom rungs of the structurally stratified labor market. They are forgotten. How else can we explain how leaders, such as those of Pittsburgh I wrote about earlier, can say that we—a community, a country, an economy—has or will recover when there are people chronically unemployed, homeless families living in parks and cars and sleeping on the heating grates of our cities, or children to whom we deliver an inadequate education? We have said to them, just as some young people say to the opportunity for a life toiling in the secondary sector, "Forget you!"

5

"Life in the Hood"

How Social Context Matters

John Edgar Wideman did not explain the differences between his accomplished life as a scholar and writer and that of his brother Robby, serving a life sentence, by blaming those differences on their parents, family, or on the two brothers' intellectual abilities. The family remained strong and vital and in the eyes of the brother on the faculty of Brown University, his younger brother is very intelligent. It was Homewood, their community, which changed from the community that had nurtured their parents and differences in how these two bothers interfaced with it.

> Because Homewood was self-contained and possessed such a strong personality, because its people depended less on outsiders than they did on each other for many of their most basic satisfactions, they didn't notice the net settling over their community until it was already firmly in place. Even though the strands of the net—racial discrimination, economic exploitation, white hate and fear—had existed time out of mind, what people didn't notice or chose not to notice was that the net was being drawn tighter, that ruthless people outside the community had the power to choke the life out of Homewood, and as soon as it served their interests would do just that. During the final stages, as the net closed like a fist around Homewood, my mother couldn't pretend it wasn't there. But instead of setting her free, the truth trapped her in a cage as tangible as the iron bars of Robby's cell.[1]

They still expected me to be like my sister and brothers. They didn't know I thought youns was squares. Yeah. I knew I was hipper and groovier than youns ever thought of being. Streetwise, into something. Had my own territory and I was bad. I was a rebel. Wasn't following in nobody's footsteps but my own. And I was a hip cookie, you better believe it. Wasn't a hipper thing out there than your brother, Rob. I couldn't wait for them to turn me loose in Homewood.[2]

Mrs. Wideman, their mother, recognized the problem and implications of the changes she observed in Homewood. Speaking to John of Robby and his friends, including one named Garth who had recently died, she said:

Out there in the street doing wrong, but that's where most of them are. What else can they do, John: Sometimes I can't blame them. No jobs, no money in their pockets. How they suppose to feel like men? Garth did better than most. Whatever else he was into, he kept that little job over at Westinghouse and helped out his mother.[3]

Sociologists have long emphasized the importance of community context as an influence on what the people who live there do. I know of no sociologists who have argued that social context is destiny, but the notion that social contexts matter is fundamental to the discipline's theoretical tradition. To a social science student John Wideman's attribution that changes in the character of Homewood are partly responsible for the pattern of life that Robby pursued do not come as a surprise or seem unlikely; rather, we would be shocked if major community changes did not affect the behavior in some who came of age in rapidly or dramatically changing places. To be sure, individuals have agency, and they are a part of the authorship of their own lives, but they do not write that script alone. Their social setting is their coauthor.

We know that the rates for the most serious common crimes are higher in poorer neighborhoods than in those where more financially comfortable people live.[4] We know too that this is in part because individuals from poor families are more likely to commit some types of serious crimes,[5] and there is anecdotal evidence, mentioned in the previous chapter, that people who are not poor sometimes come to distressed neighborhoods to find illegal goods and services, potentially getting involved in others crimes as well as both victims and perpetrators. There is, however, something more to the influence of social context than simply the additive accumulation of individual behaviors. When marginalized people live with similarly situated people, it makes a difference. These differences need not be negative, but some of them are. During the Great Depression the uneven changes in crime, some types increasing and others decreasing, was possible because people out of work or otherwise struggling to survive or feed their families could look about them and see many others in the same circumstance. They were in the same lifeboat together, struggling together to hold on until help arrived or the economic circumstance engulfing them subsided. It may turn out that the same phenomenon occured in the Great Recession of the first decade of the twenty-first century.

Until the economic crisis of 2008, as the US became more of a postindustrial economy there were not as many people put out of work. Now the unemployed and underemployed ranks have increased substantially, and as those people look about them instead of seeing those in the broader society suffering along with them, they see others doing very well. After decades of steady increase, labor force participation in the US began dropping in 1999.[6] And in the past three decades the ratio of CEOs' to workers' wages has gone from about forty to one to nearly four hundred to one.[7] One cannot really expect many to have the Great Depression-era "lifeboat together" definition of reality with the coincidence of these trends. And it is not just the relative income of chief executives that causes comparative pain. While low-skilled, working-class jobs have disappeared, jobs for more educated people were created in formerly industrial centers (see chapter 2).

The Great Recession has accelerated another trend in the US, called by some the "hollowing out of the middle class": the decline of many and the stagnation of other middle-class incomes as the wealthy grow increasingly richer. In 2009 American incomes fell, except in the highest income brackets. There, income grew substantially even as unemployment rates stayed high and the federal government struggled to stimulate economic growth.[8]

Early in the twentieth century, University of Chicago sociologists argued and offered data that, unlike the fears popularly expressed about the negative behavior and character of immigrants, "pathological behavior" was a characteristic of the neighborhoods they inhabited and not of the people themselves.[9] In recent years the social disorganization theory espoused by the Chicago School sociologists has been renewed and extended.[10] Robert Sampson and his colleagues have focused on the collective efficacy of communities. High-collective efficacy neighborhoods have that characteristic where residents are willing to look out for their neighbors and to act in furtherance of informal social control. That might mean interceding if children are acting badly or calling the police to report drug dealers. Collective efficacy is a resource necessary for effective social control of both residents and those passing through. Criminologists Robert Bursik and Harold Grasmick emphasized, in what they call a systemic approach to neighborhood social disorganization, the concept of institutional interconnectedness, which when not developed and fostered leads to more criminal behavior. Their point was that in reality we have to see neighborhoods as existing in wider social, economic, political, and institutional environments. What proponents of both versions of modern disorganization theory agree on, among other things, is the importance of social context as a determinant of behavior.

Labor Market Contexts

As I described earlier, we have found that the relationship between work and crime is influenced by the employment of those living nearby.[11] In that study of young adults, we found that men and women who spend more time out of the labor force are more likely to engage in both violent and property crimes. Importantly, though, this effect is only observed where unemployment rates are higher than average. The county, which can be thought of as the local labor market, is an important context for adults who are working or seeking employment. This is likely very different for children who, even when bussed to schools, are less mobile than their adult counterparts. For them, the neighborhood may be the more important venue from which the friends and acquaintances who influence their lifestyle and behavior are drawn. Of course, as teenagers grow older and learn to drive their "friendship catchment areas" will expand, especially if they have ready access to cars or effective public transportation.

Larger political entities such as counties, cities, states, or even the nation state are important in that the latter constitutes a labor market and the smaller units constitute some form of localized labor markets. In a discussion of how the economy affects common crime through the structure of labor markets, it is important to acknowledge national economies and the emergence of globalization as an economic force makes requisite the consideration of the worldwide economy and changes to labor markets resulting from the migration of and the internationalization of both capital and jobs (but less so workers).

To a large extent the current circumstance of American workers occurred because of a combination of the globalization of markets and the United States' national economic culture; where quarterly profits, short-term planning horizons, and a take-the-money-and-run ethic appears to rule. Such a philosophy allows mortgage bankers to engage in predatory lending, for banks to foreclose on homeowners without bothering to take requisite legal steps, and the rewarding of big bonuses to CEOs and executives even when the company has accepted government bailouts. These and other patterns shocked the American public when they came to light in the Great Recession, but as of today few signs are evident that a new ethic is emerging. By national economic culture, I mean that the focus on short-term profits and payoffs that characterize both management and unions, corporations and government set the stage for what occurred. Corporations are driven to meet Wall Street's quarterly profit expectations. Elected officials begin running for reelection as soon as they are elected. And union officials negotiate the biggest packages that they can for their members, even when doing so threatens the competitiveness of companies and sometimes even entire industries. To fully appreciate how the economy leads individuals to engage in crimes, or for neighborhoods or cities to have higher or lower crime rates, we have to recognize that the local processes are occurring within larger national and international contexts.

What occurs at the national and international levels in turn determines how regional and local economies fare. I wrote earlier of how Rust Belt cities and states suffered as a result of deindustrialization. We should not make the mistake of attributing all of the closed plants and lost jobs to globalization. True, some American corporations moved out of the cities and continue to move sizable portions of their operations offshore to take advantage of offers of lower worker costs or tax incentives, and others struggled uncompetitively with non-US companies, but there were domestic shifts that cost jobs in the old industrial states as well. The Sunbelt states of the South and West encouraged and cajoled executives to consider them as sites for new, modernized plants. A number of these states have "right to work" laws (and there are movements in some northern and midwestern states to do the same): or there are rules disallowing closed union shops and other antiunion policies, and residents and workers who believe less in organized labor. Consequently, unions that were critical to the wages and benefits of industrial workers in the Rust Belt states are less able to wield power or influence the economic welfare of workers in some of the states where industries moved. Also, these states tend to have lower tax rates. Many could provide land in uncongested areas where companies might build new facilities, thus dropping their costs for bringing in raw materials or shipping finished product. The result of these states' abilities to offer good weather, cheaper workforces, weaker unions, and other financial and quality of life (for executives) incentives, made them, if not as easy as some non-US locations, certainly appealing. Big Steel and Big Auto both opened new plants that were cleaner and more efficient in Southern states.

The General Motors Corporation's sighting of its now-shuttered Saturn plant in Smyrna, Tennessee was a good example. After considering a number of possible locations, GM made Tennessee the winner of the competition—a competition with a number of potential locations actively bidding to lure the new plant. And after a bidding war, Tennessee lost out on a new Toyota plant to neighboring Mississippi.

The open competition for manufacturing facilities continues, even though the nature of manufacturing in the US has changed dramatically. Today it is more likely that states are competing for modern "clean" industries. Politicians in many locals have convinced their constituents that they are about to become the new Silicon Valley. States, counties, and cities compete to be the new hi-tech, biotech, or green industries capital, bringing high-paying jobs and businesses that are less likely to pollute (another local cost averted). And even though resulting jobs frequently do not go to current residents but instead attract highly trained workers from elsewhere, these new residents contribute handsomely to local tax bases and enlarge government coffers, and they bring substantial purchasing power—also a good thing for the local economy.

In the 2008 presidential election, candidates argued that they would provide good, clean jobs in an emerging green economy. If high-energy prices and global warming do produce the political will that leads to the development of new industries, we can look forward to increased fevered competition to determine where companies locate. An important theme in 2012 presidential politics was how the federal government encourages, and might discourage the movement of jobs off shore.

Several years ago, when Boeing Aircraft announced that it would move its national headquarters out of Seattle, the cities of Chicago, Dallas, and Denver fell over each other to land the corporate prestige and jobs that would come with the relocation. Chicago won. In 2003 Boeing kept both states and nations waiting anxiously while various locations repeatedly upped their bids to obtain all or part of the assembly facilities for a new generation jet liner. The company rewarded several of the nations (and states within the US), where they have major customers, with commitments to complete part of the assembly in their plants. Final assembly of the 787 aircraft was won by the State of Washington, with an incentive package to Boeing of tax breaks and other benefits totaling more than three billion dollars.[12] But then Boeing opened a second production line for the 787 in South Carolina, with a less skilled but cheaper labor force, after receiving incentives from that state. Why are nations and states willing to invest so much in such competitions? The answer is simple: jobs.

Several times I have returned to the example of two young men invited by friends to spend an evening socializing: the secondary sector employee joins them and later is susceptible to getting in trouble, while the primary sector worker, a steelworker, declines, citing the need to be at work the next morning. Later I described the Seattle metropolitan area as a twenty-first century city, in part because of Boeing's presence as a major manufacturer and employer (there is also considerable employment in other modern-day industries such as software and computer technology manufacturing, and biotechnology). As a result of competition from Europe's Airbus and the downturn for airline companies in the wake of the September 11 terrorist attacks on the World Trade Center and the Pentagon, Boeing laid off in excess of thirty thousand workers in the Puget Sound region. Boeing's employment has since bounced back.

If we change the example so that instead of a steelworker it is a Boeing worker, it becomes a good contemporary example of how world politics, international competition, the policies of both the US government and the governments that comprise the Airbus consortium, and the government of the State of Washington, are critical for what happens at the local level. In the city of Seattle and in the imagined neighborhood that our two young men live in, these faraway occurrences affect lives. When I initially used this example it was to draw attention to the long-term investment that one young man was making in his entry-level job. In 2002 and 2003 he was more than likely laid off—last hired is first fired, not unlike the laid-off workers of United States Steel or General Motors Corporation several decades earlier.

Although the Seattle area economy is not as dependent on Boeing as it once was (in the early 1970s when aircraft production was in an extremely deep and prolonged slump, there was a billboard outside of Seattle-Tacoma International Airport that read "Would That Last Person Leaving Seattle Please Turn Out the Lights"), the post-9/11 bad economic times for airline companies and for Boeing have not had as an extremely negative effect on the local economy (bad, but not catastrophic). But if Boeing had not rebounded or if its high-quality jobs were not replaced, then the ripple effect through the metropolitan area and its neighborhoods might possibly have increased crime because our young would-be Boeing worker would have had to find work in a McJob, if at all.

There are two issues that we must now explore: how are the effects of employment or labor market distributions on crime in local environments such as neighborhoods conditioned by industrial and economic forces of nations, and, how do variation in these local environments condition the relationships between individuals' work experiences and their involvement in crime? The descriptions above illustrate that these two issues are not separable, but empirical links between them and analyses of the issues themselves are fairly new.

Local Labor Market Conditions and Neighborhood Crime Rates

Our earlier analyses of the capacity of labor stratification variables to explain neighborhood homicide levels in the census tracts of three large

American cities, Cleveland, Seattle, and Washington, DC, was designed to exam how three different types of local labor markets affect social processes within their communities.[13] A not inconsequential reason for selecting these three cities was that in the early 1990s all of their police departments collected and maintained crime statistics for census tracts, the local neighborhood sized units established by the US Bureau of the Census. Law enforcement in few municipalities maintained such data at the time. Since then, interest on the part of researchers and the police in crime hotspots and software and technological advances have led many more departments to collect these data. The substantive reason for each city's selection was to represent different kinds of local economies and labor markets.

One of those cities, Washington, has another very important characteristic: it was, until just the first decade of the twenty-first century, a black city. One of the early large American cities to elect a black mayor, Walter Washington became the District of Columbia's first elected mayor in 1975 after Congress approved home rule. In addition to his years of service in the federal government and his performance as appointed mayor (prior to home rule), Washington was elected because of the large majority black population residing in the District. The city did not get home rule until 1974; up until that time it was governed, like a colony of the rest of the country, by the US Congress.[14] And still today, the Congress has a very strong voice in DC governance. The social and economic structure of Washington could not be separated from its blackness. Washington, which had included slave markets early in the nineteenth century, drew many freedmen to "Lincoln's city" after the Civil War. Government jobs and civil service positions made the city a popular draw for blacks during the Great Migration, even though usually only low-level jobs were open to African Americans. After that period African Americans continued to move to Washington, because by then it had developed the reputation of being a good city for black advancement because of the large black community, the presence of black businesses, and a sizable black middle class.

As I described earlier, the labor stratification thesis effectively predicted 1990 neighborhood homicide rates in Cleveland and Seattle. But the same was not true in Washington, where we could not predict murder rates using neighborhood employment variations. What explains the variation in homicide rates in Washington is the percentage of neighborhoods' populations that are black. This one variable is such a powerful predictor that no other indicator included in the same analysis can be statistically significant—not poverty rate, not average educational attainment, not community divorce rates, not the presence of large numbers of young men, and not labor instability. On the other hand, the percentage of black residents, in addition to being a powerful predictor of homicide rates, strongly predicts other important indicators as well. That is, the high-poverty neighborhoods are also black neighborhoods. The low-education neighborhoods are black neighborhoods, as well as those with high levels of family disruption and, importantly for our purposes, so too are those places with relatively high levels of unemployment and employment in secondary sector jobs—important reasons for their high poverty rates.

One cannot say that in Washington to be African American is to live in a distressed neighborhood; we must remember that there are those black middle- and even upper-middle-class communities within the borders of the District of Columbia. But to live in a distressed neighborhood or one where many people have not obtained much education, and certainly to live among more people who are marginal to the labor market, is to live in predominantly black census tract. And we must remember that Washington, like most American cities, remains highly racially residentially segregated.[15]

Those who love the District, as it is affectionately referred to by many who live there, no doubt took exception to my earlier characterization of it as similar to the apartheid cities of South Africa, but the fact of the matter is that few cities outside of the Third World have had the level of inequality, which nearly parallels racial inequality, as did Washington before recent gentrification changed the city's complexion. An analysis of such a place predicated on a theory that explains persistent inequalities in the modern industrial world, dual labor market theory, may simply be overwhelmed by Washington's level of racial social and economic inequality that also includes considerable political inequality that was not even measured in our study.

Unfortunately, a study of three cities cannot really take into account the variations necessary to capture how the composition of local labor markets condition neighborhood patterns, but now that census tract crime rates for a large number of cities are available through National Neighborhood Crime Survey (NNCS), we are now able to examine how this multilevel process works.[16] The NNCS includes information on the crimes that occurred in each of the census tracts of eighty-seven American cities. There were more than 8,000 individual neighborhoods (census tracts) in these cities. Included in the survey are many large cities, but also some smaller ones such as Fort Wayne, Indiana; Akron, Ohio; and Tucson, Arizona. Included were cities of the old Rust Belt (Pittsburgh, Cleveland, Milwaukee, and Detroit), thriving cities with diverse economies (Seattle, San Francisco, Boston, Miami, and Denver), and cities with other industrial configurations.

Recently my colleagues and I used multilevel modeling techniques to study how variations in local labor markets (the characteristics of the industries and jobs in cities and the counties that surround them) affect the levels of crimes in their neighborhoods.[17] We used NNCS to study the neighborhoods (census tracts) that are nested in the eighty-seven American cities included. We found that over and above the levels of disadvantage and labor market characteristics of neighborhoods that labor instability of metropolitan (local) labor markets influences both violent and property crimes in neighborhoods. We discovered several important things. First, neighborhoods in cities with high-level service employers, where jobs are more like primary sector jobs, have lower average rates of violence than those in cities with fewer of these kinds of jobs. Also, neighborhoods in cities where low-level service industries (typically offering jobs with secondary sector characteristics) dominate the local economy, there are higher levels of violent and property crime.

Offering additional evidence that it is no longer just manufacturing that drives American social life, we found that the proportion of local labor market jobs that were in these industries had no real effect on the levels of violent crimes in neighborhoods. We think (and this is consistent with others) that this is evidence that the transformation of American industry, and its consequences that Wilson documented, may have been completed.[18] That said, we know that communities that felt the effects of the Great Recession most acutely because of plant closures are still suffering. Nationally, however, the level of manufacturing does not appear to be as important is it was when my colleagues and I studied Cleveland, Seattle, and Washington in the 1990s.

We found the same patterns for property crime. Local labor markets that had comparatively more people employed in secondary sector jobs had, in addition to more violent crime, more property offenses. Neighborhoods in cities with more high-level service industries, which hire more people into jobs that have the characteristics of primary sector work, have lower property crime rates.

Interestingly, it is not just the distribution of the primary and secondary sector workers into neighborhoods that matter. We found that neighborhoods that are within local labor markets with a disproportionate share of low-end, secondary sector workers in low-end service jobs see their crime rates go to the highest levels. It is not just the level of disadvantage and the kind of employment held by residents of neighborhoods that matter, but the character of the cities they are in as well. Governments that want to improve the lives of their citizens should recognize that maintaining and attracting employers that offer high-quality positions to workers not only benefit those workers—they benefit the local economy, and they have important consequences for the maintenance of healthy, low-crime communities.

Neighborhood Context and Criminal Involvement

What, though, of social context in which lives are lived? How important is social context? Criminologists for some time now have been trying to empirically specify the effect of social context on individual involvement in criminal behavior, but we have collectively found this to be a difficult enterprise. Often no statistically significant effects can be found, and when one is produced the effect is small, leading some to (prematurely in my opinion) conclude that the environment in which a person lives has little or no real effect on their behavior.[19] It is obvious from that last sentence that I do not share this belief, but instead strongly believe that social context is not just substantively significant, but very important. At times we struggle to illustrate this statistically because our means of measuring and analyzing contextual effects are limited, but they are improving. There are now analyses using regression techniques that show modest but theoretically important influences of social context on crime, and recent ethnographic studies offer compelling evidence as well; with the emergence of network analyses and hierarchical modeling techniques we have new tools that are by no means perfect for addressing this issue, but they are helping considerably.

We know, as described earlier in chapters 2 and 3, that poor places, be they cities or neighborhoods, have higher crime rates than do better-off areas, but also we know that we cannot attribute this solely to the poor. Enforcement practices, perhaps the diminished social capital that too frequently characterizes poor communities, or simply the fact that they may be better places to go for those motivated to commit crimes and those looking to find illegal activities, likely contribute to more crime where the poor live. But while we do not want—as every undergraduate sociology major knows—to commit the ecological fallacy when interpreting aggregate correlations, it is reasonable to expect that those living the most desperate lives are measurably more likely to commit desperate acts. Yet we know that simply looking at individual incomes or family incomes does not necessarily predict crime in the way we would expect it to if our expectations are based on simple utilitarian conceptions. In chapter 4 we saw that in some of our analyses, juvenile involvement in property crime was positively related to their family's incomes. Yet still, as was humorously illustrated on the cover of Gwynne Nettler's 1970s criminology text, not even the most liberal criminologist would dare go to the poor side of town, obviously out of place and just as obviously with a bit of money, in the dark of night because he's read the latest paper saying that crime is unrelated to income.[20] This is because even if we struggle to display it in our models, there is something that happens when real poverty is concentrated. That circumstance creates a context in which the individual's economic circumstance interacts with their environment to affect that person's propensity to criminal behavior, and where more such people live and spend time, it can be dangerous. This is what Anderson observes when people from "decent" families adopt "street" values and behavior as a defensive posture in the face of threats around them.

Young Adult Employment in Social Context

Recall that young adults who were employed during the last year were significantly less likely to have committed a criminal violation if they had a solid job. Those working in secondary sector occupations had an elevated probability to have committed criminal action in the previous year, and that this effect is present in counties with higher levels of unemployment but not those with a comparatively low unemployment rate. Counties make sense as a measure for the local labor markets, but so much of this theory as well as others are focused on neighborhoods. And counties cannot be conceived of as anything like a neighborhood or community. Which brings us to the question of how neighborhood context affects the relationship between work and crime. To examine neighborhood social context, my colleagues and I have studied labor market participation and crime by including, along with the respondents' individual characteristics, measures of their census tracts' racial composition (the percentage of black and Latino residents) and the level of social disadvantage.[21] Social disadvantage was measured by a scale that included the percentage of residents who were extremely poor, the percentage on public assistance, the percentage of the population over eighteen living in poverty, the percentage not married, and the percentage of residents who were in the workforce but not employed. Neighborhoods did not have the effects that we expected. The ethnic composition of respondents' neighborhoods and the level of social disadvantage had only very small direct effects on the criminality of individuals independently of the respondents' personal, educational, and employment characteristics. The only neighborhood effect that was significant was (and again contrary to most criminological expectations) that net of individual characteristics, those who live in neighborhoods with blacker populations were a little less involved in crime.

Consider our results in the context of the findings of our county contextual analyses summarized in chapter 3 and those presented by Massey and Denton, who argue that racial residential segregation magnifies the criminogenic circumstance in black communities because of the resultant concentration of poverty and disadvantage. Here we see again that individuals who are marginal to the labor market are more likely to become involved in crime, but for these young adults their neighborhood context does not matter so much. After their individual characteristics and circumstances are taken into account, only the percentage of the population that is black predicts crime, and it predicts that they will be less involved if they live in communities with more

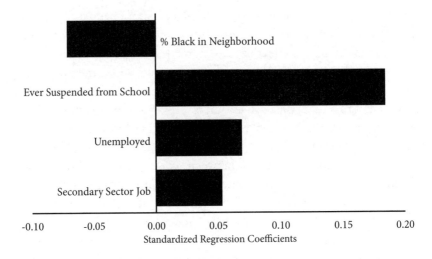

Figure 5.1. Explaining Young Adult Crime Using Employment and Neighborhood Variables
The variables in this figure are statistically significant. Also included in the regression analyses were variables measuring respondents' age,* sex,* race, ethnicity, marital status, father's highest grade completed, parental income, whether they were currently in high school, several additional employment variables, and neighborhood characteristics (percentage Hispanic and percentage disadvantaged). The table that Figure 5.1 is based on is included in the appendix.
*Indicates that this was a statistically significant predictor of delinquency.

African Americans (readers should note that we found that the race and ethnicity of individual NLSY respondents were not significantly related to criminal behavior). What we have found does not contradict Massey and Denton's findings. Segregated places do have higher crime rates, but that is a characteristic of the places, not of specific individuals who live there.[22] Our results do call into question those who would suggest that black culture in America is itself criminogenic. We do not find reason to believe that to live in a black community is to put oneself into a subculture that is crime-producing. Rather, it is the individual social and economic disadvantages that come with being marginally employed.

Our next step was to create an interaction term combining the individuals' employment variable with the social disadvantage measure of the census tract where they live so that we could consider the conditional effects of being out of work and living with others who are socially and economically marginalized. But contrary to our expectations and to the predictions of the labor stratification thesis, in the analyses for our full sample—respondents representing the US as a whole—there was no conditional effect. Employment situation was not conditioned by characteristics of the neighborhoods in which respondents live. In general, we could discern very limited environmental effects on the individual criminality of young adults.

A more complex—and I think a more interesting—picture begins to emerge as we explore subsamples. There are, not especially surprisingly, no contextual effects for rural residents. Knowing more about the characteristics of the rural neighbors of NLSY respondents did not help us to understand their criminal behavior any more than we already had based on their personal characteristics. In a national sample it is unlikely that we would have sufficient proportion of the sample from rural areas that are characterized by concentrated and isolated poverty and deprivation. Clearly there are people living in socially isolated communities of concentrated poverty (for instance on Native American reservations or in pockets of Appalachia), where people live just as desperately and some times more so than those of the worst of urban slums. A study of these places would likely find contextual influences that will not be visible from our analyses of the relatively small available NLSY rural subsample.

Social life, as everyone who has moved from farm or village to the city can attest, is different in the metropolis. When we analyzed the data for respondents who lived in metropolitan areas, as reported for the full sample, individuals who lived in the neighborhoods with more black people reported engaging in slightly less crime than others after we took into account other factors, and those living in more disadvantaged tracts reported more criminal involvement. These findings are modest, but they are significant. We again did not, however, find a neighborhood conditional effect in this analysis of young adults living within metropolitan areas, which of course includes those living in central cities and in more suburban environs.

Then there are the central cities themselves. Here again I am not referring to inner-city ghettos, but to the core cities of metropolitan areas. There we do find evidence of the importance of social context. More of those living inside the city are worse off occupationally.

When ecological influences on the criminal behavior of city dwelling respondents are considered, we find that the environment matters more because no work or low-quality work is more likely to occur for a larger group of the people who live there and consequently for the people who live in proximity to them. We think that context shows up here as important because there are sufficient numbers of similarly situated people—marginal to the labor market—to affect lifestyles and consequently criminality.

The net effect of living in communities that are more disadvantaged, even after we take into account individual family, education, and occupation differences, increases criminal behavior. For a long time some have interpreted the positive correlations between the percentage of blacks and violent crime in analyses across cities as a product of the presence of a subculture of violence in the black community. These results indicate that that interpretation is erroneous. After we take into account individual economic situations (e.g., employment), living with African Americans does not induce, but to the contrary *reduces*, criminal involvement—while in contrast, living among the disadvantaged increases it. This analysis was not designed to assess the presence or absence of subcultures, but these data at least suggest that if we are to look anywhere for procrime values and social influences that will, above and beyond individuals' own circumstance, propel them to break the law, we should focus on collective disadvantage and not on racial distribution. This is consistent with other recently published research. Of course we should not forget that to be black in America means that you are considerably more likely to live in the sections of cities with other black people and in disadvantaged neighborhoods.

Introducing the interaction term into our analysis, which measures the extent to which neighborhood ecological characteristics condition the connection between respondents' employment and crime, introduces yet another complexity. Unlike in the full sample or other subsample analyses, in the central city subsample the interaction between individual respondents' employment and the level of disadvantage in their neighborhoods is significant and negative. Having a job, any job, is most beneficial in an anticrime way for people who live among the disadvantaged. Having work protects young adults from the deleterious criminogenic effects of living in the most disadvantaged neighborhoods. This also obviously means that there is a contextual boost into crime for unemployed people who live in socially and economically disadvantaged neighborhoods. In other analyses we considered contextual effects for the quality of employment (in the primary versus secondary sector) and found that it did not matter; where life is most socially and economically difficult, simply having work reduces the criminal involvement of young adults.

Let's consider these results and their meaning for cities and their residents. For young adults in general, those with jobs and especially good jobs are less involved in crime, but simply working in any job is important for those living in distressed neighborhoods. At one level this sounds like good jobs are important for those living outside of poor communities and that any old job will do for those residing in slums and ghettos. This is certainly not the message. We must remember that these analyses are necessarily conservative because of the data that are available to us. Not included in our measure of social context is an indicator of the number of adults who would officially be considered discouraged workers (those who have given up on looking for work). Also not included are those earning their living in the illegal economy or in the marginal world of off-the-books labor—day workers, for example. So a young man or woman who is marginally employed in such settings is more set apart here, even when they are working in a McJob. That they are working at all may indicate something of their orientation to the world of work and to their future. The question remains open whether those who are in secondary sector work will continue with this orientation after prolonged experience with the mind-numbing, low-paying jobs of this nature. But for now, they are working, and therefore not likely to be as frequently contributing to street culture with their presence as much as their friends who have little else to do but hang out on the corner.

Neighborhood Context and Delinquency

In chapter 4 we looked at the results from our study of juvenile delinquency. What is important in determining which children are most likely to become involved in delinquent activity is their experiences in school—in particular how well they are doing, measured by their grade point average, and how, in the vernacular of control theory, attached to school they are. Children with good grades and those who are more attached to school are less delinquent. Also, their parents' (and here the focus was necessarily on mothers' education level) involvement in their school affects delinquency; mothers who had more education were more involved in their children's school, which reduces delinquency. On the other hand, mothers who worked were more likely to have children with lower grades, which of course increased the likelihood of delinquency. The other notable result was that family poverty, more so than neighborhood characteristics, promoted violation of the law. Essentially children who are having a good experience in school and those whose parents are well educated and involved in their children's school are, as most would expect, less delinquent.

The direct effects of neighborhood characteristics on delinquency were, like those for young adults, modest. Racial composition had a net negative effect on individual involvement in juvenile delinquency. Juveniles were less criminal, after other factors are taken into account, when they live where the Latino population is larger, and to a slightly lesser extent in neighborhoods where the black population is larger.

We used two strategies to see if social context mattered in a more complex way in the determination of juvenile delinquency: we constructed path models to consider the indirect effects of neighborhood characteristics, and we constructed a series of individual characteristics by census tract characteristics interaction terms and entered them into regression models. We did not find powerful indirect effects of the neighborhood characteristics on delinquency. Mothers who live in disadvantaged neighborhoods are less likely to work, which removes a negative influence on their children's school performance, but we must remember that this is net of the comparatively strong criminogenic influence of family poverty, which of course is not helped when those mothers are not working.

The results from the interaction analyses are more interesting. Here we created interaction terms for quite a number of individual level and neighborhood level characteristics. We were particularly interested in how young people's school success, which generally reduces delinquency, is conditioned by social context. We expected that good grades and attachment to school would be most important for children in economically distressed communities, a protective factor like jobs are for young adults in disadvantaged places. After all, kids there are more surrounded by criminogenic influences. My juvenile probation caseload was populated by boys who were not doing well in school. My coworkers and I regularly implored them to work harder, because we expected and hoped that it would cause them to be less involved in crime. In my own childhood neighborhood, Pittsburgh's Hill District, those of us doing reasonably well in school were not necessarily all "choir boys," but we were less involved in troubling behavior than some of our fellows. And Hollywood has given us a steady stream of movies where the theme is that the kids who connect to school are the ones who walk away from gangs, drugs, and trouble. Though all of the above are only anecdotal data, they are the stuff of urban knowledge, and I suspect that many of my fellow sociologists would have the same expectation. This is not what we found.[23]

The most important finding is that the children who live in disadvantaged areas are not protected from delinquency by being good students (see Figure 5.2). Figures 5.3 and 5.4 tell dramatically different stories for children depending on where they live. Figure 5.2 presents the relationship between grades (on the x axis) and delinquency for all of the children in the NLSY sample. The solid line is the relationship for those who live in neighborhoods with the average level of social and economic disadvantage (for most Americans, this is very little). Consistent with expectations, as their grades improve their involvement in delinquency goes down. This pattern has been observed in a large number of studies, some of which I described earlier. The dotted line is for students who live in census tracts where the level of disadvantage is considerably lower than average (one standard deviation below the mean level of disadvantage). Here, the effects of doing well in school are even more dramatic. Those doing well, living with few if any people who are disadvantaged, are most unlikely to get into trouble. The dashed line represents the relationship for young people who live in communities with above-average levels of disadvantage (one standard deviation above the mean). There we see no relationship between grades and delinquency; those who get good grades are not any less likely to violate the law as those who are poor students.

Something disturbing comes out when we look at juveniles living not just in different kinds of neighborhoods, but in different levels of

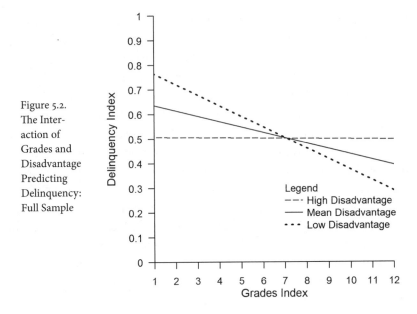

Figure 5.2. The Inter-action of Grades and Disadvantage Predicting Delinquency: Full Sample

urbanization. In rural areas we did not find any appreciable difference for those living among varying levels of disadvantage; there was no significant interaction between grades and disadvantaged neighborhoods among the rural NLSY subsample. But when the analyses focus on metropolitan areas (Figure 5.3) and on those in central cities (Figure 5.4), unexpected patterns emerge. When we studied only those in metro areas (leaving out rural respondents), good students living where more people are disadvantaged actually report higher levels of delinquency than those who do less well. And for the central city subsample this pattern is even stronger. Not only does school not appear to protect juveniles living in disadvantaged neighborhoods from criminal involvement, but for reasons we can only speculate about, they appear more delinquent.

We observed similar patterns when we consider those getting higher grades where relatively more of the adult population is marginally employed, and in metropolitan areas where more adults do not have high-school diplomas.[24] It appears that getting good grades is not protecting juveniles there from delinquency. Again, there does not seem

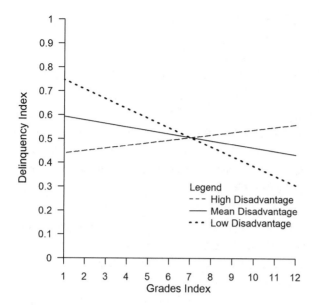

Figure 5.3. The Inter- action of Grades and Disadvantage Predicting Delinquency: In SMSA Sample

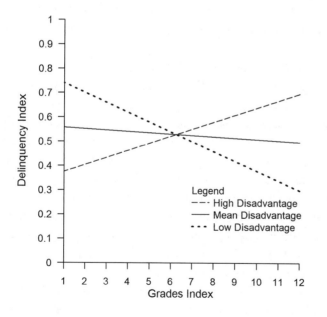

Figure 5.4. The Interac- tion of Grades and Disadvan- tage Predict- ing Delin- quency: Central City Sample

to be a positive benefit afforded from school success among children in the most distressed neighborhoods.

How could this be? It is so at variance with what is expected, and contrary to research that has been conducted on individuals and in varied types of communities. And these findings are certainly inconsistent with popular conceptions of how we should go about fighting crime and delinquency in distressed neighborhoods. First, let me stress that these results may be wrong. That is, they are what respondents said to NLSY interviewers, but those reports may not accurately represent the behavior of some children. Good students may exaggerate their delinquency. While I don't know of any study that has found this to be so, it may be that kids who do well in school and who live in disadvantaged communities overreport their criminal involvement. Why? Maybe it is their way of compensating for what they perceive as their difference from many around them. Perhaps in the midst of popular culture that glorifies "gangstas," they want to be cool too. It does not take too much imagination to also see how good students in bad neighborhoods might have some difficulties with their peers; they may be more picked on if they are bookish. Maybe they have to fight more because they are different. But then maybe they are just more delinquent than we would have guessed.

Perhaps they aren't just "representin'" to NLSY interviewers. Maybe they are actually compensating in the eyes of their friends for getting good grades by doing crimes. Perhaps they want their friends to know that even though they are good students, they are "down" like everybody else. There is, however, a more sinister interpretation. In these settings, it's possible that good students recognize that even with their academic talents, they are not likely to achieve the culturally legitimated good life via legitimate means (to borrow language from anomie theory).[25] It is possible that their talents make these young people good manpower for the illegitimate opportunities.[26] Stevie, a thirteen-year-old I supervised on probation for a few months, began his "criminal career" around the age of five. Quite bright (his school-administered IQ test scored in excess of 150 and I'm sure, knowing him, that he didn't take the exam seriously), Stevie learned early on that he could shoplift candy with impunity because he was also "so cute." Unfortunately older children also discovered this, and throughout primary school he stole for them in exchange for the attention he received. Stevie ended up on my caseload when his mother petitioned the court because he was "incorrigible." He received good grades because, as he explained, the school was so bad that he got good grades without even trying. Delinquency was just fun and entertaining for him by that time. I inherited another kid, Gary, from the PO that I replaced. Though just thirteen, he'd been on probation for more than a year. His older brother was doing time in a juvenile institution and Gary remained on probation because of a series of minor violations of his court-ordered conditions. His grades weren't great, but they were better than most others in his school. I always believed that Gary's delinquency was fueled by anger because his father had left, his brother had been taken away, and because of his generally disrupted and dysfunctional family. His school, to be generous, was weak. I was able to place him in a foster home in a nearby community where the schools were better. His grades suffered a bit in the more competitive environment, but his behavior also improved.

These two stories are reminders that we should be wary of simplistic notions about schools, performance, and delinquency. The unequal quality of schools and the disadvantaged circumstance of many of the schools attended by children from deprived communities complicate those relationships. And it must be remembered that all schools function within and cannot be held apart from the conditions from which their students come.

We have to consider that the schools that are available to children living in disadvantaged communities are not necessarily the same as those in other neighborhoods. Political scientist Gaton Alonso and his colleagues, writing about the failure of urban education, quoted Shawn, a New York City student.

> I classify myself as a good student trapped in an all right school. I am a good student 'cause academically I am strong and I get mad support from home. But I do well 'cause I have other things going for me. The thing is, a lot of kids go to bad schools and are doing bad too. Plus they are not getting real learning. So that's what's messed up. But I am a good student. I just focus on getting through the classes and passing the exams. I do what I got to do, you know. Go to class, take my notes, and bust the exams out. I just do what I have to do and pass the tests.[27]

Perhaps those many kids that Shawn is speaking of who go to bad schools are getting good grades by just marking time. Being in such schools may not only be damning their futures, but getting good grades in places that students know are bad schools may not afford the delinquency protections that good students get in stronger schools. As Alonso and colleagues point out, the schools in inner-city, disadvantaged neighborhoods are frequently a part of the troubled social ecology, and not an island from the despair around it.

In addition to the evidence that levels of neighborhood disadvantage conditioned teenagers' school performance and effects on delinquency, we found that neighborhood conditions interact with other features of juveniles' family lives as well. We know that when parents were more involved in their children's schools that this indirectly inhibited delinquency (see chapter 4 for discussion of this finding), and we also find that the involvement of parents whose families live where more adults have not finished high school especially boosted their offspring's chances of avoiding delinquency. Interestingly, this finding is the only one where we found substantial contextual effects in our rural subsample. In both urban and rural settings parents can add protection from the negative influences of undereducated neighborhood environments by demonstrating the importance of education by maintaining substantial involvement in the schools. Remember that earlier I posited that when neighborhood adults were unsuccessful in school or at work that this would send a negative education message to teenagers. Here we take note that parents can counteract this negative modeling by their own behavior that sends a message that they care about their children's education.

Might the No Child Left Behind program of the federal government be changing this? Of course much depends on how local districts have implemented it, and which aspects of the program are emphasized. It may do some good to impress upon students that they must work to achieve a minimum level of competency, and that a test must be hurdled before they leave high school with a diploma. It may also be beneficial to turn up the pressure on school districts, schools, and teachers where too many children are failing. But bringing the heat in education alone is insufficient to improve educational performance, and will certainly not alone succeed as a delinquency prevention strategy.

There are environments outside of school that must be taken into account if we are to understand what goes on in the school. Children from disadvantaged and distressed neighborhoods are far more likely to come to school not ready to learn.[28] They are more likely to be hungry, to be from homes where they cannot rest adequately, or from homes that are sources of stress. They are from neighborhoods where norms do not encourage academic achievement and their parents may say the right things about education, but their actions may convey something quite different.

The shameful little unspoken secret in the national debate on school achievement is that the schools themselves are far less important in determining students' academic outcomes than what takes place at home. We have known for quite a long time that what parents—who are also voters, and therefore a bit immune from the criticisms of political leaders hoping to get their votes and campaign contributions—do and the home life that they create are more important than teacher actions and school programs.[29] School success is, in part, dependent on the learning atmosphere at home. Do children see their parents reading? Are there books in the home? Are children encouraged to read, be creative, and take academic chances? Do they have a quiet place to study? Do parents check to see if they have homework and make sure it is done well? It is very likely that the reason we found a positive correlation between mothers' educational achievement and our respondents' grades is that the answers to more of these questions are in the affirmative in households where parents have higher academic achievement. What this means, unsurprisingly, is that the home is an important context conditioning children's success in school and in turn their likelihood of becoming delinquent. This means, that as argued earlier, parental success in education and employment help to determine juvenile delinquency. We must realize that in disadvantaged neighborhoods, where families are already severely tasked with making it day to day and where there will be fewer households with well-educated adults, that the environment will be hard for children and teachers alone to overcome.

We know that there currently exist substantial inequalities in school funding. In 2011 the Center for American Progress released a report that documented both interstate and intrastate differences in school funding.[30] As might be expected, there are considerable differences in what is spent to educate a child across the states. The report states that "the dramatic differences in per pupil expenditures between states should give us pause. The education received by children in a state such as New York that spends an average of $15,012 per pupil may be different than that of children in Tennessee who receive only $8,507 per pupil."[31] Unfortunately, within state differences are also dramatic, with some districts receiving considerably more per pupil than others. The author of the report, Diana Epstein, wrote:

> Numerous studies demonstrate that school districts in many states are not funded equitably; that is, within a state some districts receive more state and local money per pupil than do others. This paper focuses only on state and local funds because most federal funding (for example, Title I) is designed to provide supplemental resources on top of whatever the state and district are already providing. An analysis of 2004 data by The Education Trust demonstrated that the highest-poverty districts in 26 states received less state and local per pupil funding than the lowest poverty districts. The differences varied widely among states; for example, while Illinois provided $1,924 less per pupil in the highest-poverty districts, Minnesota provided $1,349 more.[32]

If education reform is to have any hope of success, then we must recognize that adequate funding for every child should also not be left behind.[33] Although No Child Left Behind is not designed for and has not been put into place as a delinquency prevention strategy, we should recognize that latent benefit of real and meaningful educational reform may be to reduce crime for two reasons. First, more children are likely to develop stronger attachments to school, which we have seen to decrease delinquency involvement in most communities. Second, improved education is likely to also improve the human capital that young people take with them to the job market as they transition from student to young adult roles. While improved human capital will not help them to get quality jobs that do not exist, they will be better prepared to compete for such jobs if and when they are created.

The problem is that the emphasis on testing and aggregate school performance may lead to student behaviors or administrative outcomes that promote estrangement from school and increased delinquency. Students who become convinced that they will not pass the test have little incentive to keep trying, and some involvement in school is likely better than none if we hope to minimize criminality. Also, when school districts are at risk of facing real decreases in their budgets if too many students fail, then who will be surprised to see students with high probabilities of failure pressured out of school so that they do not bring down the school or district average test score?

Journalists reported that children in Houston, New York City, and the State of Massachusetts who were likely not to pass were possibly forced out of school to protect schools' overall test performance and the jobs and bonuses of administrators.[34] Research by Rice University education researcher Linda McSpadden McNeil and her colleagues buttresses the anecdotal evidence provided by journalists.[35] Whether or not students leave because of pressure associated with testing, our research indicates that in some communities their chances of becoming involved in delinquency are enhanced, and this is especially so if they do not secure jobs shortly after leaving school.

Earlier I described the results of our analyses that indicated that when mothers worked their children tended to do less well in school, and were consequently more likely to engage in delinquent activity. There is an important exception to this pattern. In our central city subsample, we found that the sons and daughters of working mothers living in disadvantaged neighborhoods were less likely to have broken the law. We could only speculate that the main effect of children of working mothers having poorer school performance suggests that in such circumstances children might be less supervised, resulting in poorer grades and higher probability of delinquency. But the results for working mothers in disadvantaged urban communities suggest that we should not too hastily light on this conclusion. There the opportunities for serious delinquency are probably greater, although admittedly the distractions available to unsupervised teenagers in more advantage communities are probably better (a result of cars, allowances, etc.), and the opportunity for general delinquency are also inevitably present. But in disadvantaged neighborhoods where serious crime is more present, working moms somehow seem to insulate their children a little bit from criminal involvement. While this may not make sense at the surface, it does if we think about the model that these women are presenting to their children in the face of economic hardship. Lower delinquency among such children may well be a byproduct of having a parent who models commitment to the world of work even though the community around them is socially and economically distressed. And, though it requires even more of a leap of speculation, there is another possible explanation. In the 1960s of my youth, numerous women in my project community worked outside of the home. It was a necessity. Kids from some of those families did run wild, but many more of us had what we thought of as draconian rules put in place to make up for the lack of parental supervision. Recognizing the danger in some inner-city distressed neighborhoods, some parents elected to heavily regulate their children; their motivation was to protect their offspring from the palpable dangers of the streets.

While the results for working mothers generally may seem like an indictment of them and of a society where this is increasingly the case, I think that the pattern of these findings suggest this to be an overly simplistic interpretation. When taken in total, the role of the working mother must be seen within the broader context of the community in which a family resides. Perhaps it is that overall community context whose importance is too seldom appreciated in our haste to attach blame for delinquency to children or their parents alone.

Peer Networks, Social Context, and Delinquency

Would my Hole in the Wall Gang have broken into barns and garages if not for each other? Might Robby Wideman, or his rap partners for that matter, have engaged in the hustling life and the robbery that ultimately sent them to prison, without the influence of each other? I could not have definitively answered the question about the Hole in the Wall Gang even as I supervised them on probation, but I was pretty sure that this was a case of mutually reinforcing peer influence. And John Wideman's account of his brother's behavior is not conclusive either on this point; it does seem that Robby with his buddies was a criminogenic combination.

The criminology literature has long indicated that having delinquent peers substantially increases the chances that a juvenile will get involved in delinquency, and that literature and my anecdotal observations of juveniles on my probation caseload and young adults when I moved to State Parole tells us that crime by the young is, most often, a group phenomenon. This is the case for middle-class delinquents as well as those from more distressed social and economic backgrounds. But living where more people are marginal to important institutions such as school and work gives greater opportunity for marginalized, unbonded peers to find each other. The context of neighborhoods where more adults are out of work or underemployed sets up a circumstance where the influence of ordinary peer networks on delinquency is heightened.

This is not the place for true confessions, but I will say that the inner-city neighborhood of my adolescence provided great opportunity for law-violating behavior, because there were always nonworking young adults and wayward youth around urging me and my friends to "have a bit of fun" or "let's go get [steal] a car." How might the scene around our local basketball court, where those young adults gathered to shoot craps, smoke dope,[36] and occasionally invade our games, have been different if they had had quality jobs to go to the next day? Of course some of them would have been there still, but many of them likely would not have been.

What Then of Social Context?

There are those of my colleagues who will conclude that I've made too much of too little in the data in coming to the conclusion that social context matters. I confess that I have. The results that I use to support my argument are modest and at best suggestive, but they do not exist in a vacuum. Of course our capacity to measure social influences are compromised by the nature of quantitative data collection as it is practiced by the social sciences of the late twentieth and early twenty-first centuries. Much of what we know of social behavior is the result of survey data, necessarily the questioning of individuals. In and of itself there is nothing wrong with this, but it does limit our capacity to analyze processes that are supraindividual: those affecting individual people, but necessarily the consequences of social forces around us and the respondents to our surveys. We need to remember that because current techniques and technology make it difficult to measure these processes does not mean that they do not operate, so we should look at the results appreciating that they should be understood as companion to other sources of knowledge.

When I write that the modest results suggesting the significance of social context shaping the criminal behavior of teenagers and young adults do not exist in a vacuum, I am thinking that they must be viewed along with recent ethnographic work, in the context of social theory, and not without appreciation of the value of observations that we each make as we move throughout lives. This last bit, this "personal" evidence, is appropriately and notoriously suspect. Too many of us have had family members or students discount empirically based knowledge with a wave of the hand and a sentence that begins, "Well, that can't be true I know someone who . . ." Of course such anecdotes do not constitute disconfirming evidence, but at the same time some such tales (observations) can assist us in understanding social processes where we have modest empirical evidence.

I began this chapter recounting John Edgar Wideman's attribution to the interactions of his younger brother Robby's personality, and the changes in their neighborhood of Homewood between the years when the two siblings came of age. Wideman's account is one such anecdote. A keen-eyed social observer, it is not inappropriate for him to bring those things that he has witnessed to bear in trying to account for the differences in their lives. And it is also appropriate that we use those observations along with our modest quantitative results to make sense of how social and economic forces in communities influence individual behavior.

Envisioning the Homewood of Robby Wideman's youth and then bringing that picture forward to include the changes to places like inner-city Pittsburgh during the last decades of the twentieth century is a way that we can connect the findings of our quantitative analyses with that which we have learned from recent urban ethnographies. Homewood of the 1960s was not unprosperous, but it was clear to young men that the promise of the Great Migration to the Promised Land was tainted by the North's de facto version of Jim Crow. Smart young men of Homewood, like Robby Wideman, had options. They could work hard in school and possibly go on to college, but perhaps more likely find a job after high school in either the steel mills, their ancillary industries, or in the secondary sector as restaurant busboys or janitors or security guards. Or, as Cloward and Ohlin described, just before Robby became an adolescent, young men of Homewood could, in the face of Jim Crow opportunity structures, elect to build a street reputation and maintain a tough reputation,[37] or they could pursue the illegal alternatives to the legitimate pursuit of the good life that were available to them. Robby chose the latter.

The difference between John's Homewood and Robby's (remember that ten years separate them) is that the hope that accompanied the Great Migration was alive in postwar Pittsburgh. Black families could move out of The Hill, but more frequently *up* The Hill, to nicer houses and pleasant neighborhoods, like the Homewood of the 1940s and 50s, keeping alive the promise that had motivated their parents to leave the legally Jim Crow South. By the late 1960s Homewood was not terribly distinguishable from The Hill and in Pittsburgh, like everywhere else in America, black people were tired of waiting for their investment of hard work and hope to be paid off as promised. Homewood became the social context in which many young people did not develop attachments to schools and teachers, concluding instead, "What's the point?" Homewood and The Hill were places where marginally employed or unemployed young men could find each other hanging out on the corner singing doo-wop, smoking reefer, shooting hoops and craps. The streets of these communities provided the social context for teenagers and young adults to have the situation of company that allowed their alienation from the labor market to find a ready setting for situations conducive to crime, because it could fuel its maximum expression in the collective alienation of others who were also marginally employed if they were working at all.

John describes Robby as wanting things and wanting them more immediately than he himself had. Quoting Robby in *Bothers and Keepers*, he writes:

I'd think, Go on and love those square turkeys, but one day I'll be the one coming back with a suitcase full of money and a Cadillac. Go on and love them good grades. Robby gon do it his own way.

See, in my mind I was Superfly. I'd drive up slow to the curb. My hog be half a block long and these fine boxes in the back. Everybody looking when I ease out the door clean and mean. Got a check in my pocket to give to Mom. Buy her a new house with everything in it new. Pay her back for the hard times. I could see that happening.[38]

Robby was of the streets and so opted, with two friends, to rip off a fellow hustler, ending in the killing of their victim. To Banfield this account seems classically like a young person unable to defer gratification, the short-time horizon of the lower class.[39] Instead, I hear young black men saying, "I'm tired of this stuff, always working hard, for what? For nothing!"

Not many years after Robby Wideman began his life sentence at Western State Penitentiary, the steel mills that lined the riverbanks to the north and south of that prison began closing. Deindustrialization hit Pittsburgh and surrounding communities hard, and it was hardest felt in its segregated black ghettos. Unemployment had always been higher in those communities and among those who did have work, too many of them labored in secondary sector jobs like the thirty- and forty-year-old busboys of one downtown coffee shop who made ten cents more per hour than this high-school boy, who put in a few evening hours each day (and they had worked there years longer and would be there still when I left for college). When the mills left they threw out of work not only members of the United Steel Workers of America, but also the service workers who served them their coffee on the way to the plant and those who poured their Iron City Beer after the shift. The ripple effect that caused former primary sector workers to push secondary sector workers out of their janitorial jobs left black communities with an even more marginal workforce than the one that appeared to offer little reason for hope to the Robby Widemans a decade earlier. In this setting, the code of the street, which had existed earlier, gained full flower. The violence that Bourgois chronicled in Brooklyn had its Pittsburgh version too, and black middle-class communities like Wilkensburg and Penn Hills, which bordered Homewood, suffered from this proximity in the same way that Pattillo-McCoy's Groveland did in Chicago.[40] Those middle-class communities subsequently began the long slide that Homewood took a generation earlier. In Pittsburgh, parts of Wilkinsburg and Penn Hills shifted in the 1970s and 80s from being middle-working-class enclaves to being more like the urban ghettos.

When we consider modest statistically significant interaction effects, they should be interpreted within the context of these ethnographic descriptions and in the light of this urban history. There are families of Anderson's Philadelphia who, against the odds, successfully inculcate in their children "decent values" and the passion and skills necessary for higher academic achievement. Some of these children, as a result, make it out. But for some other families, for reasons that we can only speculate about, the stories of hope that comes with school success appear to lead to more delinquency. In the 1980s, Edmund Perry's academic promise led to him being plucked out of Harlem to attend Phillips Exeter Academy in Exeter, New Hampshire. Just days after his graduation from Exeter, Perry was killed in an alleged ill-fated mugging attempt. The story was that he and his partner selected an undercover cop for their unplanned, heat-of-the moment robbery. Had the events of that evening not ended in Perry's death he would have attended Stanford University on a full scholarship the following fall.[41] Before you conclude that you can take the kid out of the ghetto, but you can't take the ghetto out of the kid, read Robert Sam Anson's account of Perry's life and try to understand his frustration that accompanies living a life in two worlds after first being subjected to a life of inner-city desperation.

There are too the children, who of their own accord manage to academically distance themselves and as a result insulate themselves from the prodelinquency forces around them. An HBO production, the Oscar-winning *I Am a Promise*, broadcast in 1993, was a documentary about the struggles of the children and staff of one inner-city elementary school.[42] It included the story of ten-year-old Nadia, who, faced with a bad home situation, essentially adopted an older man in her neighborhood as her grandfather. He commented that "she just showed up, like a kitten that wouldn't go away." At the time of the filming she lived with him and was doing very well in school. A touching scene is recorded when she learns from the school's principal that a short story she'd written was to be published. Nadia, too, is one of those cases that add perspective to our results and the observations of ethnographers.[43] There are contrasting stories in underclass neighborhoods, and they are hidden in our statistically modest results.

In such circumstances it is not just complicated for the children—it also is complicated for the parents who try to negotiate a difficult world

on their offspring's behalf. As I considered our findings that demonstrated that both when mothers are more involved in their children's
schools in communities where more adults didn't finish high school,
and that working mothers in central city distressed neighborhoods
inhibit delinquency, I was put in mind of women raising their children in housing projects against the odds and also at variance to some
popular images. Sociologist Winona Rymond-Richmond writes about
women battling not only the gangs and streets of Chicago but the Chicago Housing Authority, who don't "get it," to protect their children
from becoming involved in or victims of the thug life.[44] I have witnessed
mothers in Pittsburgh's projects who gave up a day's pay (and keep in
mind that there are no personal days for women doing domestic work)
to be at annual parent visitation days and parent-teacher conferences.
Alex Kotlowitz's *There are No Children Here* is the true story of a Chicago mother raising her children in the Henry Horner Homes, encouraging them in school, trying to keep them from trouble, and trying to
instill positive values. At least one of her children seemed to be having
some success at the time of the book's publication.[45]

It is easy to socially canonize such mothers, and by doing so implic-
itly castigate others who do not measure up to these examples. These
women deserve all of the credit that we can heap upon them, but
using them to conclude that other mothers of troubled neighborhoods are failures is simply unfair. There is in the inner city the full
range of human possibilities—from the altruistic social activists to the
narrowly self-interested tenant representatives of the Chicago projects
that Vankatesh describes, from the women heading "decent" families
to those given over to the "street" that Anderson writes about, from the
women of Pittsburgh's Hill District who are models and rule makers
to their sons and daughters, to the women living next door to them
who had children while they were yet children and never had a chance
themselves.[46] The failures are not the women who cannot overcome
their social environment to shield their children from neighborhood
distresses and delinquency, but rather the failure of the social system
that requires superhuman Madonnas or saints of the ghetto to allow
their children even a chance.

Something similar may be said for the children themselves. We
should challenge those who lay the blame on teenagers who do not do

the monumental in the face of few or no opportunities and bad schools, or those who cannot find decent work where there are few jobs of any sort. Blame casting gets us nowhere. We should instead seek to find the means to fund schools that might give better preparation for the world of work or additional education, and dare to consider developing an industrial policy that creates the good jobs that inner-city parents need and their progeny may aspire to. Doing those two things would be the ultimate antipoverty program.

The Poor Do Not Control Their Neighborhoods

Obviously, when we conclude that social context matters in determining delinquency and criminality, then we are saying that forces external to the individual are important in determining who violates the law and how much crime a neighborhood, city, or nation will endure. This is neither a new nor a particularly interesting insight, but it is one rather routinely ignored when we consider criminal justice, welfare, and educational policies. Those with the fewest resources are expected to overcome the most difficult social circumstances, and generally on their own—and they are the least capable of rallying forces outside of their communities to address the problems there.

In *American Project* Venkatesh describes the emergence of residents' councils in Chicago's now demolished Cabrini Green projects. The idea was that the interests of families living in the projects could be voiced to the Chicago Housing Authority through these representative bodies. But the unresponsiveness of the Housing Authority created the structural contradiction that allowed these bodies to be corrupted by some residents and eventually by the gangs that came to occupy and essentially control the projects. These women of the tenant councils, like poor people everywhere, function within social and economic contexts where their ability to affect real change in their own environments, is extremely limited.

As we have seen, important limitations are created by both the neighborhoods in which they live and by the local labor market. By the very label "local labor market" we indicate that these too fit within larger labor markets, which until recent history were frequently thought of as nation states. Technological developments in communications, transportation, and manufacturing have fueled the economic processes frequently described as globalization, the internationalization of production and markets.

In a world of increasingly globalized economic forces workers are inhibited by international borders, but jobs are not. When auto manufacturing jobs moved from Detroit to Smyrna, Tennessee, more mobile workers could presumably pull up stakes in pursuit of jobs at the then-new, now-shuttered Saturn plant. When call centers open in India, people who might have staffed such jobs within the US cannot elect to chase the jobs.

This development has produced a net decline in jobs that we have described as primary sector jobs in the US and in some other industrialized economies. When they are not replaced or are replaced with jobs of lesser quality, we can expect negative consequences for both communities and individuals. These consequences will include both a decline in lifestyles and potentially, increases in crime.

Globalization, however, does not just affect states that lose jobs. The introduction of new industries, new opportunities, and the social changes that come with them affect the places where these jobs land as surely as the Industrial Revolution changed Durkheim's France, Weber's Germany, and Marx's Britain. I cannot begin to predict how these changes will influence crime in these new settings. A first step, though, is to begin to consider the limits of the thesis that I have argued for regarding places both inside and outside of the US. To date my analyses and that of most of my colleagues have been limited to American urban settings. In the next chapter I will consider how this argument and other economic considerations might apply elsewhere.

6

Lessons from the Hole in the Wall Gang

So far, the labor stratification and crime thesis has been shown to support efforts to explain some important variations in both individual criminality and in crime and delinquency rates. But I should note two very important limitations so far. The first is that the places where most of this research has been done has focused on metropolitan areas within the United States. While I have used some examples from rural areas, the Hole in the Wall Gang, and my former parolee Steven, perhaps some important aspects of the relationship between work and crime can be learned from a broader empirical consideration. Along this same line, we may learn from an examination of research outside of the US that may not have necessarily used the same theoretical frameworks as American scholars, but which nevertheless may inform the search for understanding how jobs are associated with crime.

Another limitation is the failure to find support for the thesis in Washington, DC. I think at this point, rather than taking that as evidence toward disconfirmation of the labor stratification and crime thesis, that perhaps we can learn from that empirical failure to improve our understanding of how work, employment, and perhaps the broader economy affects individual criminality and crime rates. In this chapter I will focus on the rural US and then on cities, like Washington, where a broader consideration of employment, economic, and stratification forces may aid our understanding. I will also consider some studies that have been conducted outside of the United States. In the next chapter, I will take what we have learned in previous chapters and what will be discussed here and lay out a broader labor stratification and crime thesis.

Rural Places

Rural America is a good place to begin. Much of the labor market and crime research, like much of modern criminology, has reasonably focused on urban places, but how might employment patterns in the hinterland affect criminality? In chapter 4 I introduced you to the Hole in the Wall Gang, the name I gave to a group of unsophisticated juvenile burglars that I inherited on my Western Pennsylvania juvenile probation caseload. They were a small group of kids who were disaffected from school. In some ways they were like my city charges in industrial Sharon and Farrell Pennsylvania, or the kids I grew up with in inner-city Pittsburgh. But in some important ways they were different. My naïve urban ears were surprised to hear that what they wanted from life was to be farmers. I had gone to college with young people from rural areas, but they had the same kinds of career aspirations as me. The kids in the Hole in the Wall Gang, in one respect, were like some urban working-class kids: they expected to have the kinds of jobs that their parents held. But they were different from other kids in the city. The urban working-class and poor kids that I grew up with either wanted to escape the mills (the hope of me and my friends), or longed for apprenticeships in skilled trades and crafts, or they were willing to go into the mills, make a solid wage, and root for the Steelers; the latter group had similar aspirations to the Hole in the Wall Gang members. The difference was that at the time, the urban kids had role models who had that pretty good Pittsburgh working-class, root-for-the-Steelers, life. In the late 1960s and early 70s those options were available for my classmates. None of us expected that the mills would begin disappearing just a few years later. The Hole in the Wall kids' options were more limited. Yes, some of their contemporaries escaped, like my college classmates and others, and like their urban cousins, who targeted skilled trades. But the equivalent of the mill aspirations for them was farming. The problem was they lived in rocky, hilly, Western Pennsylvania and not the productive farmlands of Iowa or Indiana or even other sections of their own state. Farming in their county was a hardscrabble life, and the land gave up few rewards. Essentially that farming option was not the equivalent of the steel mills of the time before deindustrialization. Their farming option did not hold the promise of an economically prosperous working-class life that steel mill workers enjoyed; their predicament was more similar to those who could not land the good blue-collar, unionized mill positions. In a sense their circumstance was more like the situation faced by young people in some less developed countries than it was even for the working-class children of Pittsburgh, Cleveland, and Chicago. And these mid-twentieth-century kids, other contemporary children from Appalachia and tribal lands, and the offspring of peoples from the less developed regions of the world sometimes have more in common with the pre–Industrial Revolution children of Europe than many of us would like to admit.

I recognize that this last statement cries out for explanation, maybe even justification. How can I say such a thing? First, I want to be clear that I am not alleging that all American farmers or rural area residents live a life that is even remotely like Chinese villagers or European peasants of the early nineteenth century. Second, it must be emphasized that the reality for people who live on farms, in small towns, and villages in some parts of the US is very different from others. For instance, my Hole in the Wall clients parents' farming reality was considerably different from the soybean, corn, and wheat farmers of the Midwest and West, and even from many dairy farmers who lived and worked relatively close to them. Many of them did not own their own farm, but were the hired help of others. For most of those who did have their own place, the farms were of modest size and very limited production. They regularly confronted problems associated with nearby extraction industries in and around Titusville and Oil City Pennsylvania (coal mining, oil drilling, and today, natural gas extraction). And they were in a state where, even though a substantial share of the population lived in rural counties,[1] the politics tended to focus on urban and industrial interests. So this particular group of Western Pennsylvania farmers was demographically a small group, with limited financial and political resources, working land that has limited capacity in the foothills of the Allegheny Mountains. This area is not considered Appalachia by most, but for some the life circumstances and chances for both the adults and the children were not unlike farmers and small-town people of the hills of West Virginia, Kentucky, and Tennessee.

This is not to cast them as a collective, uniformly despairing lot of modern day strugglers, like those of Steinbeck's *Grapes of Wrath*. They are no more that than are poor, urban inner-city dwellers uniformly like the stereotypic welfare cheats. It was wrong for politicians and activists to paint the poor in this way during debates about welfare reform, and it would be wrong for me to characterize the parents of my Hole in the Wall Gang delinquents and people like them in some similar fashion. That said, many of us who work or who have worked in rural Pennsylvania know that when Barack Obama said during the 2008 presidential campaign that some people in rural America were bitter, he was not wrong. Many of them are, because they are left at the margins of the economy, they don't think they are heard by urban elites in their state capital or in Washington, and their way of life seems to be under siege. Interestingly, the urban poor feel the same way, as do some Native Americans who are living on impoverished reservations. This is why I write that in some abstract but important ways, they have more in common with some people in less developed countries and with the people of preindustrial Europe and North America who early sociologists wrote about than we would like to admit.

A lesson that we can learn from the Hole in the Wall Gang is that underneath the macro economic changes that are taking place for the entire society, the social lives, including crime, of individual people changes in very important ways, and this change varies dramatically for subsets of the population. Of course this happens for the breadwinners, some of whom are parents; but, as we documented in the previous chapter, it also has very profound effects on children. We know this about the cities. We know that economic collapse has wreaked havoc on the lives of schoolkids in the projects and other inner-city neighborhoods. We must remember that it too happens to the kids that make up the other Hole in the Wall gangs in rural America.

In our analyses of the Mothers and Children of the NLSY we found that for the children in the rural portion of the sample, like their metropolitan counterparts, their school experience was the most important predictor of delinquency (except for those living in central cities, where gender was the strongest predictor, with of course girls being substantially less involved than boys, which was also the case in all of the subsamples, but the difference was greatest there).[2] In fact, school performance was more important predicting delinquency in rural areas than it was in either the metropolitan or central city subsamples of the NLSY data. But most important for our purposes is how much more significant family poverty is as a predictor of delinquency outside of cities (see Figure 6.1). In our rural subsample, poverty was substantially more important in helping us to understand delinquency than it was in the other subsamples, and fully four times stronger as a predictor of delinquency than it is in central cities. That is, poverty increases the likelihood of delinquent involvement considerably more in rural areas than it does in the cities, where poverty was a more modest predictor.

In contrast, we do not see the contextual influence of social and economic disadvantage in rural areas that is observed in the metropolitan areas and center cities. Remember that in nonrural areas, the delinquency inhibiting the effects of good school experiences was attenuated

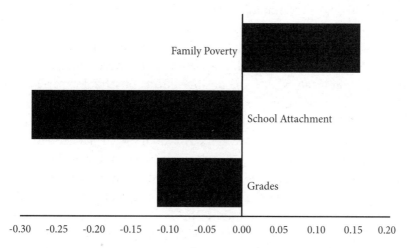

Figure 6.1. Explaining Rural Delinquency Using Family and School Variables
The variables in this figure are statistically significant. Also included in the regression analyses were variables measuring respondents' age, sex,* race, ethnicity, father present, mothers' education and employment, parental involvement in school, juvenile employment, and characteristics of the census tract in which they lived. The table that Figure 6.1 is based on is included in the appendix.
*Indicates that this was a statistically significant predictor of delinquency.

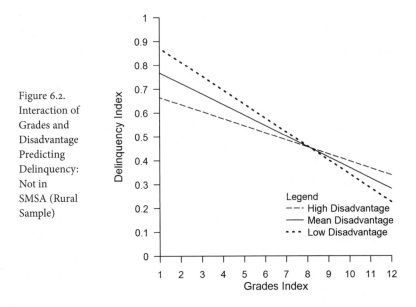

Figure 6.2.
Interaction of
Grades and
Disadvantage
Predicting
Delinquency:
Not in
SMSA (Rural
Sample)

for kids living in communities where disadvantage was high. Figure 6.2 displays the same analyses that I showed in the last chapter for the metro and center city subsamples, but here for the rural respondents of the NLSY. Readers can see that variation in the disadvantage context does not significantly alter the positive effects of school experience as an inhibitor of delinquency.

We can draw from these analyses several things that help us to understand children like those in the Hole in the Wall Gang. First, positive engagement in school is critical everywhere, but especially in rural areas, if we are to lessen delinquency. Second, the income of the family is more important than the broader social and economic community contexts in the lives of rural kids. This is not surprising. In the rural areas there is not the residential concentration of poverty and disadvantage that exist in underclass urban places. Members of the Hole in the Wall Gang were not as socially isolated from the middle class as are the children of Pittsburgh's Hill and Homewood neighborhoods, or many of those living in parts of Chicago's South Side. Where my elementary school was all black and nearly all poor, and my middle school (they were called junior high schools then) mostly the same (there was a sprinkling of whites and some middle-class kids from the more middle-class "Sugar Top" section of The Hill), those schools today have fewer whites and many fewer people who would be considered middle class. The Hole in the Wall Gang's schools had a broader range of children with whom they came into contact. Nevertheless, their delinquency was substantially influenced by the economic circumstance of their families, even if not so much by their broader community. So it is likely that the members of the Gang became involved in delinquency because of their lack of engagement in school and because of their families' poverty, the result of trying to work marginal, unproductive farmlands. And while I cannot say for certain, it is likely that the quality of their schools, because it had middle-class students, was probably higher than those in many inner-city urban neighborhoods.

What of adults in rural areas? Using the National Longitudinal Survey of Youth 97 data, we examined the association between employment and crime.[3] For respondents who live within metropolitan areas, work does matter. Remember, for both those within Standard Metropolitan Statistica Areas (SMSAs) as well as the subsample of respondents living in the central cities of metro areas, both those who were unemployed as well as those working in secondary sector occupations were more likely to have engaged in criminal behavior (see chapter 3). This is not the case for NLSY, young adult respondents who lived in rural areas. Neither the unemployed nor those working in secondary sector jobs were any more likely than others to commit crimes in rural places.[4] The only substantial crime predictor for this group (in addition to gender, women being less likely to be criminals) was having a record of school suspension. This is also an important predictor for those in the cities. We interpreted this variable as a measure of past trouble or behavior problems. So the less than stunning finding is that bad kids are more likely to turn out to be bad young adults, but what is interesting is that this is all that seems to matter for rural young adults— whereas for their city cousins, work matters too. This finding is different from results reported by researchers Matthew Stark and Tim Slack, who found that in nonmetro areas secondary sector employment, as it does in urban areas, is linked to higher rates of violence in nonmetropolitan places.[5] In contrast to findings that my colleagues and I have reported and that I summarized in earlier chapters, Stark and Slack find that jobs with low hours of work and seasonal work repress criminality outside of cities. They speculate that there, these jobs structure social life in noncriminogenic ways that are similar to what we have described for primary sector jobs in urban settings. So although we did not find that work matters in the hinterland as much as poverty does, these scholars' work indicates that it actually does, and that even jobs with lower hours and those that are seasonal represses criminality. These patterns of results suggest that this is an area of research in need of additional study.

In chapter 2 I introduced you to Steven, a resident of a rural county whom I supervised on state probation for a period. He lived outside of a small rural village with his parents (he was in his twenties) and had a very modest job, but had continued to engage in breaking and entering (the offense that placed him on probation). At the time I, of course, hoped that this kind of behavior was in his past, but I had doubts; in hindsight I suspect that I was a bit naïve. He'd been convicted of burglary and done a little time. Looking back now, he seems to me to have been locked into the same irresponsible pattern of behavior that got him in trouble before he dropped out of school. He was somewhat dependent on his parents, and didn't seem motivated to do much beyond work on his car and hang with his buds. That he had a job didn't seem to matter much. Perhaps this is because so many of the jobs occupied by him and other young adults living in the small communities and the countryside around them are secondary sector jobs. Of course if jobs like Steven's are predominately what are available to those in our rural subsample, then we might be less likely to get statistically significant results based on marginal employment when we try to predict who engages in criminal behavior there. Clearly, however, when our results and those reported by Stark and Slack are taken together, there is indication that we need a more nuanced understanding of how employment affects crime outside of cities.

Other American places, as well, are unlike the urban word when it comes to work and crime. The easiest examples, such as the reservations of Native American tribes, are semisovereign entities (subject to only some externally created laws), self-governed under treaties and acts of Congress. Historically, reservations have been marked by the neglect of the federal government, high levels of unemployment, and poverty. Few jobs existed on or near many reservations, so people were frequently constrained to live on welfare or work for whites who owned or leased land nearby. Indians working for white ranchers or in small businesses are generally in powerless relationships with their employers. The large pool of nearby unemployed workers, the geographic isolation of much of the tribal lands (which means the existence of few employment alternatives), and largely anti-Indian sentiments of many neighbors means that many Indian workers have as few resources to affect their workplace and working conditions as industrial workers prior to the existence of labor unions. Their plight is more akin to workers in colonial settings. As a consequence, until quite recently nearly all of the limited employment in or near the reservations of American Indians has been jobs with secondary sector characteristics.

Some change has occurred in recent years as a result of court decisions upholding the sovereignty of tribes and treaty rights included in old agreements with the federal government. The Boldt Decision ensured that Indian fisherman in the Pacific Northwest were entitled to a share of wild fish stocks as agreed to in a nineteenth-century treaty.[6] Court decisions have also upheld treaty rights providing that coastal Indians are allowed up to fifty percent of tideland shellfish harvests in the Northwest. Both decisions allowed Native Americans to participate more meaningfully in the seafood industry. Unfortunately, as salmon stocks dwindled and pollution limited shellfish production, Indian fishermen, like white fisherman, have suffered economically.[7]

The more important economic and job related developments for the tribes have been a series of decisions that ensure Indians the rights to open gaming casinos on their property, which can only be regulated by state governments in a limited way. A number of tribes have opened casinos, some with but marginal success, but there are important exceptions. In the states of California, Connecticut, and Washington, for example, tribes have been able to increase social services, provide jobs, and, importantly, make political contributions with legally received gambling revenues.[8] Although the tasks of casino workers have many characteristics of secondary sector work, that the casinos employ people from a population who had little or no work opportunities, and because of the link to the tribes and their governments, it may be that some of the negative criminogenic effects of such work are mitigated. This may be akin to the results reported for rural part-time and seasonal workers by Stark and Slack.

A very interesting natural experiment occurred in western North Carolina when a casino was opened on the Eastern Cherokee Reservation.[9] The casino opened midway through the Great Smokey Mountains Study of Youth (GSMS). Equalized profits from the casino were distributed to adult members of the tribe regardless of their income. The study team's data show a substantial income increase in families with at least one Indian adult. The expectation of some (likely some of the same types of people who spend a great deal of effort worrying that some inner-city mother might work at McDonalds while receiving welfare) was that the windfall would result in increased alcohol and drug abuse, domestic violence, and crime more broadly. There is no evidence that this has happened. To the contrary, the GSMS team found that the children living in the households with the enhanced incomes were more likely to graduate from high school, had lower involvement in minor criminal offense, and were less likely to become involved in drug sales.[10]

How employment on reservations that have successful gaming operations and those that do not affect crime is an interesting and important empirical question that to my knowledge has not yet been addressed by researchers. Similarly, the overall impact that these and other tribally controlled industries have on alcoholism, domestic violence, and other social problems that have plagued native communities is a rich opportunity for researchers who would approach tribal leadership about studying there. Those electing to do that should take care to be sensitive to the troubled relationship that has historically existed between native communities and academic researchers.

Anomalies?

Rural America is not the only place where a more nuanced consideration of how employment affects crime is needed. As I described earlier, Washington, DC stumped my colleagues and I a bit in our earlier analyses. In chapter 1 I stated that the beginning of my answer to the question of how the economy influences people toward or away from crime was that most individuals touch the economy through their relationship to the labor market, through their job, or because of their the lack of a job. In the past few chapters I have been articulating an argument and marshalling evidence in support for the thesis that

marginal employment and joblessness creates lifestyle patterns conducive to criminality. I have called this the labor stratification and crime
thesis. But Washington, DC's homicide rates were difficult to explain
using this approach. I speculated that the relationships of Washington's
people to the labor market and to each other may be more similar to
such relationships in parts of the less developed world than to those in
other American cities, the nation as a whole, or to most other places in
the industrialized world. To be fair to the District of Columbia, I must
point out that it is not alone in this regard. A colleague at a university in New Orleans once pointed out to me, in a surprisingly positive
tone, that living there was like living in the Third World in that it had
a few predominate industries—oil and natural gas production, as well
as shipping, which was in a steady but not expanding state—and the
city was trying to make up for the economic gap with tourism. And he
said, it had the "added benefit" of being in the continental US. Other US
cities as well may be economically and occupationally structured more
like locations in the Third World than the First. And this colleague's
statement was before the hurricanes of 2005. Who suffered most when
hurricanes Katrina and Rita hit? Disadvantaged minority communities,
where tourism's secondary sector workers disproportionately lived, and
saw more death and property loss. To be sure, many others were hurt
as well, but the storms and the slow recovery has fallen hard on poor
blacks and whites. Now, as New Orleans crawls back to be more like
it was (remember, Third World-like, according to one sociologist), the
inequalities that were there may well be recreated.[11]

We can take several things from our observations of rural areas,
Native American reservations, Washington, DC, and other cities where
the association between labor market patterns and crime may not be
the same as in cities where the perspective generates good explanations. First, racial segregation or racial stratification may not cancel the
important effects of employment on crime, but there segregation and
stratification effects may so dominate social life that all else must be
analyzed or considered within separate racial spheres—therefore any
consideration of how the economy or employment affects either individual criminality or crime rates should take place at two levels, across
racial categories and within. In Washington, geographic categories align
strongly with racial groupings because of racial residential segregation.

The extent of the correspondence of geographical categorization with race varies on Native American tribal lands depending on the number of whites living within the boundaries.

In segregated societies it is important to study not only the distribution of occupations across the broader labor market, but also within racial groups. The occupational distribution in black American communities provides a useful example. As others have described, the jobs that African American workers have held have been disproportionately likely to be in the secondary sector of the economy, so the distribution of employment within black communities is typically less balanced than in the broader society.[12] When social life is as defined by race as it is in the District of Columbia, as well as on Native American reservations, then so too are the local labor markets. Within such places even dual labor market theory (which was developed to explain persisting economic disadvantage of some groups within a society, notably but not limited to racial and ethnic minorities) cannot adequately capture the social and economic marginalization within racially marginalized groups. The theory does aid in explaining the experience of such groups on the national level, but in these highly segregated local labor markets its explanatory power to explain crime, as I am using it here, is overwhelmed by the level of racialized social inequality visited upon the local populace. We need to be able to take into account a redefined conception of the labor market in such situations. The relative positioning of jobs and the expectations of people will be influenced by both the allocation of jobs in the broader society and within their segregated enclave as well.

To an extent, we have already recognized this. When Franklin Frazier wrote in the 1950s of the "Negro middle class," he described a group that emulated the white middle class in some behaviors although their jobs, their income, and certainly their wealth did not come close to equaling that of their dominant group counterparts.[13] Members of the black middle class of the 50s were frequently postal employees, teachers, municipal workers, and low-level managers in government or social services. Their incomes may have corresponded to these occupations, but of course in many places they got "Jim Crow reductions" from their pay. And if they had wealth, it was ordinarily limited to the equity in their homes (a great many middle-class African Americans rented their homes). The same is to an extent true today.[14] Also, the unionized industrial blue-collar jobs of cities like Detroit, Chicago, Cleveland, and Pittsburgh also helped to establish a black middle class in the 1960s and 70s. Clearly today there is an important segment of America's black population that is as solidly middle-class, by the same standards, as middle-class whites.[15] But at the same time it is still the case that African American employees of the post office or fire or police departments enjoy a class prestige within their community that their white coworkers may not, and this is simply a consequence of their relatively better-off employment circumstances when compared to those living around them. Black professionals in occupations that do not enjoy large incomes, such as teachers and nurses, enjoy a public definition of the status of their positions inflated beyond similarly situated whites and more like the status of people bringing home larger paychecks in the broader society. And some secondary sector workers are accorded more standing than their jobs ordinarily would receive simply because their occupants have work. Many African Americans of my generation knew of elders in the community or in our churches who had standing and respect and were seen as having a good job because they'd held them for a long time, even if they were janitors. Similarly, Native Americans working in low-level service jobs in tribal casinos may define themselves and be seen by others as in a more preferred situation because around them are neighbors living amidst 50 percent unemployment rates.

We must be clear, though, that this internal status scale exists within the context of the dominant society's definitions of prestige. Middle-class blacks and Native Americans may enjoy the relative respect received within their communities, but they know where they stand in America. It is the positioning of secondary sector jobs in the broader American view of occupational prestige that leads young men and women to say, "I don't want no damn slave job." In high racial or ethnic segregation settings, jobs and their occupants exist within two prestige hierarchies simultaneously. The relative value of people's jobs for their incomes, quality of life, and stake in conformity will depend upon both prestige hierarchies, with individuals varying on which they place the most emphasis. For example, the young whose expectations and hopes have not been tempered by racist opportunity structures are more likely to look to the broader society's prestige allocation, for in valued jobs there is a route to the prosperous lifestyles that they see outside of their immediate environment. Older people, worn down by the experiences of competing in a game where the cards are stacked against them, may take somewhat more comfort from success as judged by the less stringent standard of the segregated community. One way that Robby Wideman differed from his parents' generation is that he was probably less likely to frame his expectations based on the circumscribed occupational distribution of the inner-city black community, or the rural South from which much of the older generation moved, than on the national labor market. To the extent that this dual system of stratification exists, when we are predicting crime rates the distribution of jobs will include both the young who experience the full force of their disadvantaged marginalization in the labor force and those a bit more placated by having lowered expectations—making it more difficult to explain our dependent variable (crime rates) when we are measuring the stratification of labor by a standard more applicable to the society at large than the more complex layering that exists for people living in segregated communities.

If we focus too much on residential segregation, however, we run the risk of missing another important complexity of social life and labor force stratification. New Orleans, like many cities, towns, and villages in the Southern US, has had a different pattern of segregation than northern places, and while Washington, DC is a southern city its residential patterns are, and have for some decades been, more like cities of the North. In the South, there was not as much need for residential segregation because of the rigid norms of social segregation. White and black children could play together when young, but it was universally recognized that as they reached adolescence they would assume the socially prescribed social distance. Without the need for rigid geographic distance, places like New Orleans developed a housing pattern that allowed some of the black servant class to live conveniently near the white homes of their employers—that is, it was convenient for those being served. Thus today you will see some very humble abodes quite near rather grand mansions, albeit off of the stately, tree-lined boulevards and avenues and out of direct view. For our purposes this cautions us against too lightly aggregating residential districts in our frameworks and analyses, because the social lives and opportunity structures for those living close at hand may be very normatively stratified in such places.

A lesson from the shortcomings of our analyses thus far is that in multiracial or multiethnic societies, racial stratification and housing patterns are not just variables that must be taken into account, but they are instead important determinants of both patterns of social life and labor market opportunity that is central to our conceptualization. For example, to explain the relationship between the economy and crime in South Africa, we would have to consider it in the context of the legacy of apartheid. Likewise, it will be useful to consider the changing ethnic composition of European states for those who study crime there, and the influences of these factors on the relationship between the economy and employment there.

Some may also see a shortcoming of the labor stratification and crime thesis in the observed changes in Seattle during the last two decades of the twentieth century. In each of three analyses the labor stratification theses effectively predicted violent crime. To be specific, the models predicted neighborhood violent crime rates in 1980 and 2000, and neighborhood homicide rates in 1990. In the first analysis census tract labor market instability was the central variable used to represent the labor stratification thesis. It was a standardized combination of census tract unemployment rates and the percentage of employed workers who were in secondary sector occupations. But the correlation between the percentage of workers in the secondary sector and the unemployment rate in 1980 was higher than it was in the 2000 data. This change does not simply represent statistical messiness over a twenty-year period; the Seattle labor market has changed, and these changes are emblematic of changes that have taken place throughout the United States.

Twenty years ago secondary sector workers—those employed on the margin of the city's economy and not in Seattle's booming aerospace industry or on her docks, or in the city's manufacturing concerns—tended to live in the same census tracts where there were a lot of unemployed people. This fit with expectations of dual labor market theorists.

By 1990 more hi-tech, medical technology, and the nascent biotech industries were bringing new types of jobs to the metropolitan area, some of which were located in Seattle or, if not actually in the city, employing people who lived there. Many of the people working in these industries were either drawn from outside of the Northwest or were young, recent college graduates. High salaries and the stock options of some companies dramatically changed some neighborhoods as well as the city as a whole. Boeing was going strong, and the diversified local economy was nearly at full employment in the early 1990s.

The 2000 census of the population reported some housing patterns that differed from those we observed in 1980. No longer were secondary sector workers living primarily in communities with higher unemployment rates. The two were still correlated, but at the end of the decade a smaller portion of the city's workers were in manufacturing and a higher portion was in secondary sector jobs. A subtle shift had taken place in the local labor market as well as in some neighborhoods in this city that I earlier referred to as a "twenty-first-century city."

In earlier chapters I described how Cleveland had gone from a thriving manufacturing city to one of Rust Belt decline, to a city that is now attempting a regeneration of its central core area. My colleagues and I speculated that the labor stratification thesis model worked slightly less well in Cleveland than it did in Seattle because there were large sections of the inner city, just outside the central business district, that were largely abandoned—a consequence of declining population and poverty. Downtown Cleveland has since been revitalized. The city now sports the Rock and Roll Hall of Fame beside new baseball and football stadiums that are home to the Indians and the reestablished Cleveland Browns. Not far away is the basketball arena where fans used to flock to see then-local favorite and hometown hero Lebron James and the Cavaliers.[16] While I cannot say that the city has gotten its money's worth out of their investments in these facilities (cities routinely believe that they do, but many critics are convinced that they do not, but that issue is beyond the scope of this volume), one does see the restaurants and street life that accompanies these developments. With time, the neighborhoods that were decimated by the loss of population in the 1980s and 90s have attracted new residents through the process of gentrification that many cities are experiencing. Gentrification is certainly not without its problems, but it certainly changes the residential distribution of employed people.[17]

My colleagues and I (see chapter 5) found consequences of the shifted labor market nationally. Today, the presence of manufacturing workers has given way as a crime-inhibiting factor to the presence of high-end service sector workers. This is not to say that manufacturing is unimportant, and it is likely very important in some cities, but clearly the occupational structure of the US has shifted and so too have the effects of employment on crime patterns.

In both Seattle and Cleveland we see evolving cities coping with changes in local labor markets. As it has in earlier eras in response to changes in economies and structural arrangements, social life, including crime and the social relations that cause it, change in response. An early founder of sociology, Emile Durkheim, predicted that eventually a new form of social organization would emerge out of the social chaos wrought by the Industrial Revolution.[18] How might cities, their neighborhoods, and residents be changing as the shift toward postindustrial society continues? Perhaps crime is responsive to the distribution of employment most acutely during times of economic change, when both jobs and expectations are dashed by the disappearance of employment opportunities that had been expected. Perhaps an enduring despair takes place later in places relegated permanently, or at least semipermanently, to the margins of local labor markets or the larger national labor market. Maybe in these later places the street cultures and their values take root and develop a self-persisting quality, but in those places, like some of Seattle's and Cleveland's neighborhoods, there emerges an accommodation to the new structure of labor markets and the persisting disadvantage that comes with it.

This is not to say that people necessarily come to accept their disadvantaged position in the social structure, but instead that some become resigned to it, others elect to fight it, and still others react angrily, though at times not purposefully, in response. People having any of these adaptations may contribute to the critical mass in a neighborhood that allows for or encourages the emergence of street cultures, which may provide the situation of company where labor market marginality finds its fullest criminogenic influence or the emergence of cultural systems like those described by Anderson or Venkatesh or Jones.[19] So thus far, it appears that a more fulsome explanation of how labor markets influence crime needs to take into account both persistent economic disadvantage and the demography of race and ethnicity.

My earlier discussion of our more limited knowledge about labor markets and crime in rural places and on tribal land also guides the way toward a more nuanced version of a labor stratification and crime thesis. As in the inner cities, the meaning of work is different there than for the wider national labor market. In rural communities there is certainly a stratification of labor, but much also depends on the nature of the farming in particular areas. The local labor markets in productive agricultural areas are substantially different from those where farming yields less. Also, these areas will be affected by nearby industries in two important ways. First, as in the case of cities, manufacturing or service concerns within commuting distance provide additional jobs. Second, the externalities of nearby industries can influence agriculture, and consequently jobs there in important ways. The places where the Hole in the Wall Gang's parents worked were negatively affected by nearby extraction industries. The same has been true in the coal producing regions of Appalachia and will probably be increasingly the case in the West. The battles between National Parks and Forest advocates and environmentalists affects what is happening in the forest products industries in the west as well, and I would be surprised if a part of the arguments between environmentalists and ranchers over the reintroduction of grizzly bears and wolves in northwestern states is not argued at some level about jobs.

These same factors influence the economy, and consequently the jobs on tribal land. But for those tribes that have successfully established thriving casino businesses they have introduced many new jobs, many of which have secondary sector like characteristics. For those tribes they have probably created a local labor market that is somewhat like what black urban communities were like in the 1950s and 60s: jobs that the wider America thinks less of (because of the relative pay and how we rank occupational prestigious), but that are defined as middle-class by locals. For those tribes without successful gaming industry, their lot likely follows the course of other rural areas; in some places things are all right because of other opportunities, but elsewhere jobs are very hard to come by. Of course for the latter it is all the more difficult because of isolation, poverty, and the racism that is the status quo.

From rural and tribal areas we can find additional arguments for building in not just how we might classify jobs into the primary and secondary sector, but how the local populace defines the jobs that are available to them. If a job as a card dealer or waitress in a casino restaurant is viewed as valuable, if those positions are steady with decent benefits, and if they are occupied by people who not long ago saw few prospects, then those jobs will very likely inhibit lifestyles that generate crime. Both in these areas and in the inner cities during the Great Migration it is important to consider the timing element, because individuals holding jobs, those in their community, and their offspring trailing them will very likely define the jobs differently.

Labor Stratification and Crime Outside of the United States

Before more fully considering these conceptual changes, I think it is helpful to consider research that has been done outside of the United States, which might either raise additional questions or help to frame an improved theoretical approach. Two studies of labor markets in Italy are useful for our purpose. Paolo Buonanno examined crime and unemployment in two distinct regions of Italy between 1993 and 2002, the North-Central and the South.[20] The former is more industrial and has historically had a more robust economy. The South, by contrast, has been characterized by less economic growth, more poverty, and less industry. Buonanno found unemployment had a large effect on crime in the South, substantially increasing crime there. By contrast, in the North-Central part of the country, with lower overall levels of unemployment, there does not appear to be a relationship between unemployment and crime. Remembering the inconsistency of studies which consider the association between unemployment and crime in the US (see chapter 2) we should be cautious to not overinterpret these findings, but they are consistent with our suggestion that people being out of work is most problematic in settings where larger numbers of others are also displaced or marginalized in the labor market (see chapter 3). Researchers Luciano Mauro and Gaetano Carmeci also used Italian regional data and concluded that unemployment and crime together helped to perpetuate regional poverty.[21] Studying both property and violent crimes in Korea between 1982 and 2004, Kim Dongil found that unemployment increased both theft and assault over and above the effects of income.[22] Lorenzo Blanco and Sandra Villa studied the role of female labor force participation on crime in the Mexican state, Veracruz.[23] They found that labor force participation reduces crime in general. But while female labor force participation reduces overall violence rates, both rape and serious assaults increase as women's wage distribution increases. What we can draw from these studies is affirmation that the association between the labor market and crime are both robust and complicated.

Of course both my explanation and the interpretation of these research results are not the first time that social scientists have looked to labor market shifts to explain social life, and sometimes problematic social life. The discipline of sociology was born during the Industrial Revolution. Central to the ideas of the first sociologists in both Europe and America were the changes in social life that were taking place around them that resulted from economic transitions. The shift from societies that were primarily agrarian to industrial meant the movement of populations from villages and farms to urban areas where new jobs could be found. Today many western nations have or are moving toward what some have characterized as postindustrial economies, and although a great deal of manufacturing continues to take place there, substantial production is occurring elsewhere. Latin American and especially Asian countries in particular are major producers and exporters. To think seriously about the connection between employment, other economic characteristics, and crime we must move beyond thinking just about the people who live (or at least lived) in places where the jobs moved from. We must also begin to think about those who live where jobs have been created, and the consequent changes in the social and economic arrangements there. How are the transitions from agrarian to modern manufacturing economies affecting the people of countries that are on the receiving end of globalization's moves of plants and jobs across borders? And the same needs to be asked about formerly rural areas within the older industrial nations, when companies move production in. Finally, what happens to people and places, both in new or old industrial economies, where so-called progress passed them by but they remain stuck, dealing with the externalities of activity around them? This is the situation that the parents of the Hole in the Wall Gang and their offspring faced. Just as increases in crime and deviance were byproducts of the first Industrial Revolution, it is likely that the localized industrial revolutions that are taking place with more recent changes may well do the same.

Obviously, important changes have taken place elsewhere in recent decades too. The collapse of the Soviet Union and the transition of some Eastern European states from nations in Moscow's sphere of influence to membership in the European Union, the continuing evolution of the EU and its dept crisis, the end of apartheid in South Africa, and the move by China, India, and Brazil to become fast-growing, productive economies all constitute major social changes with very substantial economic ramifications, which we might expect to influence crime for better or worse.

These transitions have an additional complication. Historically, the move from totalitarian regimes to democracy and more open social life leads to higher crime rates.[24] This observation may run counter to popular expectations that the latter provides greater opportunity for human fulfillment and the good life, but if we think about the nature of such transitions independently of the rhetoric and propaganda of some western nations, increases of crime in "liberated" states makes sense. Along with new opportunities to express one's self politically and entrepreneurially, there are increased opportunities for crime. Police states need not bother with troublesome niceties like the rights of the accused and due process of law in repressing both dissent and ordinary common crimes. It is quite a bit easier to clamp down on common street criminals as well as organized crime if police are free to use any technology available to them, any and all sources of information, and preemptive arrests. When the rights of the governed become more respected by the state then it becomes easier for some among them to get away with crime.

For our purposes, this complicates the consideration of how the economic changes or labor market patterns in these countries might affect crime. It is difficult to untangle the increased crime that comes with the opening up of societies from any changes that might be the result of changes in labor markets and the economic lives of the people. South Africa represents an interesting example. South Africa has long been the industrial workhorse of Sub-Saharan Africa, but as a result of apartheid policies its draw for job seekers was more limited than it is now, since liberation. In recent years migrants from South Africa's hinterland as well as from other nations of southern Africa (especially Zimbabwe, which is experiencing political and economic turmoil) have moved in order to find work in South African factories, farms, and mines. At this same time the crime rates appear to have increased. It is difficult to have confidence in this last statement, because the nature of crime statistics will differ in a democratic state than those produced by the preceding oppressive regime. Certainly the perceptions of the people, white, black, and Coloured, are that the South African crime rate has gone up.

Two explanations are popular. Many blame the new migrants, especially those from other African nations. They look to squatter settlements outside of both the cities and historically black townships, or to those townships whose populations have been swelled by immigrants, as the source of their crime problems. Others blame the continuing economic inequalities within South Africa. While the African National Congress, the dominant political party, continues to work slowly toward meeting the promises of liberation, a great many people are out of work or employed in unpromising positions. Most people recognize that delivery on the promises will take time. The second popular explanation for the perceived crime increase is the actions of those who are insufficiently patient.

Summary of Work and Crime Study Results

To summarize what is currently known about the connection between employment and crime is to say that: (1) the association between unemployment rates and crime rates is inconsistent; (2) the quality of employment is related to crime, especially in urban areas, and at times it predicts criminality in rural areas as well; (3) an association between employment and crime has been observed both within and outside of the US, and in both cases there is evidence that context matters; (4) poverty is a consistent predictor of crime, but it is especially important in rural areas, while neighborhood disadvantage is important in urban areas; (5) race dynamics are an important part of the explanation, both in urban and rural areas, and especially in and around tribal lands; (6) gender patterns, especially the working life of mothers, should be taken into account; (7) work as a criminogenic force in postindustrial economies is different than it was during deindustrialization; and (8) social, economic, and industrial context matters to how work affects criminality and crime rates. These patterns and anomalies could spell the end for the labor stratification and crime thesis, but instead I think they provide opportunity for an expanded perspective that can offer improved theoretical understanding, and may point the way toward productive social policy alternatives.

What occurred in the United States in the 1960s was an expanding economy but increasing crime as well. At the surface this would appear to run counter to the labor stratification thesis. After all, Great Migration migrants had, on average, better jobs and a better economic outlook than they had in the South, and new jobs were being created. But places like the Southside of Chicago, Harlem, Black Bottom in Detroit,[25] and The Hill in Pittsburgh were by then showing the effects of long-term disappointments in the reality of the move to the Promised Land. And there was a younger generation who had little or no experience of the South, of Jim Crow, or cotton fields. To answer the question of why crime increased during this period of economic and job growth we have to remember that chronic labor market marginalization had set in within many black communities, and second-generation African American Northerners were not as content as their parents. Rather than being exceptional, this has been a repeatedly observed phenomenon among migrants. Essentially Robby Wideman, in his impatience for the good life, was not alone among the children of the Great Migration, and they as a group are not unique in the ongoing demographic saga of America.

Now in the twenty-first century, we have the Great Recession. Persistent national unemployment rates hovered around nine percent for an extended period and are receding very slowly, yet a substantial crime decline, which began prior to the recession, seems to continue. This is another anomaly that must be accounted for in order to have a better understanding of how labor market patterns affect crime. In the next chapter I will propose an expanded labor stratification and crime thesis that does that.

7

Toward a More General Explanation of Employment and Crime

A more general explanation—that is, one that is similar to the basic labor stratification and crime thesis—must be able to explain both the apparent anomalies such as rising crime during plenty and falling crime rates during economic distress, as well as crime in societies that have moved beyond the industrial economies that began to falter at the end of the twentieth century. At the same time, that more general thesis should retain the basic explanatory model that holds that socially structured labor stratification and its consequent inequality is criminogenic. This can be accomplished by more explicitly moving social and economic disadvantage into the thesis. This intellectual direction is not new. It is fundamentally what William Julius Wilson, Douglas Massey and Nancy Denton, Elijah Anderson, and others have argued. And please remember that in chapter 5, social and economic disadvantage is a central part of the contextual argument that I used to examine how neighborhoods condition the relationship between juveniles' school experience and delinquency. What I want to do here is be explicit about the ways that taking disadvantage into account helps to explain seeming anomalies and provides the basis for a thesis that can be used more broadly to explain crime patterns under different economic and industrial conditions, and in places other than urban places in modern states.

In chapter 1 I wrote that nearly all of us interface with the economy based on our relationship to the labor market, via the job we have or do not have. Not just our incomes, but our benefits and future prospects,[1] are determined by where we work and the characteristics of our jobs. And of course, if one does not have a job that particular connection to the economy is especially problematic. This was precisely the logic we used in parole work. Encouraging and helping our clients to find and hold jobs was central to our efforts to keep them from returning to prison. It was the sudden surge in joblessness that drew Wilson to argue that an urban underclass was created by the demise of the industrial base in the American Rust Belt. Of course, as articulated by dual labor market theory, it is still the case that we must distinguish good, primary sector jobs from not-so-good secondary sector jobs. Even with substantial changes in US, European, and some Asian economies, this distinction is still worth making.

There remain jobs that are well paid, with decent and even good benefits, and with greater security and opportunity for upward advancement than many others enjoy. Among these are still the professions, and, though some political forces now want to roll them back, public workers, but this new primary sector category notably contains many people employed in technology and upper-level service sectors. Examples of the latter are the technicians who keep our far more technologically dependent business and personal worlds functioning. With fewer manufacturing jobs in mature capitalist economies like those of the US, Canada, and Europe, those who seek employment who have few marketable skills and minimal education are frequently limited to opportunities in an expanded secondary sector. These jobs have the characteristics of the McJobs that I wrote of in earlier chapters. They are poorly paid, frequently at or just a bit above minimum wage, there are few or no benefits, and workers there enjoy little job security and few if any opportunities for advancement. As was the case for secondary sector workers in the last decades of the twentieth century, employees holding jobs with this set of characteristics do not have jobs that bond them to their work and a future at the place of employment that pays them at the moment. Without such a bond, these employees, just like the jobless, can be expected to pursue lifestyles more conducive to crime. There is no more reason to expect this of mature workers than there was in earlier years, but now, in the postindustrial economies, we can expect that young adult marginalized workers, those who are unemployed, the

jobless, and those working in the expanded secondary employment sector to have a heightened probability of becoming involved in criminogenic lifestyles and consequently criminality. And, when adolescents live
in communities where there are concentrations of adults who are marginal to the labor market, as we have seen in the past, these are criminogenic environments that make it more likely that the young will become
involved in delinquency. Of course this is essentially the same argument
made earlier, with a bit of an adaptation to what are defined as primary
sector jobs, but I now want to make the case for two new and important
changes: the new complexity of manufacturing jobs, and a more explicit
place for social and economic disadvantage in the thesis.

Manufacturing in the United States and in other advanced economies has changed. For the first three quarters of the twentieth century,
workers with few or no skills and those with no or minimal education
could find work in heavy industries. Those jobs, very frequently union
jobs, were classic primary sector jobs. They paid well, had good benefits,
and after workers achieved some seniority, they had a degree of security. Those willing to work hard in back-breaking, sometimes dirty mills,
foundries, factories, and meat packing plants could provide a good middle-class life for their families. Fewer of those jobs are a part of our economy today. A growing number of manufacturing plants have elected to
locate in right-to-work states, where unions have not been able to gain a
foothold. Workers there may have quality benefits, but sometimes lower
salaries, and fewer job protections than their unionized brethren. But
another fundamental change has taken place in modern manufacturing.
In many companies there is no longer a place for the poorly educated,
low-skilled, hardworking employee. Robotics and automation provides
cheaper—some say higher quality—outputs. A colleague of mine who
recently had the opportunity to tour a European auto plant reports that
the workers on the floor were skilled technicians who keep the robots,
which are actually building the cars, working.

So when my colleagues and I discovered that the percentage of neighborhood residents who worked in manufacturing was neither positively
nor negatively associated with crime rates using 2000 census data and
crime statistics (see chapter 5), it should not be a surprise.[2] Manufacturing is a much smaller part of the US economy and of neighborhood
life than it was when I began testing the labor stratification and crime

thesis in the 1980s. Some manufacturing jobs—like those held by members of United Auto Workers Union in Michigan, who still have jobs, and the European robotics technicians that my colleague observed—are primary sector positions. Unfortunately, a substantial number of manufacturing workers now are employed in jobs that increasingly have some characteristics of the secondary sector.

The scholars who formulated dual labor market theory sought to explain the ongoing disadvantage of portions of the population not exclusively of subjugated minority group members (though largely so), but also of dominant group members who were perpetually consigned, by traits such as social class, to the lower rungs of the economic stratification ladder. I have sought to use the notions of labor market segmentation to explain how marginalization from the labor market creates crime. This was in lieu of explanations that argued that poverty caused criminality. The latter was, in my view, too dependent on utilitarian motivations. To be sure, some people are motivated by utilitarian, I-need-money kinds of concerns, but that does not, as explained earlier, help us to understand a great deal of crime, especially violent crimes. An alternative to the utilitarian linkage between poverty and crime were arguments that a subculture of poverty existed where people held values and beliefs that were different from the rest of us and that were criminogenic. Earlier I took those who make such arguments to task for failing to acknowledge, or centrally place in their explanations, how people become poor. When they did, it was generally argued that they became poor because of their failure to be motivated to work. Never mind that for many of the people counted among the poor, no jobs were available and the ones that were, secondary sector jobs, generally do not pay a family wage, and at times do not even provide a living wage for the toilers themselves.

In contrast, sociologists have documented how social structural conditions such as joblessness or racial residential segregation can lead to social conditions where cultural patterns, values, norms, customs, and practices can emerge in disadvantaged communities that make crime and delinquency more likely. This is explicit in Anderson's description of inner-city Philadelphia where he observed "decent" families who adhere to traditional norms and values, and "street" families that adhered to the code of the streets. The latter are subject to be more involved in both violence and property crimes as a result of internalizing beliefs that insist that one reacts strongly and quickly when faced with insults, or that one must be aggressively entrepreneurial in one's own behalf, even if that entails illegal activity. Also, even the children of decent families cannot ignore the code of the street, because they will be subject to it when they are out and about in the community. Most importantly for our purposes, these codes emerge in a situation of ongoing, deep, concentrated disadvantage that occurs when residents are jobless or otherwise marginal to the labor market.

Wilson, Massey and Denton, and Anderson each have a different focus, but are exemplars of how the poor or disadvantaged become that way or remain that way as a result of social structural conditions: joblessness, racial segregation, and concentrated poverty. Yes, cultural patterns do emerge that perpetuate disadvantage, but they emerge from structural conditions. For example, beliefs among young people that do not encourage remaining in school may be directly related to dropout rates, but these beliefs are a consequence of the structural, neighborhood, economic, and social conditions in which some children come of age. Two related critical structural conditions that perpetuate such disadvantage and the cultural patterns that flow from it are labor market segmentation and joblessness.

It is critical that we not simply think of the disadvantaged as people with low incomes or in poverty. Disadvantage includes both economic circumstances and social conditions. Factors such as family structure (single parent families, teenaged parents), housing (condition of housing stock, whether people rent versus living in houses they own or are buying, or homelessness), education (the proportion of people in a community who dropped out of high school), and so on help us to distinguished the disadvantaged from those living in poverty. Neighborhoods where there are high levels of single parent families, substandard housing, high dropout rates, and elevated levels of labor market marginality can be thought of as disadvantaged. Some of my colleagues include the percentage of residents who are African American in their calculations of disadvantaged neighborhoods, but I choose not to do that, believing that being black in America can contribute substantially to a person's chances of living in a disadvantaged place and being black can cause one to experience discrimination and disadvantage, but absent the racism of society, being black in and of itself does not constitute disadvantage. And here I am especially interested in people who live in circumstances that can be described as concentrated disadvantaged. Sociologist William Julius Wilson wrote:

> If I had to use one term to capture the differences in the experiences of low-income families who live in inner-city areas from the experiences of those who live in other areas in the central city today, that term would be *concentration effects*. The social transformation of the inner city has results in a disproportionate concentration of the most disadvantaged segments of the urban black population, creating a social milieu significantly different form the environment that existed in these communities several decades ago.[3]

It is the residential concentration of the economically and socially disadvantaged that exacerbates their situations, creating a social context where good jobs (see Wilson's discussion of how people in underclass neighborhoods do not benefit from personal network links to job opportunities[4]) and quality education are far less available to them, perpetuating their status and unfortunately making it likely that the disadvantage will be intergenerational. This problem is made even worse when the people of such communities are isolated from the wider society and their interactions are primarily with others who are similarly situated. Again, the base problem for the people of these communities is that too many adults are marginal to the labor market.

Most of the scholars who have written about these issues have focused on urban communities, but there is no reason why if social and economic disadvantage is concentrated and the people are isolated that it may not also create problematic living and criminogenic conditions in rural areas. Thus, in the US, on Native American reservations or in Appalachia, or in the black townships of South Africa or the "high-density" areas of Zimbabwe, the same processes perpetuate disadvantage and produce both oppositional cultures and criminality. Here too the base of the problems is the population's marginal—perhaps even nonexistent—relationship to the labor market.

Labor Market Marginality in Postindustrial Economies

The occupations that were in the primary sector during the twentieth century in the US, Western Europe, and other modern economies still are. Two things have changed. First, at least in the US and in a number of other economies, the manufacturing sector, the basis for upward mobility into the middle class for many low-skilled workers, is a far smaller portion of the workforce. Second, new occupations in high-level service sectors have emerged. These are services of the sort offered by the financial services companies and the many concerns that have sprung up to keep our more technologically dependent societies operating. Many of these jobs are different from traditional service sector jobs, many of which were classic secondary sector jobs, because they have primary sector characteristics. They are reasonably well paid (some "workers" in these sectors are incredibly well-paid), they come with benefits, there are opportunities for advancement, and positions are comparatively secure.

What is important for a more general labor stratification and crime thesis is not the title of the positions that people in either national or local labor markets occupy, but rather the characteristics of the positions they are employed in. Just as was the case with the manufacturing workers of inner-city Pittsburgh, Cleveland, and Detroit of the twentieth century, their jobs gave them something to bond to, jobs that conditioned their lifestyles and repressed not only their criminality, but their children's as well. The same is now the case for the many who labor in the high-level service occupations of the later twentieth and early twenty-first centuries. What remains important is the quality of the jobs available to people; what is still the case is that a proliferation of high-quality jobs with primary sector characteristics will inhibit criminality, and low-quality work or no work at all—labor market marginality—is criminogenic.

Not Just the Inexorable Effects of Globalization and Technology

We might easily fall into the trap of thinking that the movement of jobs to cheaper labor markets at home and abroad is simply a function of the inevitable process of globalization that is characteristic of the world economy in the current era. That trap would also include the presumption that the emergence and increasingly prominence of technologically sophisticated jobs, like many of those primary sector-like high-end service jobs, and the US's heavily financial services based economy, are also inevitable. This image ignores policies and practice choices that the US and state governments have made that encourage or exacerbate the effects of both globalization and technological changes have had on people and communities. The same can be said of some other Western industrialized nations.

It is widely acknowledged that a substantial cause of the Great Recession was deregulation of financial markets. This was a part of a decades-long set of changes that included shifting tax burdens increasingly to the middle classes, the accumulation of wealth among the already richest Americans in the belief that they are the "job creators," and negative pressure on labor unions, a powerful force in turning industrial jobs that were exploiting workers early in the twentieth century, to an important contributor to the growth of the middle class after World War II. All the while, a growing number of the jobs that have been created have the characteristics of secondary sector employment. Yes, prior to the Great Recession there was job creation, but too few of them were like the primary sector jobs that were being replaced. In the US there are quality job prospects for some, but increasingly these are reserved for the most trained among us. The stagnate US economy has made finding work a challenge for most job seekers during the Great Recession, but the unemployment rate for college graduates is less than half of the US overall unemployment rate. The recession, as we might guess, has hit the hardest those who are less skilled, who used to be able to find quality employment if they were willing to work hard.

This has always been so. We call folks residing at the bottom of social hierarchies the vulnerable for a reason: they have less capacity to weather economic storms. Of course this lessened capability is a function of many social factors, including education and training, but, very importantly, where they sit in the labor market as well. Firms employ secondary sector workers in part because that portion of the work force is easier to shed than highly trained or more valued employees. The labor stratification and crime thesis that has been our basic argument would contend that expansion of this portion of the labor market makes more workers, and also their children, susceptible to crime-conducive lifestyles. It also means that more communities exist on the margin of disadvantage, potentially falling into the much more dire circumstances than their previously more vulnerable neighbors. More people become like my urban parolee Walter or his rural counterpart, Steve. More children are subject to the delinquent life of Gary or the members of the Hole in the Wall Gang.

Why Do We Accept These Arrangements and Their Consequences?

One need only to listen to the rhetoric of major political party candidates at the national, state, or local levels to get an important lesson in foundational American values that allow for policies that have led to more joblessness and labor market marginality. First is a belief in—even a pride in—the dominance of individual rather than collective concerns. Individualism is woven into the fabric of many Western nations, but it is especially so in the US. Second, as is argued convincingly by sociologists Steven Messner and Richard Rosenfeld,[5] our national focus on material gain and wealth accumulation at nearly all costs is not just allowed by our national values, but encouraged by them. These values are supported by heroic narratives of up-by-their-bootstraps economic heroes, people who by their own individual perseverance and hard work were able to accumulate great wealth. Such narratives rarely acknowledge the extent to which these successes were supported by family capital in the form of income, wealth, education, or position; frequently our heroes have benefited from all of these, or, in the case of some, by the support of government. Cheap leases for mineral exploration on public lands, agricultural practices that enrich agribusiness (many designed to help family farmers), and federal expenditures that provide substantial profits for select companies and their stockholders (e.g., defense spending for Boeing and Lockheed-Martin, and taxpayer support for the Federal Aviation Administration, which keeps airline companies from having to pay the full cost of operating) seem not to concern politicians who overly hype the American up-by-the-bootstraps mythology. And among many of today's established families are those whose landholdings began via homestead acts, the government giveaways of land taken from Native Americans. The counternarrative is that those who are not so successful are there by virtue of their own failings.

Because of this belief system we are collectively deeply suspicious of those who have not accomplished so much, and we worry that such people might get more than they deserve based on our perception of their investment of blood, sweat, and tears. How else do we explain a social welfare system that is designed less to help those in need than to make sure that no one is ripping that system off? Or that the reason that manufacturing has left the US is because union workers' income and benefits were too good, even though some important industries in right-to-work states have also lost jobs? Or how did a political narrative emerge in 2011 that blames teachers, firefighters, and police unions for the budget struggles in some states?[6] After the 9/11 attacks we collectively couldn't praise enough our first responders, and spoke in patriotic terms of their sacrifices. But ten years later, some politicians have come to blame them, along with public school teachers, for state budget shortfalls.

Of course it is not just values and attitudes; it is action. Deregulation of important institutions (banking, media, etc.) at the national level, and short-sighted local decisions, are examples of such actions. They benefit some already well-heeled individuals and companies, but they may have deleterious effects on working people and their communities, and ultimately they have real consequences for both national and local labor markets and these in turn affect crime.

Political and economic policies and choices made in the US in recent decades have dramatically increased the concentration of both incomes and wealth. The Congressional Budget Office found that between 1979 and 2007, for the top one percent (in terms of income) of households incomes grew 275 percent, but only by 18 percent for the bottom 20 percent of earners. Incomes for those in between grew between 40 and 65 percent over this nearly thirty-year period.[7] The processes that have increased income and wealth inequality have been underway for several decades, but they have accelerated as a result of the Great Recession, in no small part because of fundamental changes in the structure of the American labor market.[8] In large measure these processes have been linked to declines in primary sector jobs (especially blue-collar jobs) and where jobs have been created, a disproportionate share have secondary sector characteristics. And as we have seen in earlier chapters, these changes have important ramifications for communities, for crime and delinquency rates, and for the individual criminality of some people constrained to these jobs, for their children, and for their neighbors.

The Walmart Contradiction

A concrete example of how this can happen may be useful for some. The Walmart Corporation provides just such an excellent example. Walmart, the largest retailer in the world, presents an interesting set of opportunities and problems for local communities. It brings economic activity, and it brings a reliably inexpensive option for local shoppers. On the other hand, Walmart is notorious for the low pay and limited benefits provided to their employees, notwithstanding their television commercials featuring employees extolling the wonderful benefits they receive from the company.[9] The problem is that this is only the case for a very small subset of those who work for the Walmart Corporation. For most, low pay and minimal benefits are the realities of working for the world's largest retailer. Consequently, most Walmart workers do not enjoy family wage jobs, and they are at times compelled to be dependent on the state. A University of California-Berkeley Labor Center study titled "The Hidden cost of Walmart Jobs: Use of Safety Net programs by Walmart Workers in California" reported evidence supporting this contention.[10] The authors of the study, Arindrajit Dube and Ken Jacobs, found that Walmart workers received substantially lower pay than other retail workers and were less likely to receive employer-based health care benefits. As a result many Walmart workers relied on state supported food stamps, Medicaid, and subsidized housing, functionally shifting the employer's labor cost to the citizens of California. Dube and Jacobs report that the results cost the state $86 million dollars annually. Thus the people of the State of California are essentially subsidizing the profits of the Walmart Corporation.

This, however, is not in and of itself the Walmart contradiction. As a result of their low labor costs and combined with its global bulk buying advantage, the company is able to drastically undercut the prices of potential local retail competitors. Dube and Jacobs point out that other retailers have tried to cut their own pay scales and benefits packages, citing competition from Walmart. In fact, this competition was cited by grocery retailers as a reason for the position they took that led to the 2003–2004 strike by 70,000 members of the United Food and Commercial Workers union.[11] Those retailers cited union concessions that they extracted because of competition from Walmart as the basis for settling the strike. The contradiction is created because Walmart's wages and benefits package are not only low for their own employees; their practices depress local salary and benefits for other blue-collar workers, who are in many ways similar to their own employees. The problem is that such workers are an important market segment for Walmart, and as their practices cut into the discretionary incomes of those workers they cut into their own customers' capacity to buy. It is those workers, and similarly situated working people, who provide a substantial share of Walmart's profits. Their practices are sowing the seeds of threat to their own long-term profits—thus the Walmart contradiction. On a wider scale, this is a problem for the American economy. The expansion of secondary sector jobs will reduce the discretionary income of the working classes, which negatively affects the consumer economy and has additional costs. Such a circumstance is likely to increase crime rates while decreasing local tax bases. It is a recipe for long-term increases in income inequality, increased crime, and decreased societal capacity to respond to that crime via either criminal justice or social welfare solutions.

Summary of Labor Stratification and the Contemporary Economy

Important economic changes have taken place, which have substantially changed labor markets in the US and around the world. Globalization has moved manual jobs from the formerly industrial world to new, developing economic powers in Asia and Latin America. There is growing labor market inequality, with new jobs being created in highly skilled professions and other primary sectors of the labor market and in an expanding secondary sector. In the US continued high unemployment is a consequence of both the Great Recession and these fundamental changes in national and international economies.

The Great Recession has accelerated the process of hollowing out the middle class, increasing the income and wealth of those on top of the economic stratification pyramid and growing the distance between them and those in the middle and lower categories. Poverty in the US has grown as a result of these changes. Now, according to the National Center for Children in Poverty at Columbia University, more than 21 percent of American children are growing up in families whose income is below the federal poverty level of $22,000 a year for a family of four.[12]

Federal, state, and local governments are being asked to cut back on safety net programs in the name of "responsible budgeting" and the need for austerity. So when more people are jobless and an increasing share of the labor force can only find work in the marginal secondary sector, the capacity of governments to provide stopgap support is being reduced (keep in mind that welfare reform in the US has already stepped substantially back from providing a safety net such as unemployment compensation for much of the population). Additionally, states are cutting back on support for public education, from kindergarten through state colleges and universities. So when it is greatly needed, our capacity to support those currently struggling or to prepare skilled workers for primary sector jobs the funding for these programs has been stalled.

Labor Stratification and Crime in the Twenty-First Century

According to the basic labor stratification and crime thesis that we began with, crime should be increasing. Marginal employment is expanding, unemployment is high, and state investment in education is low and in many places declining. With these economic changes and the housing crisis that is a central feature of the Great Recession, measures of social and economic disadvantage are likely to show that they are expanding too. But the US remains, by most indications, in a long-term reduction in crime rates, referred to be criminologists as "the crime decline." I know of no empirical criminologists who disagree that national (and for that matter most subnational) rates of crime have been dropping in recent years. There have been brief upticks in some years, but the long-term trend of declining or flat crime rates appears to be holding. Figures 7.1 and 7.2 are taken from a 2011 Bureau of Justice Statistics Report titled "Criminal Victimization, 2010."[13] They illustrate fairly steady declines in both violent and property crime victimization between 1993 and 2010. This is on top of fairly steady decreases since the mid-1970s, except for a brief period in the late 1980s and early 90s when there was a bit of upsurge in violent crimes that has been attributed to conflicts associated with competition for crack cocaine territories and markets (other

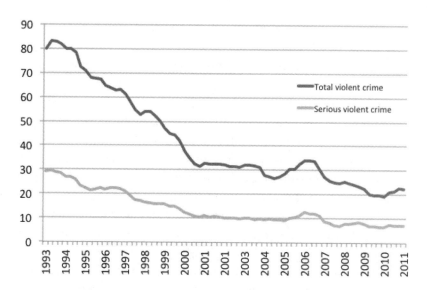

Figure 7.1. Total Violent and Serious Violent Victimizations, 1993–2011: Rate per 1,000 Persons Age 12 or Older. Source: Bureau of Justice Statistics, National Crime Victimization Survey, 1993–2011. Author: Jennifer L. Truman and Michael Planty. Date of version: October 12, 2012.

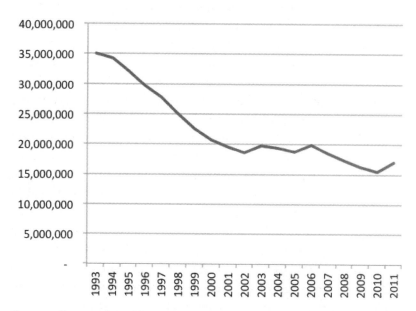

Figure 7.2. Property Crime Victimizations, 1993–2011: Rate per 1,000 Households. Due to methodological changes in the 2006 NCVS, use caution when comparing 2006 criminal victimization estimates to other years. Source: Bureau of Justice Statistics. Generated using the NCVS Victimization Analysis Tool at www.bjs.gove. 12-Apr-13

sources indicate that homicide rose for a few years then too; see Figure 1.1 in chapter 1). Thus there seems to be yet another anomaly, seemingly joining the somewhat confusing patterns of decreasing crime observed during the Great Depression of the 1930s and the increases in crime during the economic boom years of the 1960s. Dropping crime rates during the 1990s have been attributed to the generally expanding economy during that period, criminal justice changes (community policing, broken-windows policing strategies, and a massive increase in the proportion of the population locked in prisons and jails), and likely other social changes such as the increasingly aging American population. The anomaly seems to be with the continued decrease in criminal victimization since the start of the Great Recession in the late summer and fall of 2008.

But perhaps this anomaly is no more so than the actual realities of those first two earlier seeming anomalies. While it appears that some crimes (e.g., homicide) did not increase substantially during the Depression, recall that economists Phillip Cook and Gary Zarkin did find that burglary rates went up then. And the seeming anomaly of increases in crime in the 1960s occurred in the context of two phenomenal demographic changes that dramatically changed American social life, the coming of age of the second generation of the Great Migration and the crime-prone age tsunami of baby boomers. Who is to know how the economy would have affected the overall crime rates in the 1960s if these two simultaneous events had not taken place? Also, there are indications that there was unevenness in that economic boom. I will address that below. For now, though, there are two lessons that I tried to take from those two earlier seeming anomalies that are important to apply here. First, there were important collective emotions present in both cases. During the Depression there was a sense of shared burden and struggle in the population, and in 1960s inner-city America, that first Northern generation of young African Americans were frustrated by the realities of the Promised Land. Second, the patterns of criminality then were not evenly distributed across the geography of the country. While crime rates went up in American cities in the 1960s, they did not go up to the same extent everywhere. It is important to recognize both of these lessons in the development of a more general labor stratification and crime thesis, and, by doing so, I can make some sense of the seeming anomaly of continually dropping crime rates during the Great Recession. I will consider the crime drop first.

The crime drop has been attributed to a number of forces. To a large extent these explanations should not be seen as competing, but rather as a set of social forces that complement each other. Researchers have varying opinions about which of these factors or sets of factors are most important. Frequently mentioned reasons for declining crime rates (and especially drops in homicide since the peak years of the early 1990s) are: the more than quadrupling of imprisonment rates and other get-tough-on-crime strategies;[14] changes in drug markets, notably the decline in street crack cocaine markets;[15] and the improving economy during the 1990s when the crime drop was most precipitous, though of course the decline has slowed a bit, and continues now in the Great Recession and its lingering aftermath. Finally, changes in the age structure of the population, with a smaller portion of the population in the crime-prone teenaged years and early twenties for the most violent of crimes, likely has had an effect too.

While there is no contention among criminologists that in fact the amount of common or street crimes occurring within the United States has continued to decline at least up to the date for which we have reliable data (2011), there is important literature indicating that this overall pattern hides important variation within the country. Two such patterns are important for our purposes: demographic variation in both criminal involvement and victimization that have been reported during the drop, and variations in crimes across micro social environments are both important.

In her book titled the *Unequal Crime Decline*, sociologist Karen Parker examines the lowering crime rate, paying special attention to the patterns based on race and gender.[16] Neither the patterns of the decline nor the factors thought to be causing the decrease in crime are the same for whites and blacks, or for women and men. The black rate of decline has been steeper than the white rate, which has been fairly stable since 1980, and among blacks who live in highly segregated places there has also been a drop, but there the homicide rate remains high compared to that for other African Americans, and especially high compared to whites. It is important to note that Parker reports increased black male homicide rates in the first two years of the twenty-first century, and this change is masked by the overall homicide rate decline. Black female homicide rates have tended to track fairly close to white male rates, and white women had a steady but comparatively low rate compared to the other demographic categories.[17] At the same time, Parker's analyses, and those of other scholars whom she cites, indicate that the industrial restructuring that began in the 1970s, shifting the economy from a manufacturing base to a service-based economy, disproportionately affected black males. Other changes, too, like decreasing racial residential segregation for a subset of African Americans, shifted economic reality for those left behind in segregated inner cities hit hardest by those losses in manufacturing jobs.

Parker emphasizes the point that a number of factors—some that we have a relatively good understanding of, others that we do not—have caused the crime drop, but the decline has not been equally distributed, and that for a complete appreciation of what has happened we need a more nuanced, multifactor consideration. After comparing the effects of a number of social forces on homicide rates between 1980 and 2000, Parker writes:

> Comparing these two cities brings to light some important points. First, no single indicator captures the complexity of racial stratification in labor market structures. Though scholars tend to focus on the most visible effects of the economy, for example, poverty and unemployment rates, doing so may lead to a serious misunderstanding with regard to local economies and the potential relationship between economic conditions and the crime drop. Second, the path inequality takes differs based on an area's industrial mix and level of ethnic diversity . . . Finally, even though crime decreased in both Detroit and Dallas in the 1990s, the nature of the crime drop differed in each city.[18]

So the effects of the decline are not the same for all groups; we need to develop a theoretical approach to explaining these relationships that are both more complex and more nuanced, and we need a multiple factor approach to explain not only the crime drop, but any real changes in crime rates. Also, there is the suggestion that in some segments of some inner cities, crime may now be increasing. The need for more complex and nuanced consideration are bolstered by research that indicates that we need to look even more closely within cities and even within neighborhoods as we seek to understand crime distribution patterns and how to explain them.

Similar to the themes articulated by Karen Parker, John Klofas, discussing the challenges before police officers in the inner cities, argues that the continued economic distress in those communities is linked to higher crime rates than show up in city wide police statistics.[19] While the stories one hears from social service providers in distressed communities is not evidence of this pattern, they feel that something is increasingly wrong in the places where they work that is contrary to the national crime decline. In an effort to confront the problem of juvenile delinquency in their distressed communities, Kathleen Falk, the former County Executive of Dane County Wisconsin, feels that the problems will only improve if confronted by systemic intervention. Toward that end they have mounted an effort to not only improve policing, but to intervene in the lives of entire families where children are considered at risk. This includes efforts to find jobs for the parents in the belief that unless something changes for the future outlook of families and communities, delinquency will only continue to be a major problem.[20]

In a conversation with Marvin Prentice, chief executive of the Hill House Association, a nonprofit serving Pittsburgh's Hill District, I mentioned the continuing crime decline. He responded, "Not from what I'm seeing on the street." He did not argue with the city's data so much as with any suggestion that there was not continuing high levels of crime in sections of The Hill, and a disturbingly high level of gun violence. While Prentice remained unconvinced that the overall crime rate was dropping, he argued, based on what he sees on the streets of Pittsburgh, that if it is dropping than the form or nature of crime has changed. The Hill House Association is attempting, like Dane County, several systemic interventions to address crime and delinquency in their service area.

There is evidence that the form of crime has changed in some communities. In particular, gang activity has changed things in some places. Historically there have long been "gang cities," places with long histories of sustained substantial gang activity. Notable among these are New York, Chicago, and Los Angeles. But recent decades have seen an expansion into suburban counties and smaller towns.[21] According to data collected by the National Gang Center from law enforcement agencies gang problems declined in the 1990s, but increased steadily in the early 2000s. While these patterns were observed in the suburbs and in smaller towns, still the lion's share of gang problems are in cities of 50,000 residents or more.[22] More to our point, there are also variations in the seriousness of gang activity. Using gang homicide as an indicator of serious gang activity, James Howell and his colleagues found a steady level of youth gang killings in most large (100,000 or more people) cities, but substantial increases among a small subset. Among that subset was Pittsburgh. Speaking generally of changes in gang homicides between 1996 and 2009, while the nation as a whole was experiencing the continuing crime decline, Howell writes:

> Overall, more than 7 out of 10 very large cities reported a consistently high level or increasing proportion of gang-related homicides over the 14-year period. Second, a remarkable degree of consistency in the rate for gang-related homicides across trajectory groups is observed. Third, none of the trajectory groups found in these cities displayed a pattern consistent with a decline in the prevalence of gang homicide.[23]

So in addition to variation in the extent to which some populations have benefited more and others less from declining crime rates, the form and nature of crime changed more on the streets of some cities than others in recent years. What about within metropolitan areas? As Howell and his colleague document, there is a growing gang problem in some suburban places.

Recent research clearly indicates that there is also great deal of heterogeneity within cities and even within neighborhoods about how much crime there is.[24] We have long known that some neighborhoods within cities contribute most of the crime to the city crime rates—that fact is much of the point of some of the earlier chapters of this book. But we know now that even within bad neighborhoods there are specific hotspots, street intersections and blocks where a lot of that crime occurs, and others where there is very little. David Weisburd and his colleagues studied crimes in Seattle street segments between 1989 and 2002 and found stability in most parts of the city, but a distinctive group of places where crime declined and others where it increased.[25]

There were increases in the downtown business district and just to its south (a nightclub zone and the stadium district) and in the University District, while decreases were observed in the Central District (CD), the historic heart of the African American community, and in southern areas of the city that have views of Lake Washington. The former experienced significant gentrification during this period, and the latter, which already had high-end housing, became even more so. Both the gentrification of the CD and the increasingly high cost of housing in the south Lake Washington neighborhoods shifted the characteristics of the population, contributing to a very local crime decline. It is interesting to consider those results along with others produced by the University of Maryland research team using the same data set. Interestingly, an examination of the maps that they published shows that except for the downtown business district, most of the highest crime street segments are in the Central District (part of which experienced gentrification and other sections of which remained disadvantaged) and in the Rainer Valley ("The Valley"), which borders those high-end, Lake Washington view neighborhoods where crime decreased. Both the CD and The Valley contain some of the city's most disadvantaged neighborhoods.

An important exception to this observation is that there are several high-crime street segments in the University District, which is not a high-disadvantage area but is characterized by the anonymous street life that is typical of high-traffic student areas.[26] This research makes clear that contained in the overall trends in crime reduction are very different differential patterns. For instance, Anthony Braga and his colleagues have demonstrated that a major source of the crime decline is that substantially less crime in some of Boston's major hotspots has contributed disproportionately to the city's overall reduction in recent years.[27]

It appears that to an important extent, fluctuations in crime rates are linked to changes in especially volatile cities and in especially volatile places, down to crime hotspots, which may be as small as a street block or even an intersection. While large societal forces such as demographic changes, state imprisonment policies, and the economy and labor markets are no doubt important, there are also important micro place forces that cause crime rates to go both up and down. Among the factors that may have important effects on within city efforts to lower violence, drug behavior, and crime in general are efforts by citizens or coalitions of activists, such as those that occurred in Boston, resulting in what's been called the "Boston miracle." There groups, led by religious leaders, worked to get "problem people" jobs, to reduce guns on the streets, and to broker nonviolent settlements, resulting in quite substantial decreases in violence.[28] Police strategies may also elect to target particularly problematic places and the people who live in or frequent such places. Klofas, writing about increasing metropolitan challenges for police departments as opposed to classic urban challenges, notes that increasing poverty and racial residential segregation of core cities need to be of concern.[29] In particular, he notes forces like poverty that will increase crime, offers new challenges to important social institutions such as schools, and calls for more crime control on the part of some segments of the population. The latter is likely to bring officers into conflict with poor, minority populations who are marginalized from both the labor markets and power structures of metropolitan governments.

To conclude this section, I believe that once we accept that which has been obvious to social scientists observing all manner of social patterns, that a number of factors will effect changes in crime rates— not just one factor, such as the economy. Some important factors will increase crime, and others will suppress it. Important social forces in the latter category include an aging population, the massive increase in the proportion of the US population currently held in prisons and jails, and changes in interaction patterns such as those associated with drug selling. I and others who have conducted research on economic factors and crime believe that a sizable body of evidence has now accumulated indicating that joblessness, labor market marginality, a weak economy, and social and economic disadvantage are important social forces that lead to more crime. The empirical challenge before us is to simultaneously weigh the effects of crime-reducing forces and those that are criminogenic for the period just before and during the Great Recession. While the requisite crime data will soon be available, they are not yet, at the time of this writing. Furthermore, it is likely that the effects of changes in disadvantaged communities resulting from the Great Recession will take additional time to play out. Why that might be is the subject of the next section.

Labor Markets, Disadvantage, and Crime

It is not new news to say that joblessness leads to disadvantage. That is the central point of Wilson's two important books, *The Truly Disadvantaged* and *When Work Disappears*. Also, writing with Robert Sampson, Wilson makes a strong link between urban disadvantage and crime. What I and others have added to this explanation is the connection between not just joblessness, but also how work in low-end jobs, secondary sector jobs, and unemployment influences crime, and some specification of the mechanisms that link marginal work, joblessness, and criminality. Here I would like to elaborate a bit more on how employment and disadvantage affect crime and crime rates. Anderson, in his discussion in *Code of the Street*, has contributed significantly to our understanding of this connection. Here I would like to focus on four important factors: education and child rearing, gender, residential patterns, and imprisonment.

Education and Child Rearing

In chapter 5 I noted that research has long shown that children who do well in school are significantly less likely to become involved in delinquency. Unfortunately my analyses and those of Paul Bellair and his colleagues have found this not to be so for urban children who live in disadvantaged neighborhoods.[30] There those who are getting better grades report more criminal involvement than those performing less well. Of course, those who have dropped out of school altogether are the most crime-prone (see chapter 4). We do not really know why we are observing this pattern—why children from disadvantaged places are not benefiting from the antidelinquency force that education has for other children living in more prosperous places. I hope that my colleagues who qualitatively study disadvantaged communities can begin to help us to understand what is going on with these youngsters and their school experiences.

What we do know is that education in the inner cities of the US is generally not on par with what children in affluent suburbs experience, and this has consequences for their job market prospects. Joleen Kirschenman and Kathryn Neckerman found that employers in the

Chicago metropolitan area used race to sort who they would hire; employers expressed that they felt those educated in the Chicago public schools would be lower quality workers, and they presumed that most of the black applicants were from those schools.[31] Serious problems documented by Jonathan Kozol did exist in the Chicago schools, and the district was eventually put into receivership in an attempt to ameliorate the inadequacies.[32] And these problems do not just exist in Chicago. Urban schools have suffered from a wicked combination of inadequate funding and substantial challenges for a very long time.[33] Therefore, the primary institution established to help disadvantaged children to compete and change their circumstances is inadequately funded, insufficiently educating them, and does not insulate them from criminal involvement as it does for children who are already better situated.

This problem is further exacerbated for some disadvantaged children and their families. Think about this for a moment: if a teenager gets pregnant (imagine a sixteen-year-old) and elects to have and raise the child she is criticized for her choices, but as a society, we really condemn her parents. We presume that their lack of guidance or lax supervision contributed to this outcome, or that they did not model the right kind of behavior for their child, or did not inculcate the right values or stress the importance of getting an education enough. But lo and behold, we may be saying the very same thing about that very same sixteen-year-old if her child becomes a parent early. How prepared will she have been at sixteen to parent and to parent well? Of course some of these girls do all right, and the very fortunate ones have parents or extended families that help them. My point is not to either castigate or excuse these young women, but to note that if they themselves were not adequately parented and educated, then it is likely that many of them will be inadequately prepared to parent.

The point of using this example is not to take us into the realm of a wholly different social problem, teenage pregnancy, but I use it to draw attention to one of the ways that social and economic disadvantage is perpetuated. If their families or schools or communities, or their country, fail young girls and the result is becoming a parent before they are ready, we should recognized the complicity of all of the above if she cannot parent well. If parents, schools, communities, and countries do not take care of and rear their children well, those children will have a higher probability of being subject to a number of social problems including low educational achievement, labor market marginalization, and crime. And today in America we are collectively failing many children, especially disadvantaged children. Blaming parents who were themselves the victims of our collective failures one generation earlier for their children's failures does nothing to break the cycle. With joblessness and labor market marginality, we set the stage for social and economic disadvantage. In doing so, we also weaken the capacity of educational institutions, families, and children to teach and rear their children, making crime and delinquency more likely.[34]

Gender

In chapter 3, I briefly described an analysis that my colleague Kristin Bates and I conducted where we found that the basic labor stratification and crime explanation helped us to understand some female criminality, but not most. The conditionality of the associations that we observed were different from those we have seen for men in other analyses. Women who are marginal to the labor market and have weak social ties are more likely to engage in property crimes and illegal drug use. Remember that for men, the effect of employment marginality is conditioned by the employment experience of those around them. For women, work matters when they are without children, and to a lesser extent without romantic partners. We do not want to conclude that women's work experience is not associated with violence because so few women in the NLSY sample we used engaged in serious criminality, so we could not reasonably assess this relationship. What we have known for a long time is that the work women do has frequently had the characteristic of secondary sector employment: low pay, few benefits, scarce opportunity for advancement, and limited security. So it is not surprising that female responses to labor market stratification would be markedly different from that of males, who have enjoyed a much fuller array of job options.

Here, though, I would like to consider the particular circumstance of women in disadvantaged communities, which is a more narrow consideration, because our earlier analyses of women using the NLSY data included women in many different kinds of communities. In one respect this will be a broader consideration: using the work of other scholars, here I will consider not just the criminal involvement of women in disadvantaged communities, but how they negotiate their lives under such circumstances. Necessarily, this will be a very brief consideration. I recommend that readers look to the scholars I cite here (and others) to gain a full appreciation of how women and girls confront lives in places that are marked by social, economic, and political disadvantage.

Women have historically been marginalized from the labor market; therefore, the women of economically and socially challenged neighborhoods have been marginalized from the margins. Many of them have scratched out a living, if one can call it that, by doing what they refer to as "days work." My mother's Hill District contemporaries could be seen each morning boarding street cars and buses to travel to middle- and upper-class communities where they would work for sometimes as little as six or seven dollars a day. The better of these jobs included the benefits of a provided sandwich at lunchtime and car fare (the 25 cents it cost each way on the streetcar). In the evening they would return to The Hill, dead tired, to face the challenges of raising children in a tough neighborhood. Many of these women were admired by their children and by their neighbors, but while they wanted something better for their children, they could not model the American maximum that hard work paid off. No one worked harder than they did, but there was so little that could be called a payoff.

Scholars have made important contributions to our understanding of how women experience the labor market,[35] and to female criminality and victimization,[36] but until recently the literature was more limited regarding women's labor market experience and crime—especially if we keep our focus on disadvantaged women. To some extent this limit is likely a product of much lower criminal involvement by girls and women in illegal behavior and the small number of their offenses that would appear in self-reported crime studies. The lower criminal involvement of women in the frequently reported crime data, FBI's Uniform Crime Reports and the National Criminal Victimization Surveys, has made studies of this topic difficult. There are now excellent scholarly treatments of female criminal involvement more generally, but here I am especially concerned about the unique crime problems faced by women and girls in the disadvantaged communities that are consequences of the structure of contemporary labor markets.

In the same way that urban ethnographers have substantially increased our knowledge and understanding of inner-city life and behavior generally, a gap that had existed in our knowledge about women and crime is being filled by an increasing number of ethnographies that have explored disadvantaged women's experience in coping with the social and economic challenges in their lives, including work, crime, and victimization.

Some of this work was completed after federal welfare reform, so this work should be seen against the backdrop of changes in (as some might say) the destruction of the socioeconomic safety net. The consequences of welfare reform have been particularly hard on women.[37] Federal welfare reform, which was packaged in the Personal Responsibility and Work Opportunity Reconciliation Act of 1996, was passed by Congress and signed by President Bill Clinton. It was the ultimate triumph of politicians and researchers who blamed welfare for many social problems in the United States.[38] And for some in the media—and too many in the general public who too often blamed government spending on the poor for other problems, or what they saw as the demise of the American value system—it held out hope that the country was moving back toward a better day of individual responsibility and the "pull yourself up by your bootstraps" ideal. Of course that "better day" is a part of American mythology. Because of federal efforts to support writers and photographers, we have many images of what things were like for the poor during the Great Depression; while it was much worse than the standard, periodic recessions that had been a regular part of the US economy, those images express the reality of what life was like for the poor. There was no nobility in being unable to feed one's children, to clothe them, or to keep a roof over their heads. With welfare reform, pundits argued that nobility would be put back in place for the striving poor. The reality for most welfare recipients prior to reform was difficult. Most of those recipients were women with children (thus the old name Aid to Families with Dependent Children, or AFDC). And contrary to popular belief, few of these women received welfare for a long time. Most cycled on and off welfare, working at low-wage, secondary sector jobs that would disappear regularly.[39] Or the men in their lives worked such jobs, and the women would turn to AFDC when that source of support was unavailable. Sociologist Sharon Hays, who studied the effects of welfare reform, notes that even those closest to the old system, caseworkers and many welfare mothers themselves, believed some of the hype about problematic "welfare queens" and the hope and promise that would result from the new changes.[40] Writing about the poor mothers she studied, Hays says:

> They clearly understood the language of "personal responsibility." And many of them said that they thought it was about time that all those other welfare mothers they were hearing about, the ones who just "sit on their butts all day," were reminded of their responsibilities to their children and to hard-working, tax-paying Americans. When they found themselves subjected to this pressure directly, however, it often felt improperly targeted or unfairly administered.[41]

Hays points out that as a result of welfare reform and a booming economy in the years just after its implementation, the welfare rolls were more than cut in half. But the economy was no longer booming in the first years of the twenty-first century when she was doing her field work. Then many, many single women with children were no longer eligible to receive assistance, and those who were eligible were still trying to make it on less than half of the federally established poverty line.[42] These are the women who try to build lives for themselves and their children in the economically and socially disadvantaged neighborhoods produced by joblessness, unemployment, and labor market marginality. It does little good to pass federal laws mandating that these women work to take care of their families if there are no jobs for them to get.

Jason DeParle, a *New York Times* writer, has written a particularly accessible and compelling examination of welfare, its reform, and the lives of the people it was most supposed to benefit, the poor.[43] Focusing on three related women, their family history, and their children, he warns us not to oversimplify the the choices, the outcomes of reform, or the challenging lives of women who struggle to deal with social and economic disadvantage.

There are inner-city women who were thought to have turned to entrepreneurial crime in the face of limited legitimate options, crushing poverty, and violence around them. And in the 1990s one option that was available was the drug trade. Unfortunately many of the women trying to make it in the crack market were themselves victims of addiction. In her book *Sexed Work: Gender, Race and Resistance in a Brooklyn Drug Market*, Lisa Maher reported on how a racially diverse group of women confronted the realities of addiction and tried to make it in the context of very limited options.[44] Maher found that these women were not the passive victims of men working the drug trade, nor was the expanding market that occurred when crack cocaine hit the street scene a source of entrepreneurial opportunity for them. Both arguments have been made, but the lived realities of Maher's subjects were more complex than either of these options. Fundamentally, she found that the dominant forces affecting these women and their options were the same social structural forces dominating the lives of other disadvantaged and dispossessed peoples. She writes:

> The street functions as a distinct cultural and social milieu which evidences 'the same structures of gender relations as family and the state. It has a division of labour, a structure of power and a structure of cathexis' (Connell, 1987:134). For the women in this study, street life served as the principal locus of social and economic relations. The patterning of these relations is clearly linked to, shaped by, and cannot be separated from, broader cultural understandings of gender, race, and class.[45]

Comparing the lives of the women in her study with the struggles of earlier generations of disadvantaged women, Maher states:

> In addition to experiences of discrimination and occupational segregation faced by earlier cohorts of minority women, the women in this study were also confronted with a rapidly declining job market. Compared to their parents, these women had restricted employment opportunities and those with the most extensive work experience tended to be older women in their thirties. Many of the parents of the 36 minority women in this sample had been in regular employment and often at least one

parent had held a secure job. The women's fathers had been employed in a range of (mostly secondary sector) jobs.[46]

The declining job market of which she writes is the same phenomenon described by Wilson in *The Truly Disadvantaged* and *When Work Disappears*. Note that the "secure" jobs of the older generation were secondary sector positions, not the good primary sector jobs that took people out of disadvantaged neighborhoods. Maher concluded that the same intersection of racism, sexism, and class stratification was the source of the problems for these women involved in the drug trade and all the other "hustles" they engaged in to live and feed their habits, and were the same forces pressing down on nonhustling women of the ghetto.

What about the girl children of disadvantaged places? Sociologists Jody Miller and Nikki Jones have written two separate compelling ethnographies that are separated by a few years and nearly a thousand miles. Their works tell the powerful stories of life for inner-city girls. Miller's research was set in St. Louis, and Jones's in Philadelphia. Both scholars emphasize different aspects of the story, but they complement each other very well. Together they humanize their subjects and expose the lies of simple characterizations of these young women in the media and in political discourse.

In *Getting Played: African American Girls, Urban Inequality, and Gendered Violence*, Miller does not as much focus on female participation in crime as she does their victimization.[47] She does not tell a story of a group of passive victims. Instead, the girls she interviewed are actively engaged in trying to protect themselves from the multiple whammy of racial segregation and discrimination, high levels of social and economic disadvantage, and the worst of a gendered society. We know that African American girls experience a phenomenal amount of victimization that criminologist Janet Lauritsen attributes to the acute poverty present in the distressed communities that too many of them live in. Miller writes:

Research has consistently shown that women's risk of sexual victimization is at its highest in adolescence and young adulthood. This risk is heightened further for young women in distressed urban communities.

Just as scholars have documented the organizational characteristics, gender ideologies, and situational contexts associated with sexual violence in high-risk groups such as college fraternities, sports teams, and the military, I show some comparable facts of disadvantaged settings that encouraged sexual aggression against young women. As Elijah Anderson documents in *Code of the Streets*, behavioral expectations for young men in disadvantaged communities encourage cultural support for such violence, in part, through their emphasis on sexual conquest.[48]

These young women go to schools where too often neither their education nor their safety is sufficiently cared about. They live in communities where boys and men, beaten down by their own struggles in school, the labor market, and by life itself, adhere to an ideology that encourages them to strive for status in negative ways, such as crime and violence, and especially sexualized violence toward the young women who have to negotiate those same streets. A young man Miller quotes who was interviewed during her study explains this dynamic:

> Ricky said young women in the neighborhood were particularly at risk in the context of parties: "They have to be extra careful about leaving. And they have to watch what they do. [Watch their drinking] and getting high. I mean, you got some smooth talkers in our neighborhood, so." Asked why he thought the guys in his neighborhood did that to girls he explained:
>
> > I think it's just to get a image, a name. To make theyselves look big. . . . I can't really explain it. A lot of guys do it just so other guys can be like, "Aw, man, he'll do this" or "He'll do that." Like for example, "We did this and we did that, and it was [so-and-so's] gal." Most of 'em just do it for a name, many, just for a image. Try to look like something they not.
>
> Thus an important feature of girls' sexual abuse was the status rewards such behavior provided within male peer groups.[49]

Girls who come of age in disadvantaged neighborhoods suffer the consequences of disadvantage just as their brothers do, but it is considerably exacerbated by the gendered ideology carried by the men and boys who live around them. And as both Miller and Anderson point out and make a compelling case for, although it does not excuse these men by any stretch of the imagination they are who they are, and they behave how they behave, due in significant ways to the dispossessed nature of their lives resulting from inequality—including, importantly, that which results from joblessness and segmented labor markets. And this is overlaid with the racial and gendered stratification that affects the entire society.

In *Between Good and Ghetto*, Jones also points to the problems created for young women who are navigating thru communities that suffer from real, substantial, and long-term disadvantage, while also dealing with the realities of race and gender stratification in the society at large.[50] She uses concepts that parallel Anderson's decent and street families in *Code of the Streets*, contrasting "good girls" who try in their behavior to adhere to traditional conceptions of appropriate feminine behavior with girls who are "ghetto," who are like their male counterparts, willing to fight in order to get and maintain respect. But in a very important way, the word that I used, "contrasts," is not actually appropriate. While one can conceptually contrast these alternatives, Jones points out that the reality for these young women is that they are frequently somewhere in between the poles of these two behavioral alternatives. She writes:

> Of course, real people—and perhaps especially adolescents—do not fit neatly into only one or two conceptual categories. My conversations with girls about their experiences with violence, along with my observations of their actions and conversations with others, revealed that girls astutely worked the code *between* the equal and opposing pressures of good and ghetto.[51]

The problem for these girls that Jones points out and illustrates with their comments is that if their behavior is closer to the "good" pole they are more likely to be victimized in the hypermasculinized neighborhoods devastated by disadvantage, labor market marginality, joblessness, and hopelessness. If their behavior is closer to the "ghetto" pole:

> Their efforts to protect themselves put them at risk of losing access to formal institutional settings like schools or the church, where girls who

mirror normative gender expectations—girls who are perceived by others as good—can take some refuge. . . . Thus, inner-city girls find themselves caught in what amounts to a perpetual dilemma, forced by violent circumstances to choose between two options, neither of which offers the level of security that is generally taken for granted in areas outside of urban poverty.[52]

Residential Patterns

Two contemporary features of urban America are especially important in any discussion of the ways that employment and disadvantage influence crime: racial residential segregation, which is not just a feature consigned to US history, but remains a central feature of urban life; and gentrification. The latter is the phenomenon of of middle- and upper-middle-class homeowners, primarily whites, but not exclusively so, moving into poor and minority communities. Both of these social forces are important for changes in disadvantaged communities, for the people who live in them, and for crime that occurs there.

Today, many young people believe that racial residential segregation was a byproduct of Jim Crow, and that it disappeared after federal civil rights and fair housing laws were passed. Unfortunately that is not true. While in some cities segregation has softened, it still very much defines the social geography of most American cities.[53] To the extent that American racial residential segregation has diminished it has been in cities with relatively small African American populations. For most cities segregation continues, despite the passage of federal civil rights legislation and the passing of time. And that continuing segregation is an important part of the social structural arrangements perpetuating labor market inequalities, social and economic disadvantage, and crime.

In what is certain to become a landmark study, Ruth Peterson and Lauren Krivo explore the very different worlds where black, white, and Latino people live within American cities.[54] The latter are not as segregated as African Americans, but a great many of them continue to reside in distinctly Latino neighborhoods. Racial residential segregation is important because of all the other social problems that it exacerbates and concentrates onto marginalized populations, and the way this pattern translates into differential levels of crime. Peterson and Krivo write:

> Our key contention is that residential segregation is the linchpin that connects the overall racial order with dramatic racial and ethnic differentials in violent and property crime across communities. It does this be reinforcing the complicated web of social and institutional inequality that privilege white neighborhoods compared to African American, Latino, and other types of neighborhoods.[55]

A key feature of segregation is that it inhibits access to labor markets because so many potential job connections are made within established social networks. When a portion of the population has been systematically marginalized from the labor markets and that population is segregated, their networks are less likely to have contacts with those who are working and who thus are the first to become aware of job opportunities. And as many have demonstrated, a key force leading to social and economic disadvantage and all of its attendant social problems is marginalization from the labor market. Peterson and Krivo are clear about how this disadvantage causes crime in select neighborhoods:

> Neighborhoods that are highly disadvantaged have heightened crime rates for two broad reasons. First, processes that encourage criminal behavior are particularly prevalent in areas where disadvantage abounds . . . Within a context of limited opportunities, theft and other property crimes may occur in an effort to secure resources, and luxuries that are not otherwise attainable. Activities such as prostitution, drug trafficking, shoplifting, theft and sale of stolen property, and other opportunistic crimes may become regular sources of "income" and a means of acquiring wanted goods and services . . . Violence as "self-help" may also be used in these crimes, or in other social situations where conflict arises, as participants seek to protect themselves and their possessions rather than engage the police or other authorities.[56]

Segregation leads to differential access to the labor market, and to social and economic disadvantage and both of these forces increase levels of crime and delinquency. Here we begin to see why the differential levels of crime observed by Karen Parker and by David Weisburd and his colleagues occur, even if the overall national crime pattern is one of decreasing crime rates.

Gentrification is another important residential phenomenon that is changing the look of urban America and shifting the geographic patterns of both disadvantage and crime. The post-World War II period was marked by the increasing suburbanization of US metropolitan areas; the combination of GI Bill mortgages, the development of modern highway systems, and concern on the part of some city dwellers about school and residential integration led to considerable expansion of suburbs. Beginning in the 1960s and 70s, the movement of middle-class residents led to a number of cities becoming minority group majority cities: their tax bases declined, and their schools suffered from a loss of revenue right at a time when urban challenges were confronting school districts, and this process continues for some cities today.[57] Some even continue to lose population. Note our earlier description of population decreases in Pittsburgh, and the classic contemporary case is Detroit; these two cities are not alone in having this problem.

But now a new population shift has been taking place in many US cities: the movement of middle and upper-middle-class households back into central cities, or gentrification. With this process American cities are transitioning in such a way that if it continues, these places will look more like older European cities in some respects. There, more expensive urban core housing is frequently occupied by better-off residents, and poor and minority populations live more toward the outskirts and frequently in what Americans think of as the suburbs—thus the label of gentrification for this process. In many cities this process is accelerating because of more expensive oil and policies, such as the destruction of problematic housing projects that concentrated both the poor and social problems.

Just as suburbanization had major effects on social life, so too does gentrification. Anderson described these issues in *Street Wise: Race, Class, and Change in an Urban Community*.[58] There he described two adjoining neighborhoods: Northton, a desperately poor black ghetto, and The Village, a racially and socially diverse enclave that was well along in the gentrification process. Residents of both places were dismayed by both the presence and the behavior of those living in the other place. Perhaps most salient for our purpose is that The Village provided a close, proximate target for the dispossessed, disadvantaged youth of Northton. As a result, the "new" residents of the former spent considerable time and energy trying to "manage" the neighborhood by attempting to increase safety and diminish perceptions that the streets were unsafe because of their nearby neighbors. This is consistent with what other scholars who have examined the effects of gentrification have noted.[59] There is evidence that both larceny and robbery can increase with gentrification. Sociologists Andrew Papachristos and his colleagues found that crime rate changes resulting from gentrification have a racial component. It is linked to reduced homicide for white, black, and Latino neighborhoods, but is linked to increases in the number of street robberies in African American gentrifying neighborhoods.[60] Generally, gentrification should be seen as another social force that disrupts community informal social control, particularly if it happens rapidly.[61] And when it occurs in formerly disadvantaged neighborhoods or in close proximity to them, an already criminogenic circumstance is worsened. Additionally, if the circumstance usually happens consistent with what Anderson described in his two Philadelphia neighborhoods, the disadvantaged do not benefit from the influx of middle-class people. The networks of the latter, which could break down the social isolation of the former and lead to important opportunities such as knowledge of potential jobs, will rarely connect because although they live in physical proximity, the social distance between the gentrifiers and the disadvantaged remains as large as ever.

And then there is Washington, DC, which I earlier referred to as an apartheid city. I have to confess that some of the qualities that caused me to apply that label are still present in the nation's capital, but in some very important respects it has changed. As of the 2010 US census of the population, the District is no longer majority black. Gentrification has changed the demography and thus the social life of Washington. But because the metropolitan area still has some apartheid-like characteristics—residential segregation, income inequality, unequal education, and crime—these problems are increasingly moving into the suburbs along with the people who are being displaced by Washington's ongoing gentrification. Today many residents of the District of Columbia warn visitors to be wary of going into Prince Georges County in Maryland

(PG County, as it is popularly referred to) because of the crime and gangs.

Mass Imprisonment

And then there are prisons, which most citizens believe to be a consequence of crime—and of course they are, to some extent. But they may also be a cause of crime. That is what many criminologists are convinced has happened as a result of what is now being called mass imprisonment in the United States. A now well-documented product of the combination of the war on drugs and get-tough-on-crime policies by the states and the federal government has been the near quintupling of the prison population in the United States since 1980, which now has far and away the highest incarceration rate in the world.[62] This trend has moderated in the last few years, partially due to budget struggles in many states. Mass incarceration has had multiple effects that are important for any discussion of labor markets, disadvantage, and crime.

This pattern is all the more problematic because of the continuing patterns of racially disproportionate practices in the criminal justice system. It is not new news that everyone is not treated the same in either the juvenile or adult justice systems, but what too many do not understand is that the form has changed somewhat, although black and brown people still have different experiences in the criminal justice system than whites.[63] Like racial residential segregation, racial disproportionality in the criminal justice system did not go away with the passage of the 1960s-era civil rights legislation. Congress has now partially addressed the inequality with earlier war on drugs sentencing mandates that set the conviction penalty for crack cocaine (used disproportionately by minorities) at one hundred times that of powder cocaine (used disproportionately by whites), with no legal, medical, or pharmacological reason for the difference. Now the penalties are "only" eighteen times as high—still resulting in racially disproportionate sentencing, but an improvement. Police profiling does not happen in every jurisdiction and some argue that it does not occur to a substantial degree in general, but there is some evidence that argues that it is a problem, and people of color certainly perceive it to be a continuing problem.[64] What is clear is that the very large increase in the number of people in prison has had grave effects on African Americans and Latinos. For instance, Bruce Western has shown that one-third of young African American men who do not finish high school can expect to be locked up in a penitentiary at any one time, and a high percentage of African American men will at some time in their lifetime be under the control or supervision by the criminal justice system.[65]

First, we have to recognize that nearly all of those imprisoned men and women are released and most frequently return to the very communities they were sentenced from. Not surprisingly, a prison record makes it more difficult to find a job, and this is even more of a problem for African Americans who have been locked up.[66] Marginally employed people, whose work circumstance increases the chances that they will become involved in crime, are even more dramatically marginalized if their violations lead to conviction and incarceration. Mass incarceration has led to underestimates of the number of people who are unemployed and jobless, because those "in the joint" are not counted in these statistics.[67] Incarceration has negative consequences for the marital stability, family life, and the physical health of those who are behind bars. It substantially lessens their ability to fully participate in civic life, or to have access to government services that are designed to improve the lives of the poor.[68] What's more, criminal justice policy in the US has masked the level of unemployment, the degree to which there is white/black income inequality, and led to the erroneous perception that African Americans have begun to catch up to the white majority economically and socially, because so many poor black men are locked up and uncounted.[69]

In addition to the effects that mass imprisonment have had on those who are sent to jails and prisons, our corrections policies are having devastating effects on those communities that have the least resources to withstand additional assaults: disadvantaged neighborhoods. Criminologists Dina Rose, Todd Clear, and their colleagues found what they called coercive mobility, the churning of people from disadvantaged communities to prison and back, is devastating to those neighborhoods.[70] Criminal justice policies have made the labor market circumstance, disadvantage, and likely crime in already marginalized, disadvantaged communities worse.[71]

Labor Market Stratification, Disadvantage, and Crime

I am not suggesting that it is only through these four factors —child rearing and education, gender, residential patterns (including segregation and gentrification), and mass imprisonment—that labor market stratification, or the segmentation of labor, is linked to disadvantage and thus to crime, but they are important examples of how this process continues to cause problems for a substantial part of the population, those living in disadvantaged neighborhoods, and for crime and crime rates. Figure 7.3 provides a visual description of the argument. The arrow leading directly from "labor market stratification" depicts what most of the preceding chapters have been about. Segmented labor markets produce individual labor market marginality that increases criminality, and when sufficient numbers of workers are unemployed, jobless, or in secondary sector jobs, crime and the crime rate of a location will increase. Labor market segmentation also increases social and economic disadvantage because marginalized workers have limited legal incomes or lower incomes, and when sufficient numbers of people so situated are concentrated in isolated places, the kinds of underclass neighborhoods that Wilson wrote about in *The Truly Disadvantaged* emerge. Gender stratification contributes to labor market stratification because so many traditionally female jobs have been structured as secondary sector jobs. As a result, this labor market pattern both perpetuates gender stratification and, when men do not have primary sector jobs available to them, they compete for such secondary sector jobs, bringing them the poorer wages and benefits that so many women have already been subjected to.

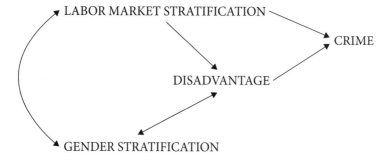

Figure 7.3. An Expanded Labor Stratification and Crime Thesis

Gender contributes to social and economic disadvantage when women are paid less, are consigned to jobs with less security and benefits, when they receive inadequate or no child support, and when they become the victims of stereotyped driven welfare reform policies. When the options of women and girls are truncated they suffer especially from the crime and violence that is an unfortunate but predictable part of living in disadvantaged places.

The other social forces affecting the life of the disadvantaged (child rearing practices and education, and residential patterns), are both consequences of and causes of social and economic disadvantage, and they are important determinants of crime. Educational inequality and child rearing practices help to create the next generation of people that Anderson called "street," who carry with them and act on the code of the street. Of course this is certainly not so for all or even necessarily most children and families of disadvantaged neighborhoods, and Anderson acknowledge this. But not educating children well, and attributing fault to families that we know are already troubled and disadvantaged by their circumstance, is what William Ryan discussed in his book *Blaming the Victim*, which he wrote in 1976. Pundits, politicians, and the general public continue to assign responsibility for nearly all of the ills of modern society on this hardly supported—if at all— segment of the population.[72] Compared to other modern industrialized nations, Americans are substantially more willing to accept the poverty of its own citizens.[73]

As scholars have shown, segregation and gentrification are powerful ongoing forces that shape metropolitan areas, influence access to both quality education and jobs, change the face of poverty, and affect crime and crime rates. Segregation increases and exacerbates social and economic disadvantage and the social problems that follow from it, including crime. Gentrification can improve the social, economic, and crime statistics of a neighborhood by displacing those who suffered from these problems, but it does not make the lot of those people better and very likely shifts the burdens of these problems to other portions of metropolitan areas.

Mass imprisonment moves those whose crimes were in part a product of the marginalized labor, poor schooling, and family and community disruption that are integral to coming of age and living in disadvantaged places into institutions—most of which do little for them, except to make them even less capable of competing in the more competitive labor market in which they were already handicapped. And since nearly all of them leave prison, most frequently returning to the same or similar neighborhoods that they lived in before they were incarcerated, they bring back labor market prospects that not only condemn many of them to labor market margins, but their communities to continuing disadvantage.

Back to Race, Labor Market Marginality, and Crime

It is my guess that more than a few readers by now have thought something to the effect of "he has moved too casually back and forth between racialized and nonracialized arguments linking employment and crime." That was not a mistake, and it has not been casual. This is not a story simply about how African Americans suffer from the effects of a segmented labor market. Many whites, Latinos, and Native Americans are also marginalized from quality work, and when they live with many people who are also jobless, unemployed, or working in secondary sector occupations they have a higher probability of engaging in crime and their residential places will have higher crime rates.[74] As I described earlier, this may well happen in rural places where there is concentrated white poverty, such as in portions of Appalachia. Also, while I do not know of research that has tested the labor stratification and crime thesis in Indian Country, I strongly suspect that such an analysis would show employment and crime patterns not terribly dissimilar to those observed in inner cities.

In some fundamental ways, however, this *is* about race because of the combined effects of labor market discrimination and marginality, concentrated poverty, residential segregation, unequal access to quality education, and the continuing legacy of Jim Crow and the disappointments of the Great Migration's move to the Promised Land. I began this chapter by saying that an expanded labor stratification and crime thesis needs to be able to account for the apparent anomalies; there are three. Actually there are two, because economists Phillip Cook and Gary Zarkin have discredited much of what we believed about low crime rates in the Great Depression.[75] The most recent apparent anomaly, that crime rates have continued to decline during the Great Recession, may not be an anomaly either. There are important empirical questions that will need to be addressed by researchers when we can look back on the period 2008 to 2013 about what effect the labor market had on crime rates, net of other important factors which influence the level of crime such as prison incapacitation and a changing age structure of the population. But perhaps more importantly, it is the point made by Parker, Klofas, and by Weisburd and his colleagues that the current decline is uneven across segments of the population and in particular, places within metropolitan areas. The third anomaly was that in the 1960s during a robust, growing economy, crime rates did increase, particularly in American cities. What that view masks is what was going on in those cities that received the Great Migration movers. And that is what brings this story back to race, and in particular to racial inequality. While the nation's economy was booming in the 1960s and in some important ways the black population was considerably better off than in previous decades, there was very high unemployment in the inner cities, particularly for young black males. Some estimates place those unemployment rates in some places in the 20 to 25 percent range, comparable to the national rate during the heart of the Great Depression.[76] Earlier I wrote about the disappointments experienced by young African Americans whose parents brought them from the Jim Crow South to the North, being told that life would be so much better in this cold but freer Promised Land. These young people did not have the experience of trying to make it in the rural South that kept a boot on the backs of both their necks and their aspirations. So while the parents may have appreciated new opportunities in the urban North, to their children who moved with them—and to my contemporaries like Robby Wideman and Cecil Rice (Wideman's rap partner and my Boy Scout mate), who were born in the North—there was no comparative improvement. There was just a nation that refused to allow them opportunities to thrive. In such circumstances, just as we have shown the stratification of labor and the consequential labor market marginalization of people in those inner-city ghetto communities, it helps to explain why crime rates increased there.

In the first of a series of talks that Martin Luther King Jr. gave for the Massey Lectures for the Canadian Broadcasting Company in 1967,

TOWARD A MORE GENERAL EXPLANATION >> 223

he addressed the criticisms aimed at African Americans and some of their communities after a series of urban riots. Critics (like those that I described earlier who simply want to blame crime on thugs) argued that the riots were symptomatic of African American's inability or unwillingness to behave correctly. King's response to those critics was to point them to socially structured social and economic inequality. As I said in chapters 1 and 4, continued inequality and disadvantage can produce individual criminality or revolution; political, social, and economic leaders would do well to heed the words of Reverend King and those of Victor Hugo, whom he quotes:

> For a perceptive and vivid expression of culpability I would submit two sentences written a century ago by Victor Hugo. "If a soul is left in darkness sins will be committed. The guilty one is not he who commits the sin, but he who causes the darkness." The policy makers of the white society have caused the darkness; they created discrimination, they created slums, they perpetuate unemployment and poverty. It is incontestable and deplorable that Negros have committed crimes. But they are derivative crimes; they are born of the greater crimes of the white society.[77]

Robby, Walter, Steven, the Hole in the Wall Gang, and Their Peers

This expanded labor stratification and crime thesis, by bringing social and economic disadvantage fully into the explanation, can help us to understand the people discussed in this book.[78] John Edgar Wideman introduced his brother Robby to you in his book *Brothers and Keepers*; there you learned of Robby's wants, dreams, and frustrations and his crime that led to a life sentence in a Pennsylvania prison. I introduced you to Walter, a young inner-city black man who had done time in another Pennsylvania prison and whom I met when he was placed on my parole caseload. Frankly, Walter did not want to work. I also introduced you Steven, a white parolee living in a rural area. He too had done time in a state penitentiary, but before that he worked in unstable jobs and moonlighted as a burglar. The Hole in the Wall Gang, the group of rural white kids whose futures held limited hope and less encouragement of dreams, engaged in delinquency simply because they did not have a good reason not to. They got no stake in conformity from school, or from an economic future that they could envision.

Their peers—who in some cases, like Robby and Walter, were also my peers—run the gamut of reaction to marginalization and disadvantage. Some of us made it out as a result of good fortune and good luck. Most continued on, some in angry desperation that led to crime, prison, drugs, or early death, but most have tried to continue to struggle against the odds that are stacked against them. What is amazing is that most are not like Walter, who did not want to work, or Steven who worked and dabbled in crime. Most are more like the members of the Hole in the Wall Gang. They want something out of life and they are willing to strive for it, but they need to be able to believe that their efforts will matter. Those who do believe will be less likely to engage in crime or participate in lifestyles that make crime more likely. Those who can no longer believe may not be as heroic as Victor Hugo's Jean Valjean, but they will be no less desperate.

8

A Tale of My Two Cities

It was the best of times, it was the worst of times, it was the age of wisdom, it was the age of foolishness, it was the epoch of belief, it was the epoch of incredulity, it was the season of Light, it was the season of Darkness, it was the spring of hope, it was the winter of despair, we had everything before us, we had nothing before us, we were all going direct to Heaven, we were all going direct the other way—in short, the period was so far like the present period, that some of its noisiest authorities insisted on its being received, for good or for evil, in the superlative degree of comparison only.

—From *A Tale of Two Cities*, by Charles Dickens, 1859

The two cities that I have called home for much of my life, Pittsburgh and Seattle, like the London and Paris of which Dickens wrote, are both alike in some ways and very different in other ways. A brief look at them will, I believe, point us in directions that the labor stratification and crime thesis will lead us for both research and public policy questions that should be asked. And as was the case in the mid-nineteenth century, some of our noisiest authorities—politicians—see in our current state either the best of times or the worst of times. To hear some speak we have turned the corner toward a brighter future with significant challenges ahead, but ones which we, as a society, have the capacity to address if we will only summon the will. While others, considering the same social and economic realities, are certain that rather than us all going to heaven, instead our society and nation is perched on the edge of falling, as Dickens called it, "the other way."

Before my consideration of my two cities, I want to briefly consider the world they exist in today. On July 7, 2005, terrorists attacked London, as they had Madrid a year earlier, and New York and Washington, DC before that. In the aftermath heads of state who were gathered in Scotland for the G8 conference made statements about standing united and fighting against the "uncivilized" actions of those who perpetrate such acts. But are these attacks really the acts of some uncivilized group of extremists? The answer from most social scientists would be a resounding "no." It is unpopular in the US to ask the question, "Why do they hate us?" It is in fact defined by many as unpatriotic, un-American, or perhaps even treasonous to ponder such a thing. But we really must, if we are to ever make real, lasting headway in antiterror efforts, take such questions seriously. In earlier chapters I speculated about what could happen if the disaffected, marginalized people living in American inner cities came under the influence of a charismatic leader, capable of mobilizing or harnessing or focusing their efforts. In fact we already have the answer to that question. If we are lucky, social movements begin. While some would say unluckily (and others would respond more positively), perhaps revolution would fulminate. Most would agree that the acts of terrorism that have occurred are among the worst possible outcome products of alienation. The attacks on those major cities, as well as those elsewhere in Europe and in Africa, Russia, Asia, and the Middle East, are byproducts of global economics, politics, and social forces rather than the purely domestic. But as I hope has been made obvious, the marginalized and disaffected of American inner cities are as well, in their particular social circumstance, in part because of those same global forces. The "they" in the question "why do they hate us" includes many who were born here or in other modern industrialized nations. They are the dispossessed. When we choose policies and practices that have little or no regard for segments of populations, why should it ever be a surprise that they resent those who make these choices or those who benefit from them? Relegating segments of society to the social and economic margins is bad for those people—and it can have very negative consequences for others as well.

Searching for the motivations of terrorists does not, as critics of the pursuit of such questions allege, seek to excuse the behavior. When criminologists explain the causes of crime we do not make excuses for criminals, as too often some of our students conclude. In both instances scholars are in search for the causes of human behavior that are harmful to others, as well as frequently to the person who engages in the behavior. The sources of these, like other human behaviors, no doubt lie in complex interactions of biology, psychology, and social forces. It is the social forces that are the focus of consideration here. For those that wish to simplify the behavior of either terrorists or of run-of-the-mill common criminals and argue something to the effect that "those people are just different," I think they are wrong by oversimplifying. Although I focus on one set of causal forces, it is with recognition that other social and economic forces, as well as the insights of biology and psychology, are important too.

To the extent that culturally supported norms and values are responsible for crime, or for that matter are one possible motivation for social movement involvement, revolution, or even possibly terrorism, I would like to suggest that we stop thinking about "cultures of poverty" and instead seriously consider "cultures of inequality."[1] By this I mean the answer to the question, How much inequality does a society have a taste for?

Within the cultural system of every group are conceptions of fairness and justice. And unless one subscribes to notions that we all contain inborn, innately centered notions of fairness and justice, the groups that we form will develop norms that define our collective beliefs (or a competing set of beliefs) about what is fair and just. Societies then may be thought to develop justice norms or fairness norms, among which will be culturally supported conceptions of how much inequality between the people of that society is acceptable. More likely, groups within societies develop such conceptions and the larger society becomes the scene of competitions between groups with different ideas about how much inequality will be allowed. Of course, these rather simple ideas are complicated further because these competing groups also differ in how they define people, or at least those who are deemed worthy of concern.

Some may worry about equality for all who live within the understood boundaries of societies, while others believe in equality for members of their or other select groups; that is, their norms can justify inequality between in-group and out-group people. Even still, norms frequently exist, and this is an important viewpoint in the US, that allow for great inequality as long as it is based on some set of acceptable criteria. For many Americans such inequality is acceptable so long as it is based on competition in an imagined meritocracy. Obviously I say "imagined," because many who hold such views do not like to accept that empirically observable obstacles to real open competition exist.

What I mean by "a taste for inequality" is the level of popular and political acceptance (and those two do not always coincide) of either unequal outcomes or unequal opportunities available to those living within a political unit. Popular tastes for inequality can be produced by general consensus, or when a competing group is successful at pushing their view among members of the society. One presumes that popular acceptance of inequality will have some substantial relationship to public policy, but that really is an empirical question. For example, it seems that the very restricted, low-value welfare benefits policies of the Jim Crow-era Southern states were a consequence of the willingness to define all blacks and most poor whites as deserving of their deep poverty. Elsewhere during that same period—especially in the Northeast and Upper Midwest, which were not the halcyon Promised Lands of the dreams of Great Migration travelers—there was more racial openness and better welfare benefits. What is the difference between those two locations? Of course there are many important differences: former slave-holding states versus free states, largely agriculture versus industrial economies, large black populations versus places where it was comparatively small. I would suggest that there is yet another important difference, and that is a relatively higher historic taste for inequality in the South.

To be fair, we should not engage in the simplistic South-bashing that characterized much Northern think during the height of the modern civil rights movement. Northerners watched horrifying black and white TV news footage of white cops putting German Shepherd dogs on black marchers. They saw the grisly visage of Emmett Till in his casket and wondered who could do that to a child. They watched George Wallace and Lester Maddox and Bull Connor put seemingly human faces on the hatred of the South. They watched all of this and smugly thought, "We are different from them; we are better people." Well, we have pretty good evidence that Northerners are in fact not better people than Southerners. And today many of the latter like to point out their belief in their own moral superiority because they were less hypocritical.

Southerners saw how white suburbanites greeted Martin Luther King and his followers when they tried to integrate segregated Chicago neighborhoods. They were appalled to see a black Boston businessman on the ground in front of City Hall being impaled with the staff on which an American flag flew. And just as we watched black children being spat upon by ugly faces outside of Southern schools in the fifties and early sixties, the news brought Southerners updated images of ugly, spitting Northerners in the late 1960s and early 70s who opposed bussing. So neither region has cornered the market on morally superior people. What differentiated the two regions was what came to be the dominant conceptions of proper civility in public life. The two factors that likely differentiated Southerners and Northerners were differences in the extent that racial prejudice, discrimination, and segregation were a part of "acceptable" individual and collective identity, and the degree to which politicians and officials could embrace such ideas officially and overtly. What I am arguing is that there was a higher taste for inequality in the South. And where there is a high taste for inequality, a culture of inequality can develop. In such a place substantial inequalities based on race, social class, religion, immigration status, or any number of social markers are widely and publicly perceived to be not only okay, but a part of collective identity.

Just as some scholars have argued that a culture of poverty leads to behavioral patterns among have-nots that make them less likely to work and more likely to commit crimes, a culture of inequality sets the stage where the social structural conditions are allowed to persist that fosters the criminogenic atmosphere that I described in earlier chapters. Where racial or class inequality is allowed to flourish, then labor market segmentation and labor inequality is more easily tolerated by officials and the general public. After all, "those people are different from us," or "if they were as talented as we are, then they might have what we have." In this last statement we can substitute "worked as hard as," or "deferred gratification," or "were as moral as" in place of "as talented." In ostensibly democratic states when more people buy into justifications for inequality (that is, they have a high taste for inequality), these cultural definitions that are expressions of norms and values of cultures of inequality, the ideological pillars that allow criminogenic inequality to fester are in place.

Along with two colleagues, David Pettinicchio and Blaine Robbins, I used data from the World Value Survey to see if we could find cross national variations in attitudes about minorities and immigrants that would be consistent with the culture of inequality, and if that variation could be connected to national welfare and imprisonment policies.[2] Two of our findings are pertinent here. First, nations do vary substantially in attitudes about how much the poor, minorities, and immigrants should be assisted, with less developed countries being more hostile to the welfare state. And second, among industrialized nations, the United States is an outlier to the degree to which citizens do not favor supporting those on the margins of society. While US attitudes are not comparable to less developed countries in Africa and Asia, it is also not as progressive as European and other industrialized nations. The US scores considerably higher on taste for inequality than the other western industrialized nations that we most frequently compare ourselves to. And, as is widely known, the US is also far and away the greatest imprisoner of its citizens. This is the context in which we should consider Pittsburgh and Seattle.

Two Cities

People know Pittsburgh, the steel city, home of the Steelers, Pirates, and Penguins. Its history as a city, as it was taught to my classmates and me as we grew up there, began in the eighteenth century when a young Virginia surveyor, George Washington, was a part of a group that thought the confluence where the Allegheny and Monongahela rivers came together to form the Ohio would make a good site for what would become the British Fort Pitt. Today, the hillside from which he allegedly first saw the three rivers is named Mt. Washington. Later, Fort Pitt was captured by the French and renamed Fort Duquesne, only to be renamed Fort Pitt again when the British took it back. Industrialists and financiers Andrew Carnegie, Henry Clay Frick, Thomas Mellon, and others led the creation of a powerful manufacturing center built on the ready access to natural resources, the rivers to transport both inputs and outputs, and the strong backs of recently arrived European immigrants and later, Great Migration movers form the American South.

Pittsburgh today is a city that, as I described earlier, suffered substantially with the decline of American industrial production at the end of the twentieth century. It lost population and its steel mills were shuttered, demolished, or left as silent reminders of a bygone era. But before that it was a vibrant city that was not only attractive to migrants, but had rich educational and cultural resources. It has excellent universities and colleges, first-rate museums and libraries. While other cities suburbanized at the expense of the downtown business and retail core, Pittsburgh's remained alive. When other cities were convinced to modernize by giving up their trolleys and streetcars, the people of Pittsburgh kept theirs in service. Now streetcars are trumpeted as a "new" green form of public transportation. When I was growing up on The Hill, streetcars were seen on nearly all of the major streets throughout the community. Many routes have given way to buses now, but still electric powered streetcars service some sections of the city.

The Hill District was filled with poor people, but it had vitality to it also. The Hurricane Lounge on Center Avenue and the Crawford Grill on Wylie Avenue featured the stars of the day; Louis Armstrong, Lena Horne, Miles Davis, Sara Vaughn, Dizzy Gillespie, and others played there. The Negro League baseball team sponsored by The Grill, the Crawfords, featured future Hall of Famers Josh Gibson, Satchel Paige, and Cool Papa Bell. The community was home to the *Pittsburgh Courier*, one of the nation's most influential black newspapers. If one wants to know The Hill and its people of the twentieth century, you should read or see playwright August Wilson's ten-play series, one for each decade.

Today Pittsburgh is a city whose largest employer is the University of Pittsburgh Medical Centers or UPMC, as everyone in town knows it. In general Pittsburgh is among the best big cities in which to search for work as the nation's recovery from the Great Recession continues. What has changed is who works in Pittsburgh. There is still some heavy industry in and around the metropolitan area, but it is not like it was. Today medical, technical, and corporate headquarters jobs are the leading opportunities for employment rather than steel and iron. Housing prices are comparatively affordable, and the overall city crime rate does not stand out compared to cities of comparable size. The Hill is experiencing some gentrification on its margins, and a very noticeable characteristic when traveling through it now is the number of vacant, overgrown lots where once stood occupied apartment buildings.[3]

But Pittsburgh's recovery, as indicated by the shift in the nature of employment that is available to residents, is uneven. Gone are the days where a strong back and willingness to work were enough, and the changes are reflected in the city's neighborhoods. Map 8.1 is taken from the Pittsburgh Police Department's 2010 Annual Report. It displays the distribution of the city's 2010 homicide across census tracts. Sixty-eight percent of murders occurred within the highlighted area. The area of high homicide extends from Homewood, on the eastern edge of the city, through East Liberty to The Hill District, and then across the Allegheny River onto the North Side. In addition to being the unfortunate communities that experience most of the city's criminal lost of life, they are also the places where black and poor people live. These are neighborhoods where residents are less likely to be employed by Pittsburgh's medical, technical, and corporate labor markets, at least in the quality jobs that are offered in these concerns. They are places of high levels of joblessness, unemployment, and secondary sector employment—that is, marginal employment. These are Pittsburgh's most disadvantaged neighborhoods. So it is little wonder that the crime decline experienced by the nation, the State of Pennsylvania, and Pittsburgh as a whole is not benefiting the residents of these struggling communities to the same extent.

Earlier I mentioned that Marvin Prentice, an executive at the Hill House Association, a nonprofit located in The Hill District, commented that the crime decline was news to him because that did not fit with what he sees on the streets. He confessed to not relying on data, but said that it appeared and felt to many of the people who live and work on The Hill that there was still a substantial amount of violence there. And according to the Pittsburgh Police Department, Prentice is accurate when he perceives a great deal more violence in the neighborhoods that his agency serves than in much of the rest of the city.

An important contributor to Pittsburgh's violence and homicides are gangs. As a high-school kid there I did not have a sense that Pittsburgh

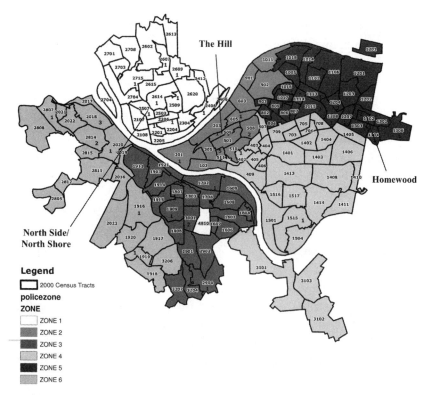

Map 8.1. Pittsburgh 2010 Homicides by Census Tracts. City of Pittsburgh, Department of Public Safety, Bureau of Police, Pittsburgh PA, Annual Report 2010 p. 51, http://apps. pittsburghpa.gov/pghbop/10_Police_Annual_Report.pdf.

was a gang city, and later this was supported when I became privy to criminal justice reports while I worked as a State parole agent. Of course there were periodic appearance of gangs, but gangs were not an enduring feature of the city. This changed in the early 1990s. Criminologists George Tita and Jacquelyn Cohen attributed the emergence of gang activity to involvement in the drug trade.[4] Other criminologists have also linked drug marketing and gangs in other American cities.[5] By late in the decade Pittsburgh's gangs were heavily involved in the crack cocaine trade and guns, and a substantial portion of the city's homicides were gang related. Criminologist James Howell attributes the decline and virtual disappearance of gangs at the turn of the millennium to a crackdown effort by the Pittsburgh Police Department, which brought a Federal Racketeer Influenced and Corrupt Organization Act (RICO) indictment against one of the more prominent gangs and that in turn had a chilling effect on gang activity.[6] But by the middle of the first decade of the twenty-first century, gangs had come back with a vengeance to Pittsburgh's communities.[7] This is probably what Prentice sees and is referring to when he says that it does not look like a crime decline to him.

The Hill House Association is actively trying to address inner-city violence problems by focusing on children in their K-12 years with a comprehensive program aimed at teaching them about violence and how to avoid it. A very important element of their program involves parents in an effort to help them deal with and counter the influences of the streets. But much of their focus is on the school and how to improve performance and engagement. What is critical is that their efforts are investments for the long haul. What is unfortunate is that one very hard-working program (and I expect that there are others engaged in such efforts too) cannot change the structure of the labor market that parents, other adults, and ultimately their children will have to confront. That segmented labor market, creating joblessness, low-quality marginal work, and unemployment, will continue to cause social and economic disadvantage and ultimately limit the effectiveness of both criminal justice and nonprofit efforts.

Seattle is a much younger city. Its urban history is traced to the landing of the Denny party on what is now Alki Beach at the base of what is now West Seattle. That original group of settlers found the rain that gives Seattle its reputation (and terribly dismayed those pioneers), and they found that they did not "discover" or even "settle" this place. Elliot Bay, the portion of Puget Sound on which their settlement and modern downtown Seattle sits, was already a place where native people lived, fished, and enjoyed a good life. Among those that early whites encountered was Chief Sealth, who, it is said, did not want the city named for him, but it was. (The city's name was what white settlers did to Chief Sealth's name.) Seattle's first major industry was timber. The Skid Road (now Yesler Way) was the road on which freshly cut logs were skidded down the hill to Henry Yesler's sawmill, which sat on Puget Sound in an area that is now part of the downtown district. In addition to performing this function for early industry, the Skid Road was where hard-edged men and women lived, drank, and struggled. ("Skid Row," the name of the sections of cities throughout the country where down-and-out people are found, is a variation on Seattle's original road.) Not long after early white settlers arrived they established the Territorial University, which later became the University of Washington, in the hope that it would help them toward statehood. The county where Seattle sits was also named King County, named for a slave-holding vice president to curry favor for the same statehood aspirations (in the late twentieth century, the name was officially changed to Martin Luther King County). But in spite of these efforts the settlement did not really begin moving toward being an actual city until the Alaska gold rush of the late 1890s. As the jumping-off place for prospectors, Seattle thrived by selling outfits to prospectors and "entertaining" them when they returned. It is said that few returned from the north with any gold, and most who did, did not leave Seattle with their riches.

Modern Seattle is said to have been launched, at least in the consciousness of the rest of the country, with the 1962 World's Fair. In actuality the city had already become a thriving port city and it had considerable industry anchored by Boeing Aircraft and ship building, both of which were boosted by World War II demands. Another wartime feature of Seattle was the internment of its Japanese population, but this was not the first time that Asians suffered at the hands of their neighbors. Earlier Seattle was the scene of anti-Chinese, anti-Japanese, and anti-Filipino protest movements and riots, which on at least one occasion ended up with local whites forcing Chinese residents down to the docks in an effort to forcibly compel them to return to China.

Like Pittsburgh and other cities, Seattle had cable cars and streetcars, and like many other American cities Seattle was convinced to give up electric-powered mass transportation in favor of gasoline-powered busses. Now the city is constructing, at considerable expense, a few streetcar lines to compliment a fledging attempt to build a light rail system. The Seattle of today is the home of some of the US's most iconic businesses. In addition to Boeing, Nordstrom's, Microsoft, Starbucks, Costco, and Amazon, all founded in and around the city, still call it home. The local economy, which only a few decades ago was primarily Boeing and shipping, is now diversified by the inclusion of many software and biotech companies. Like everyplace else, Seattle suffered with the Great Recession, but not nearly as bad as many other cities.

As is obvious from my comments above, Seattle's ethnic history is not pristine. It remains today one of the whitest cities in America. It has not been too many decades since many neighborhoods had residential covenants restricting who could live there, keeping the small black population restrained to the Central District (CD). But as was the case in Pittsburgh, that neighborhood, which was earlier and remains one of the most disadvantaged parts of the city, had its own charms, including a jazz scene centered along Jackson Street. There the early careers of Ray Charles, Quincy Jones (who grew up in Seattle), and Ernestine Anderson were nurtured, and even though Seattle was off on the edge of the continent Dave Brubeck, Charlie Parker, Stan Getz, and others found their way there. Before Seattle begat Jimi Hendrix, whose grandparents arrived as vaudeville performers in 1911, and grunge music, Seattle had a flourishing jazz scene. Today, the people of Seattle are justly proud that major political offices (mayor, county executive, and city and county council positions) have been held by people of color for multiple terms, in spite of the small minority populations.

Seattle today is 75 percent white and has a substantial Asian population, a relatively small African American population of about 8.5 percent, a rapidly growing Latino population, and sizable, relatively recent immigrant populations from Asia, the Pacific Islands, and Africa (primarily from East Africa). The population of color in Seattle has expanded where it lives beyond the Central District. Blacks, Asians, Latinos, Native Americans (a very small portion of the population), immigrants, and whites populate neighborhoods moving south from the CD, down the Rainer Valley and into the near-in suburbs. The Asian population has moved out of China Town/International District (the ID) to many parts of the city, but Beacon Hill, immediately south of the ID, is predominately Asian. One zip code in south Seattle (98118) was, after the 2010 US census, declared the most diverse in the US because it is home to Native Americans, European Americans, African Americans, Latinos, Asian Americans, Filipinos, Samoans, Ethiopians, Eritreans, Somalis, Vietnamese, Cambodians, Burmese, and others. Neighborhoods bordering Lake Washington, some of which lies within that most diverse zip code, are predominately white, but with some integration. And as is the case in other American cities, although all of the south Seattle neighborhoods where people of color live are not disadvantaged, most of disadvantaged neighborhoods of the city are located there.[8]

As I described in earlier chapters, Seattle's crime rated is, compared to many other cities, including Pittsburgh, comparatively low. But important patterns are the same. Map 8.2 is taken from the website of the Seattle Police Department. It shows the number of homicides in 2010 in Seattle census tracts. Map 8.3 does the same for the total number of reported violent crimes. Since the city's number of homicide is low, Map 8.3 may facilitate easier comparison to Map 8.1, which displays the distribution of Pittsburgh's murders. Seattle's homicides are not quite as concentrated as Pittsburgh's, but the maps document that where they occur, for the most part, they conform to the same pattern. Most homicides in Seattle occur in the CD and down through the Rainer Valley and up across Beacon Hill. The other high area is in Southwest Seattle, another area populated by poor people of color, poor whites, and the highest concentration of the Latino population in the city. Murder occurs in Seattle, as it does in Pittsburgh, where people of color live in disadvantaged neighborhoods. People there are more frequently marginal to the city's comparatively robust labor market. In these high-violence neighborhoods, one finds higher unemployment, joblessness, and secondary sector employment.

Recent high-profile murders, robberies, and assaults have led neighborhood activists to try to begin a campaign to make south Seattle neighborhoods safer. They have marched, held meetings with the police department, and are actively discussing what they might do about crime and violence. Popular thinking is that some of the violence is a consequence of renewed gang activity, but it is unlikely that the majority of serious crime that takes place there is gang-related.

Like Paris and London that Dickens wrote of, my two cities, Pittsburgh and Seattle, are very different but in some ways they are very similar. Pittsburgh is much older, but they both have an industrial history born of their locations on the water. They have both been and continue to be educational and cultural centers, and to have vibrant, comparatively healthy downtown business districts. Seattle is more of a twenty-first century industry town, but Pittsburgh is no slacker in this regard. Pittsburgh has a considerably larger African American population than

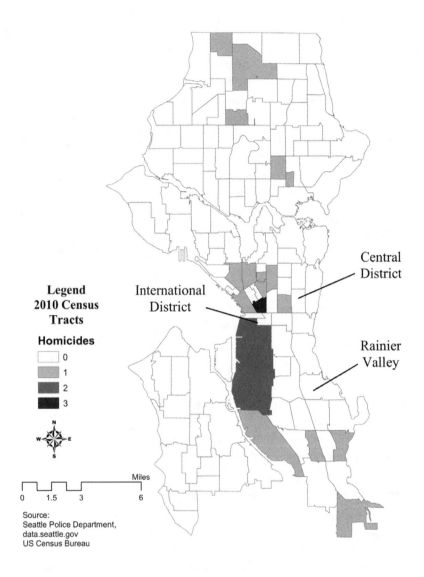

Map 8.2. Seattle Homicides 2010 by Census Tracts. Seattle Police Department website, http://web5.seattle.gov/mnm/statistics.aspx?tabId=3.

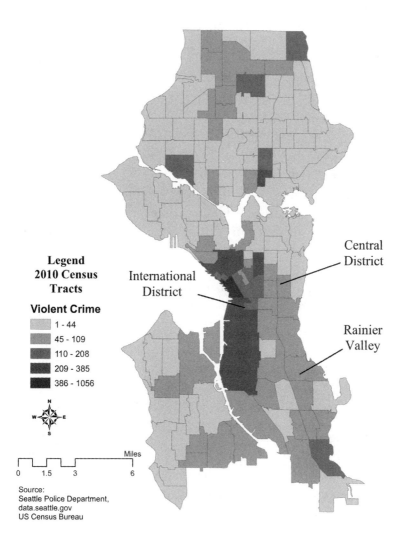

Central
District

International
District

Rainier
Valley

Map 8.3. Seattle Violent Crimes 2010 by Census Tracts. Seattle Police Department website,
http://web5.seattle.gov/mnm/statistics.aspx?tabId=3.

Seattle, but the latter, though having a larger proportion of its population that is white, has substantial racial and ethnic heterogeneity too. Pittsburgh had significant immigration streams from Eastern and Southern Europe; Seattle had significant immigration from Scandinavian countries and, of late, from Asia and Africa. Seattle has few sections that might really be called underclass neighborhoods, especially if one takes seriously important characteristics of such places as isolation from the mainstream and concentrated poverty. Pittsburgh certainly has neighborhoods that would qualify for this dubious designation. Much of Seattle's black population arrived after World War II, while Pittsburgh was a destination for Great Migration movers from World War I into the early 1960s. Homicide and crime more generally in both cities follows social and economic disadvantage. Seattle's relatively low level of disadvantage can be traced to the educational, racial, and ethnic composition of the city's residents, and importantly to the nature of the local labor market. Pittsburgh's higher level of disadvantage can also be traced to its social and demographic composition and the characteristics of its local labor market. Though they are different in many respects they are the same in that the distribution of serious violent crime follows disadvantage in both cities, and, predictably, the form that disadvantage takes in both places reflects their respective economic histories, the patterns of each city's demography, and the characteristics of the local labor markets.

I said that Seattle's crime rate is, year after year, substantially lower than Pittsburgh's. This fact is a critical difference between the two cities, and important factors that lead to this difference are worthy of note. The marginalized and disadvantaged in my two cities come from and are maintained in their circumstance by different histories and different labor market structures. The people of Seattle are fond of believing that "we are different up here"—and in some respects we are. The racial and ethnic composition, as I have described, allows the white majority to not be especially threatened, allowing for the widespread belief that the city is more culturally tolerant. Perhaps it is, but if so that is no doubt in part because of the demographic composition.

The defining feature of Pittsburgh's recent history was the collapse of big steel. Seattle suffered no such lost. In fact, while that was occurring in the East, the Pacific Northwest weathered downturns in the timber, fishing, and paper industries, but Boeing was moving forward and Microsoft was being founded. In the city that no longer has those iconic steel mills, it's hard to imagine what will break up the intergenerational disadvantage that plagues some neighborhoods. In Seattle, there are those young people unable to compete for the jobs being created. So in both places, current labor market conditions are conducive to marginalizing portions of the population, particularly young people, but Seattle has fewer of them and fewer people in and around substantial disadvantage. It may be useful think in terms of acute labor market disruptions and chronic disruptions. As is the case with our bodies, acute injuries can become chronic problems, and the same is true of social problems produced by labor market dislocations. Of course these negative effects interact with other social forces influencing social life; important among these forces are migration and racial conflict. Pittsburgh's circumstance for working-class people is more chronic, while Seattle's is more acute for most of those hoping to find work. I suspect that the crime difference between Pittsburgh and Seattle is largely due to these factors and their racial and ethnic composition (and all of the social and economic disadvantages faced by minorities) differences.

Today in both cities, new generations of Robby Widemans, or others like my parole clients Walter and Steven and my juvenile probationers Gary and Hole in the Wall Gang, are being created because too much of the adult population is marginal to the labor market and too many children are marginalized from school. In the most disadvantaged neighborhoods it is possible that even children who are doing okay in school are engaging in delinquent activity, not even being protected by their school performance. And not enough adults hold the kind of employment that inspires children or structures young adult lifestyles so that they are less criminogenic. In both cities it is too easy for some to conclude that there is work for people who want work, without recognizing how dramatically different jobs can be not only in terms of salary, but in the bonding value of employment. Still, there are adults there who were struggling even before the Great Recession who would have been happy to have even a secondary sector job. It is too easy for some in the media, some politicians, and for some of us around the water cooler or on a bar stool to write off the crime in our midst because of gangs and thugs. We do not like to recognize that crime around us and the thugs and gangsters that may be contributing to it are products of social arrangements less of their doing and more of what we all collectively allow. Crime—and many other problems, like drug abuse and poverty—will continue as it is until we take seriously the social structural causes, institutional arrangements, and resulting cultural patterns that perpetuate criminogenic conditions. Here I have focused on the criminogenic effects of labor market arrangements, but that does not, obviously, draw a complete picture of the sources of contemporary crime, though it is certainly part of it. Pittsburgh and Seattle and other cities are well advised to move beyond simplistic blaming of the perpetrators for their actions. Yes, they are a part of the answer and bear responsibility for what they do, but so too do we.

What Is to Be Done?

These are big problems, which are not likely to be amenable to short run or easy fixes. The crime and disadvantage consequences of the structure of labor markets cannot be conveniently dealt with by telling those who are marginalized from those structures to "get over it and get a job" to pick themselves up by their bootstraps, or work harder, or stop doing drugs. Structural causes will require structural change to address the problems of inequality and the crime and disadvantage which results. That said, we need not, as some with very strong feeling in the 1960s argued, wait for the revolution. Efforts large and small may result in some positive changes.

I believe that the first thing that must be done is to stop wasting precious resources on strategies that we have good evidence is likely to have little or no effect (e.g., the Drug Abuse Resistance Education or DARE program). Those resources should be deployed on projects and programs that have been effectively evaluated and found to produce the desired outcomes. I do not mean to say that we should not be inventive or creative and try some new things. Good ideas to reduce crime and to decrease social and economic disadvantage should be tried. But as they are, they should be evaluated—keeping what works, making adaptations in programs and fixing aspects that are found to be wanting, and stopping when research demonstrates that our good idea in theory did not produce the desired effects in the field. Evaluation research is neither free nor necessarily cheap, but throwing money away for no observable good is ultimately the most expensive waste of time and resources.

With those caveats in mind, I would like to offer suggestions that might address the problems that I have written about here. First, holistic efforts, like those undertaken in Dane County, Wisconsin and the antiviolence efforts in Boston, which not only directly deals with kids and young adults but includes active efforts to confront family problems and to get adults into meaningful employment, are the most likely to have success. Such approaches have the virtue of not trying to treat the individual as if they exist in a social vacuum. There is a growing appreciation among academics, some in the policy world, and others who live the street life that jobs and adequate preparation for the primary sector jobs being created is central for the long-term hope of crime reduction. Homeboy Industries is a Southern California nonprofit aimed at helping gang members get out of "the life." One of their mottoes is, "Nothing stops a bullet like a job."[9]

There are things that businesses, governments, and community institutions, notably the schools, can do to mitigate the effects of the current labor market structure. Much is made of the importance of private sector job creation, but we delude ourselves if we fail to recognize that all jobs are not created equal. Yes, nearly always any job is better than no job, but the growing literature is making it increasingly clear that too many secondary sector jobs are criminogenic. It is likely pointless to wait for most businesses to decide to endow all or even most of their jobs with primary sector characteristics (decent salary, good benefits, promotion opportunities, etc.) for the sake of the collective good. But, more businesses might take a long, serious look at their human resources policies and ask two important questions. First, is their compensation package for employees possibly contributing harm to long-term business and profits (e.g., the Walmart contradiction)? Second, might it make more sense for the bottom line to adjust employment practices? Costco Corporation is a good example of a concern that has opted to treat most of their employees as primary sector workers. They have reasoned that doing so keeps a more stable and quality workforce, which is good for their bottom line. There is no doubt that other companies have made similar decisions. If more do so, perhaps it will be good for their long-term profits—it is certainly good for their workers, their workers' families, the communities those workers live in, and for local and state governments, because primary sector workers pay more taxes and are less likely to use as many government-supported social welfare resources.

To really make the difference that that workers, employers, and communities need, we need to think in terms of what sociologist Arne Kalleberg calls "a new social contract":

> We are in dire need of a new social contract to address the consequences of the growth of polarized and precarious employment systems. This social contract requires the coordinated efforts of government, business, and labor. The example of flexicurity[10] suggests that labor market institutions matter; some countries are better able than others to address the challenges and consequences posed by the global division of labor and the tendencies toward polarized and precarious work. Tackling the sources and consequences of the polarization in job quality will enhance both the competitiveness of the American economy and the quality of work experience by Americans themselves.[11]

State and local governments should make critical assessments of tax breaks they have given or may give going forward to entities that promise new jobs in exchange for those expensive incentives. What kinds of jobs will they bring? I am not suggesting that tax breaks only be given to those that produce just primary sector jobs. That is the choice that policy makers must make in the context of their local labor market. If the local labor market is so stressed that an infusion of secondary sector jobs will help people and communities, then that may be the wise choice to make. But they should not make the mistake of using their taxing capacity up by treating prospective primary sector and secondary sector employers as if they are the same.

Local governments might also look to their public transportation systems. In some places a spatial mismatch happens: empty jobs exist and jobless workers are theoretically available, but the latter have a very difficult or perhaps impossible time getting from where they live to where they might work. When this takes place, smart governments can help the public and the employers with effective use of public transit resources. Local officials should make sure that potential workers can efficiently get from where they live to where they work. And it does little good to tell people that they should live closer to their jobs. People of disadvantaged communities do not necessarily have the luxury of moving, and even if they can, they may not be able to afford to pay the rent or the mortgages close to where they might find a job. Even an increasing number of colleges and universities have recognized that members of their faculties cannot afford to live near campus because of the cost of housing.

I wish that I had a ready suggestion of how to use schools to improve the lot of inner-city children, especially those living in the most disadvantaged places. But we don't, because we do not have a good understanding of why those performing better in school are also engaging in more delinquency in the poorest neighborhoods. I suspect, though, that the solution lies in the wisdom offered by Jonathan Kozol, who counseled that if money is not the answer, then why won't those whose children are attending very well-funded schools send substantially more money to the schools teaching disadvantaged children?[12] Yes, class size reduction efforts have not made the promised difference, but should we expect modest reductions in class size to make a major difference in the face of the abundance of challenges faced by those teaching in inner-city schools? Would substantial reductions in class size and other investments aimed at addressing the challenges to learning in many inner cities make the difference? If we do not educate these children better than we have, we can expect them to continue the cycle of dropping out of school and struggling in the job market, which will perpetuate problems like social and economic disadvantage and crime and delinquency. If they are not educated so that they can meaningfully compete in the labor market of the twenty-first century, they will be the next Robby Widemans, Stevens, and Walters.

What about jobs for kids? I do not believe that simply giving jobs to the Garys and the members of the Hole in the Wall Gang is the solution to delinquency. If we want to make a difference, I believe that we should develop efforts to do two things. First, get their parents good jobs. That alone will do more for their children and their communities than any single thing that we can do. Second, if we are going to give work to high-school kids, that work should be tied to school performance. Not simplistically by saying they have to maintain a particular grade point, but make having and holding the job contingent on their improvement or maintaining a clear standard of performance in school.

Undertaking efforts such as these will not be cheap. But is our current policy an efficient use of either money or human resources? Large segments of the population are not productively used in the economy. A phenomenally large portion of the American population is locked in prisons—more than 1.6 million in 2010, at a cost that is conservatively estimated to be $35,000 per man per year (women and children are more expensive because of the lack of economies of scale), and when we lock people in Supermax facilities the costs are estimated to exceed $100,000 per man per year.[13] Since most who are imprisoned eventually return to their community, they, their communities, and the public bear the additional financial and human cost of them being even less employable than they were when they went in, and in most instances less capable of functioning as productive, law-abiding members of society. It is not clear that other western industrialized nations will follow the US into the policy trap of believing that they can incarcerate away their problems, but the tough talk heard from some of their politicians should give their citizenry pause.

Of course, there is an alternative. I have on several occasions in earlier chapters warned that the status quo runs the risk of a substantial, perhaps growing portion of the population angrily rejecting that status quo. Then there might occur the radical restructuring of the society that some believe is the ultimate solution to labor stratification. Is that what America is waiting for?

After serving a bit more than seven years of his sentence, Robby Wideman received an associate's degree from a community college that had been running an education program in Western Penitentiary (the program was discontinued just after Robby's completion because of Department of Corrections budget cutbacks). Robby was selected to give the commencement address for the inmate graduation.

The theme of our program today is "The world shapes and is to be shaped." I find this to be very appropriate. Because the world we were raised in has helped to shape many of the attitudes of us graduates here today. Most of us grew up in the ghettos of Pittsburgh and the surrounding area. There the emphasis was, get the most you can get with the least amount of work. My education helped me to realize, though, that nothing worth having comes without hard work and concrete effort. But being shaped by the world through this "quick get-over" concept and seeing that this concept was folly, it is now time to take our lives and our world into our own hands and shape it for the better. To show our fellow citizens and our children that education is the means by which we can make a world where men and women can truly be free to dream our own destinies and work hard and learn well and see those dreams become reality.

—Robert Douglas Wideman, from *Brothers and Keepers*[14]

Data

Table A.1

Table for Figure 4.1 Regression of Delinquency Index on Respondent, Parent, and Neighborhood Variables – Mothers and Children of the NLSY, 1998 Wave, Full Sample N=1497: Standardized &Unstandardized Coefficients & St Errors

	Model I	Model 2
Background Variables		
Female	-.163***	-.165***
	-.225	-.228
	(.035)	(.035)
Age	-.035	-.036
	-.018	-.018
	(.014)	(.014)
Black	.007	.031
	.009	.043
	(.043)	(.054)
Hispanic	.003	.045
	.005	.074
	(.047)	(.059)
Father or Stepfather Present	-.030	-.026
	-.044	-.038
	(.039)	(.039)
Parental SES Variables		
Family Poverty	.080**	.079*
	.166	.165
	(.054)	(.054)

Table A.1 (continued)

	Model 1	Model 2
Parental SES Variables		
Mother's Education	-.051	-.052
	-.044	-.045
	(.023)	(.023)
School Variables		
Attachment to School	-.182***	-.184***
	-.225	-.228
	(.032)	(.032)
Grades	-.067**	-.065**
	-.023	-.023
	(.009)	(.009)
Parental Involvement in School	.022	.020
	.035	.032
	(.042)	(.042)
Youth Work Variables		
Employed	.013	.011
	.017	.015
	(.038)	(.038)
Mother's Employment Variables		
Mother Employed	.002	.005
	.003	.007
	(.039)	(.039)
Neighborhood Variables		
% Black		-.058
		-.134
		(.097)
% Hispanic		-.083*
		-.262
		(.114)
Disadvantage		.036
		.023
		(.029)
% Marginal Work Force		.005
		.002
		(.015)

% of Population over 25 with no High School Degree		.018
		.131
		(.203)
Constant	—	—
	.803	.822
	(.226)	(.228)
R Square	.080	.084

^ = p < .1
* = p < .05
** = p < .01
*** = p < .001

This table is taken from Crutchfield, Robert D., Tim Wadsworth, Heather Groninger, and Kevin Drakulich. 2006. "Labor Force Participation, Labor Markets, and Crime." Washington, DC. National Institute of Justice. www.ncjrs.gov/pdffiles1/nij/grants/214515.pdf. This work was supported by the National Institute of Justice, grant number 2000-IJ-CX-0026.

Table A.2

Table for Figure 4.2 Regression of Delinquency Index on Respondent, Parent, and Neighborhood Variables – Mothers and Children of the NLSY, 1998 Wave, In SMSA Sample N=1167: Standardized &Unstandardized Coefficients & St Errors

	Model 1	Model 2
Background Variables		
Female	-.150***	-.154***
	-.203	-.209
	(.039)	(.039)
Age	-.025	-.024
	-.013	-.012
	(.016)	(.015)
Black	.002 .003	.049
	(.049)	.068
		(.059)
Hispanic	-.008	.042
	-.013	.065
	(.051)	(.064)
Father or Stepfather Present	-.065 *	-.058^
	-.092	-.083
	(.043)	(.044)

Table A.2 (continued)

	Model I	Model 2
Parental SES Variables		
Family Poverty	.065*	.063*
	.127	.123
	(.059)	(.059)
Mother's Education	-.051^	-.055^
	-.043	-.042
	(.025)	(.026)
School Variables		
Attachment to School	-.157***	-.159***
	-.194	-.197
	(.037)	(.037)
Grades	-.048	-.045
	-.016	-.015
	(.010)	(.010)
Parental Involvement in School	.007	.004
	.011	.006
	(.047)	(.047)
Youth Work Variables		
Employed	.031	.019
	.043	.069
	(.042)	(.043)
Mother's Employment Variables		
Mother Employed	.008	.012
	.012	.018
	(.044)	(.044)
Neighborhood Variables		
% Black		-.105*
		-.224
		(.103)
% Hispanic		-.108**
		-.324
		(.125)
Disadvantage		.045
		.028
		(.031)

% Marginal Work Force		.027
		.012
		(.017)
% of Population over 25 with no High School Degree		-.013
		-.092
		(.231)
Constant	—	—
	.786	.819
	(.255)	(.256)
R Square	.068	.076

^ = p < .1

* = p < .05

** = p < .01

*** = p < .001

This table is taken from Crutchfield, Robert D., Tim Wadsworth, Heather Groninger, and Kevin Drakulich. 2006. "Labor Force Participation, Labor Markets, and Crime." Washington, DC. National Institute of Justice. www.ncjrs.gov/pdffiles1/nij/grants/214515.pdf. This work was supported by the National Institute of Justice, grant number 2000-IJ-CX-0026.

Table A.3

Table For Figures 4.3 and 4.4 Employment, School, and Juvenile Violent and Property Crime Involvement

	Violent Crime	Property Crime
Basic Model Variables		
Age	-.092c	-.024
Sex	.276c	.181c
Race	.016	-.055c
Family Income	.018	.046b
Parents' Marital Status	-.011	.117c
Central City Resident	-.041b	-.045c
Macro Variables		
Population Size	.012	.018
Percent Black	.010	-.096c
Percent in Poverty	-.077b	-.015
Median Family Income	-.075b	.039
Percent Single Mothers	.056a	.091c
Unemployment Rate	.026a	.003
Unemp/Cent. City	.004	-.045c
Interaction		

Table A.3 (continued)

	Violent Crime	Property Crime
Education and Work Variables		
Been Suspend From School	.165c	.161c
Out of School and Work	.053c	.038b
Part-Time Employment	.005	.054c
Hours Worked	.027	-.005
Amt of Education Exp.	-.047b	-.006
GPA	-.113c	-.116c
Parents' Characteristics		
Parents' Job Quality	.005	.024
Parents' Education	.018	.093c
Father Full-Time	-.013	.104b
R Square	.179	.129

a = p < .05; b = p < .01; c = p < .001

Crutchfield, Robert D., Margo Rankin, and Susan R. Pitchford. 1993. This table was also published in Jargowsky, P. A., S. A. Desmond, and R. D. Crutchfield. 2005. "Is Suburban Sprawl a Juvenile Justice Issue?" In *Our Children, Their Children: Confronting Race and Ethnic Differences in American Criminal Justice*, edited by Darnell Hawkins and Kimberly Kemph. Chicago: University of Chicago Press.

Table A.4
Table for Figure 5.1 Regression of Crime Index on Individual and Tract Level Variables – NLSY97, Wave 3, Full Sample N=2934: Standardized &Unstandardized Coefficients & St Errors

	Model 1	Model 2
Background Variables		
Female	-.142***	-.142***
	-.033	-.033
	(.004)	(.004)
Age	-.043*	-.045*
	-.009	-.010
	(.004)	(.004)
Black	-.037ˆ	-.002
	-.010	-.000
	(.005)	(.007)
Hispanic	-.026	-.011
	-.007	-.003
	(.006)	(.007)

Married	-.003	-.003
	-.002	-.002
	(.011)	(.011)
Parental SES Variables		
Father's Highest Grade	.030	.028
	.001	.001
	(.001)	(.001)
Parental Income	-.009	-.008
	.000	.000
	(.000)	(.000)
School Variables		
In High School	-.028	-.030
	-.008	-.008
	(.006)	(.006)
Ever Suspended	.185***	.184***
	.044	.044
	(.005)	(.005)
Work Variables		
Weeks Worked in Last Year	.010	.010
	.000	.000
	(.000)	(.000)
Unemployed	.069*	.069*
	.036	.036
	(.014)	(.014)
Secondary Sector	.052*	.053*
	.012	.013
	(.005)	(.005)
Occupational Status	.001	.001
	.000	.000
	(.003)	(.003)

Here and in subsequent tables the first entries are Betas, the second b, and the third are standard errors

^ = p < .1
* = p < .05
** = p < .01
*** = p < .001

This table is taken from Crutchfield, Robert D., Tim Wadsworth, Heather Groninger, and Kevin Drakulich. 2006. "Labor Force Participation, Labor Markets, and Crime." Washington, DC. National Institute of Justice. www.ncjrs.gov/pdffiles1/nij/grants/214515.pdf. This work was supported by the National Institute of Justice, grant number 2000-IJ-CX-0026.

Table A.5

Table for Figure 6.1. Regression of Delinquency Index on Respondent, Parent, and Neighborhood Variables – Mothers and Children of the NLSY, 1998 Wave, Rural Sample N=330: Standardized &Unstandardized Coefficients & St Errors

	Model 1	Model 2
Background Variables		
Female	-.166**	-.172**
	-.241	-.249
	(.078)	(.079)
Age	-.056	-.059
	-.029	-.031
	(.030)	(.030)
Black	.016	-.104
	.025	-.163
	(.104)	(.142)
Hispanic	.016	.054
	.035	.120
	(.120)	(.155)
Father or Stepfather Present	.085	.082
	.133	.127
	(.096)	(.096)
Parental SES Variables		
Family Poverty	.159**	.158*
	4265	.425
	(.144)	(.145)
Mother's Education	-.069	-.064
	-.067	-.062
	(.053)	(.058)
School Variables		
Attachment to School	-.276***	-.284**
	-.342	-.351
	(.067)	(.068)
Grades	-.118*	-.114*
	-.047	-.046
	(.022)	(.022)
Parental Involvement in School	.065	.065
	.111	.109
	(.092)	(.093)

Youth Work Variables		
Employed	-.047	-.041
	-.068	-.059
	(.084)	(.085)
Mother's Employment Variables		
Mother Employed	.003	.005
	.004	.008
	(.084)	(.084)
Neighborhood Variables		
% Black		.149
		.506
		(.326)
% Hispanic		-.047
		-.198
		(.325)
Disadvantage		.005
		.004
		(.092)
% Marginal Work Force		-.024
		-.014
		(.043)
% of Population over 25 with no High School Degree		.02834
		.203
		(.445)
Constant	—	—
	.753	.738
	(.495)	(.507)
R Square	.166	.177

$^\wedge = p < .1$
$^* = p < .05$
$^{**} = p < .01$
$^{***} = p < .001$

This table is taken from Crutchfield, Robert D., Tim Wadsworth, Heather Groninger, and Kevin Drakulich. 2006. Labor Force Participation, Labor Markets, and Crime. Washington DC. National Institute of Justice. https://www.ncjrs.gov/pdffiles1/nij/grants/214515. pdf. This work was supported by the National Institute of Justice, grant number 2000-IJ-CX-0026.

NOTES

NOTES TO CHAPTER 1

1. From Wideman, John Edgar (1984), *Brothers and Keepers*, New York, Holt, Rinehart and Winston.
2. Officially called Western State Correctional Institution by the State of Pennsylvania, it is known as Western Penn by the people of Pittsburgh.
3. Lehman, Nicholas (1991), *The Promised Land: The Great Black Migration and How it Changed America*, New York, Knopf.
4. Wilson, William Julius (1987), *The Truly Disadvantaged: The Inner City, The Underclass, and Public Policy*, Chicago: University of Chicago Press.
5. Cook, Philip and Gary A. Zarkin (1985), "Crime and the Business Cycle," *Journal of Legal Studies*, January.
6. From an interview of a North Carolina grandmother, Spindale, N.C, September 28, 1938, http://lcweb2.loc.gov/cgi-bin/query/D?wpa:6:./temp/~ammem_K74w::.
7. From a New England textile worker, http://lcweb2.loc.gov/cgi-bin/query/D?wpa:18:./temp/~ammem_K74w::.
8. For discussion of the crime-prone years see Hirschi, Travis and Michael Gottfredson (1983), "Age and the Explanation of Crime," *American Journal of Sociology* 89(3):553–84.
9. Cohen, Lawrence, and Marcus Felson (1979), "Social Changes and Crime Rate Trends: A Routine Activity Approach," *American Sociological Review* 44(4):588–608.
10. Wilson, in his book *The Truly Disadvantaged*.
11. After critics complained that the word "underclass" was a pejorative term that victimized the poor, Wilson began referring to the "ghetto poor" (1990, "Studying Inner City Dislocations: The Challenge of Public Agenda Research," *American Sociological Review* 56(1):1–14). The plight and the social processes affecting the underclass and the ghetto poor are the same.
12. Tonry, Michael (2011), *Punishing Race: A Continuing American Dilemma*, New York, Oxford University Press.
13. Western, Bruce (2006), *Punishment and Inequality in America*, New York, Russell Sage Foundation; Clear, Todd R. (2007), *Imprisoning Communities:*

How Mass Incarceration Makes Disadvantaged Neighborhoods Worse, New York, Oxford University Press; Pettit, Becky (2012), *Invisible Men: Mass Incarceration and the Myth of Black Progress*, New York, Russell Sage Foundation.

14. The first caseload, composed of boys under the age of eighteen, was when I worked as a juvenile probation officer. The second caseload was adult parolees.

15. Massey, Douglas S. and Nancy A Denton (1993), *American Apartheid: Segregation and the Making of the Underclass*, Cambridge, MA, Harvard University Press.

16. Massey and Denton, *American Apartheid*.

17. Quillian, Lincoln (2002), "Why is Black–White Residential Segregation So Persistent? Evidence on Three Theories from Migration Data," *Social Science Research* 31(2):197–229. Also see Logan, John R. and Mark Schneider (1984), "Racial Segregation and Racial Change in American Suburbs, 1970–1980," *American Journal of Sociology* 89(4):874–88 for a discussion of the complexities of metropolitan racial residential segregation in the US.

18. Leymon, Ann Shirley (2011), "Unions and Social Inclusiveness: A Comparison of Changes in Union Member Attitudes," *Labor Studies Journal* 36(3):388–407; Schutt, Rusell K. (1987), "Craft Unions and Minorities: Determinants of Change in Admission Practices," *Social Problems* 34(4):388–402; *Time Magazine* (1966), "Labor Law: Against Union Discrimination," Friday, December 2, www.time.com/time/magazine/article/0,9171,836595,00.html; Ray, Marshall (1964), "Unions and the Negro Community," *Industrial and Labor Relations Review* 17(2):179–202.

19. Readers should see Massey and Denton, *American Apartheid,* for compelling evidence of the concentrating force of racial residential segregation.

20. Peterson, Ruth D. and Lauren J. Krivo (2010), *Divergent Social Worlds: Neighborhood Crime and the Racial–Spatial Divide*, New York, Russell Sage Foundation.

21. Cohrs, J. Christopher and Monika Stelzl (2010), "How Ideological Attitudes Predict Host Society Members' Attitudes towards Immigrants: Exploring Cross-National Differences," *Journal of Social Issues* 66(4):673–94.

22. European nations certainly have sizable groups of illegal immigrants, but some of those nations also have a legitimate guest workers program.

23. Pettit, Becky and Jennifer L. Hook (2009), *Gendered Tradeoffs: Family, Social Policy, and Economic Inequality in Twenty-One Countries*, New York, Russell Sage Foundation.

24. US Bureau of the Census (2012), *Households and Families: 2010*, www.census.gov/prod/cen2010/briefs/c2010br-14.pdf.

25. Ventura, Stephanie J. (2009), Changing Patterns of Nonmarital Childbearing in the United States. NCHS Data Brief, no 18. Hyattsville, MD: National Center for Health Statistics.

26. Sampson, Robert J., and William Julius Wilson (1995), "Toward a Theory of Race, Crime, and Urban Inequality," in *Crime and Inequality*, edited by John Hagan and Ruth D. Peterson, 37–56, Stanford, CA, Stanford University Press.

27. There is a long tradition of social disorganization theorizing in sociology and criminology that in recent years has found new life under the leadership of Sampson and colleagues and Burskik and his colleagues. Later this work will be discussed more completely in a discussion of how labor market stratification affects neighborhoods.

28. Massey and Denton, *American Apartheid.*

29. Sullivan, Mercer L. (1989), *Getting Paid: Youth Crime and Work in the Inner City*, Ithaca, NY, Cornell University Press; Anderson, Elijah (1999), *Code of the Street: Decency, Violence, and the Moral Life of the Inner City*, New York, Norton; Pattillo-McCoy, Mary (1999), *Black Picket Fences: Privilege and Peril Among The Black Middle Class*, Chicago, University of Chicago Press.

30. This research will be discussed in subsequent chapters.

31. Readers should see Cantor, David, and Kenneth C. Land (1985), "Employment and Crime Rates in the Post-World War II United States: A Theoretical and Empirical Analysis," *American Sociological Review* 50(3):317–32; Parker, Robert Nash, and Allan V. Horwitz (1986), "Unemployment, Crime, and Imprisonment: A Panel Approach," *Criminology* 24(4):751–73; Box, Steven (1987), *Recession, Crime and Punishment*, Totowa, NJ, Barnes and Noble Books; Chiricos, Theodore G. (1987), "Rates of Crime and Unemployment: An Analysis of Aggregate Research Evidence," *Social Problems* 34(2):187–211; Gillespie, Robert W. (1975), *Economic Factors in Crime and Delinquency: A Critical Review of the Empirical Evidence*, Washington, DC, National Institute of Law Enforcement and Criminal Justice, Department of Justice; Hale, Chris, and Dima Sabbagh (1991), "Testing the Relationship between Unemployment and Crime: A Methodological Comment and Empirical Analysis Using Time Series Data from England and Wales," *Journal of Research in Crime and Delinquency* 28(4):400–17; and Britt, Chester L. (1994), "Crime and Unemployment Among Youths in the United States, 1958–1990: A Time Series Analysis," *American Journal of Economics and Sociology* 53(1):99–109.

32. Thornberry, Terence P. and R. L. Christenson (1984), "Unemployment and Criminal Involvement: An Investigation of Reciprocal Causal Structures," *American Sociological Review* 49(3):398–411; Hagan, John (1993), "The Social Embeddedness of Crime and Unemployment," *Criminology* 31(4):465–91.

33. Pager, Devah (2007), *Marked: Race, Crime, and Finding Work in an Era of Mass Incarceration*, Chicago, University of Chicago Press.

34. Cloward, Richard A. and Lloyd E. Ohlin (1960), *Delinquency and Opportunity: A Theory of Delinquent Gangs*, New York, The Free Press.

35. Reuter, Peter H. Robert J. MacCoun, Patrick Murphy, Allan Abrahamese, and B. Simon (1990), *Money from Crime: A Study of the Economics of Drug Dealing in Washington, DC*, Los Angeles, Rand Corporation; Staley, Sam (1992), *Drug Policy and the Decline of American Cities.* Piscataway NJ, Transaction Publishers.

36. McCall, Nathan (1994), *Makes Me Wanna Holler: A Young Black Man in America*, New York, Vintage, 120–23.

37. Clarridge, Christine (2007), "Dreams of Getting Off the Street," *Seattle Times*, September 4, http://seattletimes.com/html/localnews/2003867286_clean-dreams04m.html.

38. Reuter et al., *Money from Crime*.

39. Levitt, Steven and Sudhir A. Venkatesh (2000), "An Economic Analysis of a Drug-Selling Gang's Finances," *Quarterly Journal of Economics* 115(3):755–89.

40. Haller, Mark (1971), "Organized Crime in Urban Society: Chicago in the Twentieth Century," *Journal of Social History* 5(2):210–34; Griffin, Sean Patrick (2000), *African-American Organized Crime in Philadelphia, 1968–1984: On Exploitation and Urban Politics*, PhD dissertation, Pennsylvania State University, available from UMI, Ann Arbor, MI, Order No. DA9966814.

41. Kornhauser, Ruth R. (1978), *Social Sources of Delinquency: An Appraisal of Analytic Models*, Chicago, University of Chicago Press; Katz, Jack (1988), *Seductions of Crime*, New York, Basic Books.

NOTES TO CHAPTER 2

1. This name of this parolee, like that of other parole and probation clients that I refer to, is a pseudonym.

2. See Banfield, Edward C. (1968), *The Unheavenly City*, Boston, Little Brown and Company; and Murray, Charles (1984), *Losing Ground: American Social Policy 1950–1980*, New York, Basic Books.

3. Anderson, Elijah (1999), *Code of the Street: Decency, Violence, and the Moral Life of the Inner City*, New York, Norton.

4. Wilson, *The Truly Disadvantaged*; Wilson, William Julius (1997), *When Work Disappears: The World of the Urban Poor*, New York, Knopf; Massey, Douglas S. and Nancy A Denton (1993), *American Apartheid: Segregation and the Making of the Underclass*, Cambridge, MA, Harvard University Press; Peterson and Krivo, *Divergent Social Worlds*.

5. Sullivan, Mercer L. (1989), *Getting Paid: Youth Crime and Work in the Inner City*, Ithaca, NY, Cornell University Press.

6. Pattillo-McCoy, *Black Picket Fences*; Parker, Karen F. (2008), *Unequal Crime Decline: Theorizing Race, Urban Inequality and Criminal Violence*, New York, NYU Press.

7. Merton, Robert K. (1949), *Social Theory and Social Structure: Toward the Codification of Theory and Research*, New York, The Free Press.

8. Chiricos, Theodore G. (1987), "Rates of Crime and Unemployment: An Analysis of Aggregate Research Evidence," *Social Problems* 34(2):187–211; Yang, Bijou and David Lester (1994), "Crime and Unemployment," *Journal of Socio-Economics* 23(1–2):215–22.

9. Raphael, Steven, and Rudolf Winter-Ember (2001), "Identifying the Effect of Unemployment on Crime," *Journal of Law and Economics* 44(1):259—283; Dongil, Kim (2006), "The Effects Of Economic Conditions On Crimes," *Development and Society* 35(2):241–50.

10. Britt, Chester L. (1994), "Crime and Unemployment Among Youths in the United States, 1958–1990: A Time Series Analysis," *American Journal of Economics and Sociology* 53(1):99–109; Cantor, David, and Kenneth C. Land (1985), "Employment and Crime Rates in the Post-World War II United States: A Theoretical and Empirical Analysis," *American Sociological Review* 50(3):317–32.

11. Parker, Robert Nash, and Allan V. Horwitz (1986), "Unemployment, Crime, and Imprisonment: A Panel Approach," *Criminology* 24(4):751–73.

12. Worrall, John L. (2008), "Racial Composition, Unemployment, and Crime: Dealing with Inconsistencies in Panel Designs," *Social Science Research* 37(3):787–800.

13. Cook, Philip J. and Gary A. Zarkin (1985), "Crime and the Business Cycle," *Journal of Legal Studies*, 14(4):115–28.

14. Rosenfeld, Richard and Robert Fornango (2007), "The Impact of Economic Conditions on Robbery and Property Crime: The Role of Consumer Sentiment," *Criminology* 45(4):735–69.

15. Critics of dual labor market theory such as Rosenberg, S. (1975), *The Dual Labor Market: Its Existence and Consequences*, unpublished PhD dissertation, University of California at Berkeley have correctly argued that this dichotomy is an oversimplified, but in published research criminologists have found even this broad categorization of occupations to have utility in explaining crime rates.

16. In the early 1990s when I presented early research on this topic to a group of county officials I titled the talk "McJobs." One official issued the challenge that I was using an ethnic slur, but my defence was that the title was intended to cast aspersions on the characteristics of the fast-food jobs, not on an ethnic or national group. Then in early 2004, the McDonalds Corporation lost a lawsuit against the publishers of a popular dictionary for including "McJobs" as an entry. I, along with the publisher, felt vindicated when the courts found against the plaintiff.

17. See Anderson, Elijah (1990), *Street Wise: Race, Class and Change in an Urban Community*, Chicago, University of Chicago Press.

18. The Bureau of the Census does not classify jobs as primary and secondary sector, but instead divides occupations into categories upon which researchers subsequently impose the dual labor market categorization. CPS is a monthly survey conducted by the US Census Bureau for the Bureau of Labor Statistics. It gathers information on employment, unemployment, and a wealth of other good and useful aspects of the work force and the labor market. Information can be found at www.census.gov/cps/.

19. Crutchfield, Robert D. (1989), "Labor Stratification and Violent Crime," *Social Forces* 68(2):489–512.

20. The most widely used unemployment measure in the US is collected monthly by the US Census Bureau and the Bureau of Labor Statistics, the Current Population Survey (CPS). CPS includes a wealth of data that measures current employment. Information can be found at www.census.gov/cps/.

21. Liebow, Elliott (1967), *Talley's Corner: A Study of Negro Streeconner Men*, Boston, Little Brown.

22. One can find out more about the Millionaire Club Charity at www.millionair-club.org/.

23. Wilson, August (2011), *Jitney*. New York, Samuel French, Inc.

24. Venkatesh, Sudhir A. (2006), *Off the Books: The Underground Economy of the Urban Poor*, Cambridge, MA, Harvard University Press.

25. Fagan, Jeffrey, and Richard B. Freeman (1999), "Crime and Work," *Crime and Justice* 25:225–90.

26. Pittsburgh is a good location for this example because of its history as an industrial center where unskilled blue-collar workers could build a good, middle-class life. Obviously I could have elected to use a host of other Rust Belt cities during that period, or a contemporary city whose local labor market has weathered the shift to the twenty-first century global economy better than most in the old Rust Belt.

27. "Day turn," as mill workers called it, was the shift that began at 7:00 a.m. and ended at 3:00 p.m. In actuality, most newly hired workers on the labor crew would be unlikely to have this shift; most end up on the night shift (11:00 p.m. to 7:00 a.m.) or the swing shift, sometimes simply referred to as the "3:00 to 11:00" shift by steelworkers.

28. Cohen, Lawrence, and Marcus Felson (1979), "Social Changes and Crime Rate Trends: A Routine Activity Approach," *American Sociological Review* 44(4):588–608. Cohen and Felson argue that crime and victimization are more likely to occur with the convergence of motivated-to-commit-crime actors, the presence of potential victims, and an absence of guardians.

29. Crutchfield, Robert D. and Susan R Pitchford (1997), "Work and Crime: The Effects of Labor Stratification," *Social Forces* 76(1):93–118.

30. The now infamous case of the central park jogger, the young woman who was brutally raped, beaten, and left for dead in New York's Central Park, was believed to have been a victim of a pack of young men out "wilding"—attacking, mugging, and assaulting people at random. Five teenage boys confessed and served time, but as we now know (and has been confirmed with DNA test), the jogger was assaulted by another man and not a pack of "wilding" minority kids.

31. Crutchfield, Robert D. (1989), "Labor Stratification and Violent Crime," *Social Force* 68(2):489–512.

32. Wilson, *When Work Disappears*.

33. None of the many people that I spoke with during a six-week visit had themselves been a victim of a violent crime, but nevertheless, most felt that they were in constant danger.

34. Totalitarian governments have historically been able to keep street crime in check because they and their police forces do not need to worry about such niceties as civil liberties and human rights.

35. We should take care to remember that prosperous or middle-class has histori-cally meant something very different within the black population (see E. Frank-lin Frazier (1957), *Black Bourgeoisie*, New York, The Free Press.). While the white middle class was characterized by people in professional occupations or office jobs, black middle-class men most frequently worked in blue-collar occupa-tions or if really fortunate may have secured a post with the railroad or with the postal service.

36. Gray, John (1998), *False Dawn*, New York, The New Press, 111, cited in Kal-leberg, Arne (2011), *Good Jobs, Bad Jobs: The Rise of Polarized and Precarious Employment Systems in the United States, 1970s to 2000s*, New York, Russell Sage Foundation.

37. Kalleberg, *Good Jobs, Bad Jobs*, 14.

38. Planning is now underway to open a supermarket; the area is gentrifying.

39. Pittsburgh's North Side, another traditionally black area, is also noted. A sub-stantial portion of the North Side has now been "urban-renewed."

40. Shaw, Clifford R. and Henry D. McKay (1969), *Juvenile Delinquency and Urban Areas*, rev. ed., Chicago, University of Chicago Press.

41. Sampson, Robert J. and William Julius Wilson (1995), "Toward a Theory of Race, Crime, and Urban Inequality," in *Crime and Inequality*, 38.

42. Crutchfield, Robert D. (1989), "Labor Stratification and Violent Crime," *Social Forces* 68(2):489–512.

43. While many researchers use census tracts as neighborhoods, they recognize that they are not perfect proxies. Tracts are official designations by the US Bureau of the Census that are designed to approximate neighborhoods in size and shape; that is, they attempt to draw the boundaries by using natural and manmade obstructions such as waterways, highways, and major streets, but they certainly do not correspond perfectly to residents' perception of the boundaries of their communities. In some cities the correspondence is closer than in others. In Seattle, tracts are reasonably well-aligned with neighborhoods.

44. The census occupation categories were divided using the logic of dual labor market theory. The secondary occupational categories were service work-ers, machine handlers, equipment cleaners, helpers, and laborers. Categories placed in the primary occupations group are managers and professionals, technical, sales and administrative support, precision production, crafts, repair-persons, machine operators, assemblers and inspectors, transporta-tion, and material-moving occupations (Crutchfield, "Labor Stratification and Violent Crime").

45. Other control variables included in the analysis were the age distribution of the population (the percent of men who were in the crime-prone fourteen- to twenty-five years age range), the divorce rate, residential mobility, and whether or not the tract was within the central business district.

46. Anderson 1999.

47. Crutchfield, Robert D., Ann Glusker, and George S. Bridges (1999), "A Tale of Three Cities: Labor Markets and Homicide," *Sociological Focus* 32(1):65–83; Anderson, *Code of the Street*.

48. Vehicle theft is also accurately counted for insurance purposes, but our interest in this paper was on violence, thus the use of homicide rates as a dependent variable.

49. Downtown Cleveland has since undergone a renewal with the construction of the Rock and Roll Hall of Fame, new sports arenas, and restaurants, bars, and stores that typically pop up around such attractions.

50. Since these analyses were done using 1990 data, things have changed dramatically in Washington. Likely as a result of gentrification, the 2010 census found that the city is no longer—for the first time in many decades—majority black.

51. Though referred to as "apartheid cities," these South African cities in the post-apartheid era continue to have social and geographical patterns that are products of apartheid's residential segregation and pass laws. Under these laws blacks and Asians were required to live in separate specific areas, and they were not legally permitted into white areas without government issued passes—most often for work.

52. Unlike the previously published analyses of 1980 and 1990 data, these maps are not taking into account other social features of the census tracts (e.g., racial composition, age distribution, education, divorce rate, poverty). Nevertheless, even without controlling for these other factors, the geographic distribution of violent crime and employment are remarkably the same.

53. Wilson, *The Truly Disadvantaged*.

54. All of these maps use 2000 data rather than updated 2010 data, because the crime statistics are taken from the National Neighborhood Crime Study (NNCS) that was conducted by sociologists Ruth Peterson and Lauren Krivo (Peterson and Krivo, 2010).

55. Southeast Washington is one of the sections of the city that has experienced substantial gentrification since the 2000 census.

NOTES TO CHAPTER 3

1. Piore, Michael J. (1975) "Notes for a Theory of Labor Market Stratification," in *Labor Market Segmentation*, edited by Richard C. Edwards, Michael Reich, and David M. Gordon, New York, Heath.

2. RIF stands for "reduction in force." It is contemporary corporate speak for "laid off," a nice way of saying fired because of no fault of the employee.

3. Piore, "Notes for a Theory."

4. Crutchfield, "Labor Stratification and Violent Crime."

5. Hirschi, Travis (1969), *Causes of Delinquency*, Berkeley, University of California Press.

6. Sampson, Robert and John Laub (1993), *Crime in the Making*, Cambridge, MA, Harvard University Press.

7. Laub, John H. and Robert J. Sampson (2003), *Shared Beginnings Divergent Lives: Delinquent Boys to Age 70*, Cambridge, MA, Harvard University Press.

8. Sampson, Robert J., John H. Laub and Christopher Wimer (2006), "Does Marriage Reduce Crime: A Counterfactual Approach to Within-Individual Causal Effects," *Criminology* 44(3):465–508.

9. For discussions of the impact of incarceration on African Americans see Western, Bruce (2006), *Punishment and Inequality in America*, New York, Russell Sage Foundation; Clear, Todd R. (2007), *Imprisoning Communities: How Mass Incarceration Makes Disadvantaged Neighborhoods Worse*, New York, Oxford University Press; Pettit, Becky, *Invisible Men*. America's astoundingly high homicide victimization rate far and away disproportionately falls on young African American males. See LaFree, Gary, Eric P. Baumer, and Robert O'Brien (2010), "Still Separate and Unequal? A City-Level Analysis of the Black–White Gap in Homicide Arrests since 1960," *American Sociological Review* 75(1):75–100; Parker, *Unequal Crime Decline*.

10. Phillips, Susan D, Alaattin Erkanli, Gordon P Keeler P; E. Jane Costello, and Adrian Angold (2006), "Disentangling the Risks: Parent Criminal Justice Involvement and Children's Exposure to Family Risks," *Criminology & Public Policy* 5(4): 677–702.

11. Crutchfield, Robert D. and Susan R Pitchford (1997), "Work and Crime: The Effects of Labor Stratification," *Social Forces* 76(1):93–118.

12. Some studies of boot camps have found when they are less military styled—less drill and pseudosergeants screaming and more life skills and job training—that there can be positive results.

13. Hill, Gary D. and Elizabeth M Crawford (1990), "Women, Race, and Crime," *Criminology* 28(4):601–26.

14. Bates, Kristin A., and Robert D. Crutchfield (2001), "Family, Work, and Crime: An Examination of Labor Stratification in the Lives of Women," presented at the Annual Meeting of the American Society of Criminology, Atlanta.

15. Crutchfield, Robert D., Tim Wadsworth, Heather Groninger, and Kevin Drakulich (2006), *Labor Force Participation, Labor Markets, and Crime*, Washington, DC, National Institute of Justice, www.ncjrs.gov/pdffiles1/nij/grants/214515. pdf. This work was supported by the National Institute of Justice, grant number 2000-IJ-CX-0026.

16. Ramiro Martinez, Jr. (2002), *Latino Homicide: Immigration, Violence, and Community*, New York, Routledge; Sampson, Robert J. (2008), "Rethinking Crime and Immigration," *Contexts* 7(1): 28–33; Sampson, Robert J., Jeffrey D. Morenoff, and Stephen W. Raudenbush (2005), "Social Anatomy of Racial and Ethnic Disparities in Violence," *American Journal of Public Health* 95(2):224–32.

17. Springsteen, Bruce (1984), "My Hometown," on *Born in the USA*, Bruce Springsteen and the E Street Band, Columbia Recording.

18. Krivo and Peterson do find that older men's arrest rates go up a small bit as joblessness increases. Krivo, Lauren J. and Ruth D Peterson (2004), "Labor Market Conditions and Violent Crime among Youth and Adults," *Sociological Perspectives* 47(4):485–505.

19. I am not suggesting that explaining who among them do and do not violate the law and similar questions are not important, but rather that more delinquency accompanying a push for independence among an age cohort that finds their similar aged fellows more normatively central in their lives is not surprising. See Hirschi and Gottfredson, "Age and the Explanation of Crime"; and Moffitt, Terrie E. (1997), "Adolescence-Limited and Life-Course-Persistent Offending: A Complementary Pair of Developmental Theories," in *Developmental Theories of Crime and Delinquency*, edited by Terence P. Thornberry, 11–54, New Brunswick, NJ, Transaction.

20. Krivo and Peterson, "Labor Market Conditions."

21. Hawkins, J. David, and Joseph G. Weis (1985), "The Social Development Model: An Integrated Approach to Delinquency Prevention," *Journal of Primary Prevention 6(2):73–97*; Haggerty, Kevin P., Elizabeth A. Wells, Jeffrey M. Jenson, Richard F. Catalano, J. David Hawkins (1989), "Delinquents and Drug Use: A Model Program for Community Reintegration," *Adolescence 24(94):439–56*.

22. E.g., Steven A. Cernkovich and Peggy Giordano (1992), "School Bonding, Race, and Delinquency," *Criminology* 30(2):261–91; Josine Junger-Tas (1992) "An Empirical Test of Social Control Theory," *Journal of Quantitative Criminology* 8(1):9–28; Kimberly L. Henry and Michael D. Slater (2007), "The Contextual Effect of School Attachment on Young Adolescents' Alcohol Use," *Journal of School Health* 77(2):67–4.

23. "Less delinquent" is written purposely to convey the understanding that even groups of good kids frequently encourage each other to smoke, drink, or steal ("Who will know if you just take one?") For an analysis of the influence of peers and adults in the context of positive forces such as good families and good school performance, see Huebner, Angela J; and Sherry C Betts (2007), "Exploring the Utility of Social Control Theory for Youth Development: Issues of Attachment, Involvement, and Gender," *Youth and Society* 34(2): 123–45.

24. Rosenfeld, Richard and Robert Fornango (2007), "The Impact of Economic Conditions on Robbery and Property Crime: The Role of Consumer Sentiment," *Criminology* 45(4):735–69.

25. Parker, *Unequal Crime Decline*.

26. Worrall, "Racial Composition, Unemployment, and Crime."

NOTES TO CHAPTER 4

1. Actually, I left juvenile probation about halfway through their probation period to take the position with adult parole. With this group, I am pretty confident that they did not go on to a life of crime. Others I am not so sure of, and I came to know that some of "my kids" regrettably did get in more serious trouble later.

2. Greenberger, Ellen and Laurence Steinberg (1986), *When Teenagers Work: Psychological and Social Cost of Adolescent Employment*, New York, Basic Books.

3. Hirschi, Travis (1969), *Causes of Delinquency*, Berkeley, University of California Press; Cernkovich and Giordano, "School Bonding, Race, and Delinquency";

Sampson, Robert and John Laub (1993), *Crime in the Making*, Cambridge, MA, Harvard University Press; Jenkins, Patricia H. (1997) "School Delinquency and the School Social Bond," *Journal of Research in Crime and Delinquency* 34(3): 337–67; Hawkins, J. David, Denise M. Lishner, Richard F. Catalano (1985), "Childhood Predictors and the Prevention of Adolescent Substance Abuse," in Jones, C. L., and R. L. Battjes (eds.), *NIDA Research Monograph Vol. 56: Etiology of Drug Abuse: Implications for Prevention*, 75–126, Washington, DC, US Government Printing Office.

4. Warren, John Robert, Paul C LePore and Robert D Mare (2000), "Employment During High School: Consequences for Students' Grades in Academic Courses," *American Educational Research Journal* 37(4): 943–69.

5. Steinberg, Laurence, and Sanford M. Dornbusch (1991), "Negative Correlates of Part-Time Employment during Adolescence: Replication and Elaboration," *Developmental Psychology* 27(2):304–13.

6. Wright, John. P., Francis T. Cullen, and Nicholas Williams (1997), "Working While in High School and Delinquent Involvement: Implications for Social Policy," *Crime & Delinquency* 43(2):203–21.

7. Bachman, Jerald G., and John Schlenberg (1993), "How Part-Time Work Intensity Relates to Drug Use, Problem Behavior, Time Use, and Satisfaction among High School Seniors: Are These Consequences or Merely Correlates?" *Developmental Psychology* 29(2):220–35.

8. Ploeger, Matthew. (1997), "Youth Employment and Delinquency: Reconsidering a Problematic Relationship," *Criminology* 35(4):659–75; and Paternoster, Raymond, Shawn Bushway, Robert Brame, Robert Apel (2003), "The Effect of Teenage Employment on Delinquency and Problem Behaviors," *Social Forces* 82(1):297–335.

9. Apel, Robert, Raymond Paternoster, Shawn D. Bushway, and Robert Brame (2006), "A Job Isn't Just a Job: The Differential Impact of Formal Versus Informal Work on Adolescent Problem Behavior," *Crime and Delinquency* 52(2):333–69; Apel, Robert, Shawn Bushway, Robert Brame, Amelia M. Haviland, Daniel S. Nagin, and Raymond Paternoster (2007), "Unpacking the Relationship Between Adolescent Employment and Antisocial Behavior: A Matched Samples Comparison," *Criminology* 4(1):67–97.

10. Crutchfield, R. D., M. Rankin, and S. R. Pitchford (1993), "Inheriting Stakes in Conformity: Effects of Parents' Labor Market Experience on Juvenile Delinquency," presented at the Annual Meetings of the American Society of Criminology, Phoenix; Apel, Robert, Shawn Bushway, Raymond Paternoster, Robert Brame, and Gary Sweeten. 2008. "Using State Child Labor Laws to Identify the Causal Effect of Youth Employment on Deviant Behavior and Academic Achievement," *Journal of Quantitative Criminology* 24(4):337–62.

11. Wilson, *The Truly Disadvantaged* and *When Work Disappears*.

12. Anderson, *Code of the Street*.

13. Sullivan, Mercer L. (1989), *Getting Paid: Youth Crime and Work in the Inner City*, Ithaca, NY, Cornell University Press.

14. Heimer, Karen, and Ross L. Matsueda (1994), "Role-Taking, Role-Commitment, and Delinquency: A Theory of Differential Social Control," *American Sociological Review* 59(3):365–90.
15. Crutchfield, et al., "Inheriting Stakes in Conformity"; Wadsworth, Tim (2000), "Labor Markets, Delinquency and Social Control Theory: An Empirical Assessment of the Mediating Process," *Social Forces* 78(3):1041–66; Bellair, Paul E., and Vincent J. Roscigno (2000), "Local Labor-Market Opportunity and Adolescent Delinquency," *Social Forces* 78(4):1509–38; Bellair, Paul E., Vincent J. Roscigno, and Thomas L. McNulty (2003), "Linking Local Labor Market Opportunity to Violent Adolescent Delinquency," *Journal of Research in Crime and Delinquency* 40(1): 6–33.
16. Banfield, Edward C. (1968), *The Unheavenly City*, Boston, Little Brown.
17. Ingram, Jason R., Justin W. Patchin, Beth M. Huebner, John D. McCluskey, and Timothy S. Bynum (2007), "Parents, Friends, and Serious Delinquency. An Examination of Direct and Indirect Effects Among At-Risk Early Adolescents," *Criminal Justice Review* 32(4): 380–400.
18. Wadsworth, Tim (2000), "Labor Markets, Delinquency and Social Control Theory: An Empirical Assessment of the Mediating Process," *Social Forces* 78(3):1041–66.
19. Cernkovich and Giordano, "School Bonding, Race, and Delinquency"; Fagan, Jeffrey and Sandra Wexler (1987), "Family Origins of Violent Delinquency," *Criminology* 25(3): 643–70.
20. Anderson, *Code of the Street*, 146.
21. Milano, Fred (2000), "Cooling Out the Middle Class," Annual Meetings of the Society for the Study of Social Problems, Washington, DC.
22. Wilson, *The Truly Disadvantaged*.
23. Crutchfield, R. D., M. Rankin and S. R. Pitchford (1993), "Inheriting Stakes in Conformity: Effects of Parents' Labor Market Experience on Juvenile Delinquency," presented at the Annual Meetings of the American Society of Criminology, Phoenix AZ.
24. Bellair and Roscigno, "Local Labor-Market Opportunity and Adolescent Delinquency."
25. Crutchfield, et al., *Labor Force Participation*.
26. Crutchfield, Rankin, and Pitchford, "Inheriting Stakes in Conformity"; Crutchfield et al., *Labor Force Participation*.
27. Kozol, Jonathan (1992), *Savage Inequalities: Children in America's Schools*, New York, Harper Collins. For any reader inclined to think my experience or the accounts of Kozol are outdated, they should consider the YouTube site www.youtube.com/watch?v=JEczvyM3Boc&feature=related. It is a brief film clip about a program sponsored by Oprah Winfrey called "Trading Schools." They have a group of students from an inner-city school spend time at a much better funded suburban school, while the latter's students go to the Chicago urban school. Both groups of students are shocked by what they find.

28. "White flight" obviously has this effect, since on average white families incomes are 30 to 40 percent higher than black family incomes. But even when increased suburbanization is not because of white flight, it increases inequality because it has, in most cities, led to a decline in the tax base that local schools depend on. See Jargowsky, P. A., S. A. Desmond, and R. D. Crutchfield (2005), "Is Suburban Sprawl a Juvenile Justice Issue?" in *Our Children, Their Children: Confronting Race and Ethnic Differences in American Criminal Justice*, edited by Darnell Hawkins and Kimberly Kemph, Chicago, University of Chicago Press.
29. Parrish, Thomas B., Christine S. Hikido, and William J. Fowler, Jr. (1998), *Inequalities in Public School District Revenues*, Washington, DC, US Department of Education, Office of Educational Research and Improvement.
30. Jargowsky et al., "Is Suburban Sprawl a Juvenile Justice Issue?"
31. I (in Crutchfield et al., "Inheriting Stakes in Conformity") should emphasize here that this result was found not for what we typically label inner-city neighborhoods, but rather it was for respondents residing in the core city of counties as defined by the US Census Bureau. This will of course include slum or ghetto neighborhoods, but middle-class and quite well-off residential areas as well.
32. Wilson, *The Truly Disadvantaged*; Massey and Denton, *American Apartheid*; and Anderson, *Code of the Street*.
33. *Collected Poems*Langston Hughes, "Harlem," available at www.poetryfoundation.org/poem/175884.
34. Bonilla-Silva, Eduardo (2004), "From Bi-Racial to Tri-Racial: Towards a New System of Racial Stratification in the USA," *Ethnic and Racial Studies* 27(6): 931–50; see also Forman, Tyrone A., Carla Goar, and Amanda Lewis (2002), "Neither Black nor White? An Empirical Test of the Latin Americanization Thesis," *Race & Society* 5(1): 65–84.
35. For an intriguing historical account of how the Irish moved from a marginalized ethnic group in the US and came to be defined as "white" and the troubled relationship between Irish and African Americans, see Ignatiev, Noel (1996), *How the Irish Became White*, New York, Routledge.
36. If one types in "slave job" in an Internet search engine you will find links to blogs and discussion boards where this phrase is used by frustrated workers.
37. Sullivan, *Getting Paid*, 76.
38. Lehman, *The Promised Land*; Thomas, W. I. and Florian Znaniecki (1996), *The Polish Peasant in Europe and America: A Classic Work in Immigration History*, edited by Eli Zaretsky, Champaign-Urbana, IL, University of Illinois Press.
39. The family lived for a period in the nearly all white Shadyside, before moving back to Homewood where John had come of age. Robby looked forward to moving into a black community.
40. Wideman, *Brothers and Keepers*, 86.
41. Anderson, *Code of the Street*, 145–46. Of course some ghetto residents do not want to work hard or even work at all, but any casual or even cynical but honest observer must admit that the "lazy gene" is unique to no class.

42. Crutchfield et al., *Labor Force Participation*.
43. Martinez, Ramiro, Jr. (2002), *Latino Homicide: Immigration, Violence and Community*, New York, Routledge; Sampson, Robert J., Jeffrey D. Morenoff, and Stephen W. Raudenbush (2005), "Social Anatomy of Racial and Ethnic Disparities in Violence," *American Journal of Public Health* 95: 224–32.
44. Warren et al., "Employment During High School."
45. Hirschi, Travis (1969), *Causes of Delinquency*, Berkeley, University of California Press; Hindelang, Michael J. (1973), "Causes of Delinquency: A Partial Replication and Extension," *Social Problems* 20(4):471–87.
46. Bellair and Roscigno, "Local Labor-Market Opportunity and Adolescent Delinquency"; Bellair, Roscigno, and McNulty, "Linking Local Labor Market Opportunity."
47. Sampson, Robert J. (2009), "Disparity and Diversity in the Contemporary City: Social (Dis)order Revisited," *British Journal of Sociology* 60(1): 1–31; Sampson, Robert J. (2006), "How Does Community Context Matter? Social Mechanisms and the Explanation of Crime," in *The Explanation of Crime: Context, Mechanisms, and Development*, edited by Per-Olof Wikström and Robert J Sampson, 31–60, New York, Cambridge University Press.
48. Merton, Robert (1938), "Social Structure and Anomie," *American Sociological Review* 3(5):672–82.
49. Crutchfield et al., "Inheriting Stakes in Conformity."
50. Tittle, Charles R., Wayne J. Villemez, and Douglas A Smith (1978), "The Myth of Social Class and Criminality: An Empirical Assessment o the Empirical Evidence," *American Sociological Review* 43(5): 643–56.
51. Hindelang, Michael J., Travis Hirschi, and Joseph G Weis (1979), "Correlates of Delinquency: The Illusion of Discrepancy between Self-Report and Official Measures," *American Sociological Review* 44(6): 995–1014; Farnsworth, Margaret, Terence P. Thornberry, Marvin D. Krohn, and Alan J. Lizotte (1994), "Measurement in the Study of Class and Delinquency: Integrating Theory and Research," *Journal of Research in Crime and Delinquency* 31(1): 32–61.
52. Hindelang, Michael J. Travis Hirschi, and Joseph G. Weis (1981), *Measuring Delinquency*, Thousand Oaks, CA, Sage.
53. As middle-class kids have affected the dress styles of the street and of hip-hop culture, the use of dress to make these distinctions are likely troublingly more difficult for store detectives.
54. See Moffitt, Terrie E., Avshalom Caspi, Honalee Harrington, and Barry J. Milne (2002), "Males on the Life-Course-Persistent and Adolescence-Limited Antisocial Pathways," *Development and Psychopathology* 14:179–207.
55. Farnsworth et al., "Measurement in the Study of Class and Delinquency"; Crutchfield et al., *Labor Force Participation*.
56. Jargowsky et al., "Is Suburban Sprawl a Juvenile Justice Issue?"; Hindelang et al., *Measuring Delinquency*.
57. Farnsworth et al., "Measurement in the Study of Class and Delinquency."

58. Anderson, *Code of the Street*; Pattillo-McCoy, *Black Picket Fences.*

59. Cohen, Albert K. (1955), *Delinquent Boys: The Culture of the Gang*. New York, The Free Press.

60. Crutchfield et al, "Inheriting Stakes in Conformity."

61. Cloward, Richard A. and Lloyd E. Ohlin (1960), *Delinquency and Opportunity: A Theory of Delinquent Gangs*, New York, The Free Press.

62. Sullivan, *Getting Paid*; Pattillo McCoy, *Black Picket Fences.*

63. Anderson, *Code of the Street.*

64. Venkatesh, *Off the Books.*

65. Fagan, Jeffrey A. (1996), "Drug Use and Selling Among Urban Gangs," in *Encyclopedia of Drugs, Alcohol and Addictive Behavior Second Edition*, edited by Jerome Jaffe, 565–74, New York, MacMillan.

66. Fagan, Jeffrey A. and KoLin Chin (1990), "Violence as Regulation and Social Control in the Distribution of Crack," in *Drugs and Violence, NIDA Research Monograph* No. 103, edited by Mario de la Rosa, Bernard Gropper, and Elizabeth Lambert, 8–39, Rockville MD, US Public Health Administration, National Institute of Drug Abuse.

67. Davies, Garth (2006), *Crime, Neighborhood, and Public Housing*, New York, LFB Scholarly Publishers, 73–74.

68. Bourgois, Philippe (1995), *In Search of Respect: Selling Crack in El Barrio*, Cambridge, Cambridge University Press; Pattillo-McCoy's *Black Picket Fences*; Sudhir Alladi Venkatesh (2000), *American Project: The Rise and Fall of the Modern Ghetto*, Cambridge MA, Harvard University Press.

69. Shakur, Sanyika, aka Monster Kody Scott (1993), *Monster: The Autobiography of an L.A. Gang Member*, New York, Grove Press.

70. Sullivan, *Getting Paid.*

71. Wilson, "Studying Inner City Dislocations."

72. Gates, Henry Louis (1997), "Race and Class in America," Jessie and John Danz Lecture, University of Washington, Seattle, WA.

73. www.ncaa.org/wps/wcm/connect/public/ncaa/issues/recruiting/probability+of+going+pro.

74. Akers, Ronald; Reinarman, Craig and Harry G. Levine, cited in Mosher, Clayton J. and Scott Akins (2007), *Drugs and Drug Policy: The Control of Consciousness Alteration*, Thousand Oaks, CA, Sage.

75. Lehman, *The Promised Land.*

76. Venkatesh, *American Project.*

77. Banfield, *The Unheavenly City*; Murray, *Losing Ground.*

78. Ryan, William (1971), *Blaming the Victim*. New York, Pantheon.

79. "Forget you" is now the publicly consumable title and lyric in a popular song by rapper Cee Lo Green, and there is another version that fans can download that use the "uncoded" lyrics as well.

80. Lou Rawls, "Street Corner Hustler Blues/World of Trouble," from Lou Rawls Live, 2005 Remaster.

NOTES TO CHAPTER 5

1. Wideman, *Brothers and Keepers*, 74–75.
2. Wideman, *Brothers and Keepers*, 86.
3. Wideman, *Brothers and Keepers*, 68.
4. The linkages between poverty and a number of social problems, including crime, are discussed in Saegert, Susan, Phillip J. Thompson, and Mark R. Warren (2001), *Social Capital and Poor Communities*, New York, Russell Sage Foundation. See also Covington, Jeanette (1999), "African-American Communities and Violent Crime: The Construction of Race Differences," *Sociological Focus* 32(1): 7–24; or Block, Richard, "Community, Environment, and Violent Crime," *Criminology* 17(1): 46–57.
5. Kramer, Ronald C. (2000), "Poverty, Inequality, and Youth Violence," *The Annals of the American Academy of Political and Social Science* 567:123–39.
6. Mosisa, Abraham and Steven Hipple (2006), "Trends in Labor force participation in the United States," *Monthly Labor Review* (October): 35–57, Washington, DC, Bureau of Labor Statistics, www.bls.gov/opub/mlr/2006/10/art3full.pdf.
7. AFL-CIO (2012), "CEO to Worker Pay Gab," www.aflcio.org/Corporate-Watch/CEO-Pay-and-the-99/CEO-to-Worker-Pay-Gap.
8. Shaprio, Isaac (2005), "New IRS Data Show Income Inequality Is Again on the Rise," Center on Budget and Policy Priorities, Washington DC, www.cbpp.org/cms/?fa=view&id=746.
9. Park, Robert Ezra, E. W. Burgess, and Roderick Duncan McKenzie (1967), *The City*, Chicago, University of Chicago Press; Faris, Robert E. L. and H. Warren Dunham (1939), *Mental Disorders in Urban Areas: An Ecological Study of Schizophrenia and Other Psychoses*, Chicago, University of Chicago Press; Shaw, Clifford R. and Henry D. McKay (1942), *Juvenile Delinquency and Urban Areas: A Study of Rates of Delinquency in Relation to Differential Characteristics of Local Communities in American Cities*, Chicago, University of Chicago Press.
10. See Sampson, Robert J. (2006), "Collective Efficacy Theory: Lessons Learned and Directions for Future Inquiry," in *Taking Stock* by Sampson, Robert J., New Brunswick, NJ, Transaction, 149–67; Bursik, Robert J. and Harold G. Grasmick (1993), *Neighborhoods and Crime: The Dimensions of Effective Community Control*, New York, Lexington Books.
11. Crutchfield and Pitchford, "Work, Crime and Labor Stratification."
12. Thomas, Ralph and Dominic Gates (2007), "Aerospace Tax Break May Rest on Union Neutrality," *The Seattle Times*, http://seattletimes.com/html/businesstechnology/2003547126_unions30.html.
13. Crutchfield, Glusker, and Bridges, "A Tale of Three Cities."
14. The District of Columbia to this day only has one nonvoting member in the House of Representatives and so is substantially without voice in the national legislature, a political point strongly made by proponents of District statehood and by African American nationalists making a point about how blacks are treated in modern America.

15. Massey and Denton, *American Apartheid*.
16. Peterson and Krivo, *Divergent Social Worlds*.
17. Crutchfield, Robert D., Lauren J. Krivo, and Ruth D. Peterson, under review, "Local Labor Markets and Violent Crime," presented at the National Consortium on Violence Research, Workshop on Violent Crime in Geographic Context, University at Albany, Albany, NY, April 2005.
18. Grant, Don S. III, and Ramiro Martinez (1997), "Crime and the Restructuring of the US Economy: A Reconsideration of the Class Linkages," *Social Forces* 75(3):769–98.
19. For discussions of studying contextual effects see Blalock, Hubert M. (1984), "Contextual-Effects Models: Theoretical and Methodological Issues," *Annual Review of Sociology* 10:353–72; and Erbring, Lutz and Alice A. Young (1979), "Individuals and Social Structure: Contextual Effects as Endogenous Feedback," *Sociological Methods and Research* 7(4):396–430.
20. On the cover is a cartoon. A recently mugged middle-aged man, very likely an academic, is sitting on the ground being interviewed. He says, "How do I feel about being mugged? Well, naturally I didn't enjoy it and I certainly don't condone violence or threats of violence as a means toward social change. However, I can empathize with my assailant and realize that in his terms this is a valid response to the deteriorating socioeconomic situation in which we find ourselves." Nettler, Gwynne (1978), *Explaining Crime, 2nd edition*, New York, McGraw Hill.
21. Crutchfield et al., *Labor Force Participation*.
22. See Peterson and Krivo, *Divergent Social Worlds*.
23. Crutchfield, Robert D. and Tim Wadsworth (2013), "Aggravated Inequality: Neighborhoods, School, and Juvenile Delinquency," in *Macro Economic Effects on Youth Violence*, edited by Richard Rosenfeld et al. New York, NYU Press.
24. Those data are not presented here, but these results can be found in Crutchfield et al., *Labor Force Participation*.
25. See Merton, Robert K. (1949), *Social Theory and Social Structure: Toward the Codification of Theory and Research*, New York, The Free Press; Messner, Steven F. and Richard Rosenfeld (2007), *Crime and the American Dream, Fourth Edition*, Belmont CA, Thompson Wadsworth.
26. See Cloward and Ohlin, *Delinquency and Opportunity* and Venkatesh, *Off the Books*.
27. Alonso, Gaston, Noel S. Anderson, Celina Su, and Jeanne Theoharis (2009), *Our Schools Suck: Students Talk Back to a Segregated Nation on the Failures of Urban Education*, New York, NYU Press.
28. Heckman, James J. (2008), "Schools, Skills, and Synapses," *Economic Inquiry* 46(3):289–324.
29. Coleman, James S., Ernest Q. Campbell, Carol J. Hobson, James McPartland, Alexander M. Mood, Frederic D. Weinfeld, and Robert L. York (1966), *Equality*

of Educational Opportunity, US Department of Health Education and Welfare, Washington, DC, US Government Printing Office.

30. Epstein, Diana (2011), "Measuring Inequality in School Funding," Center for American Progress, Washington, DC, www.americanprogress.org/wp-content/uploads/issues/2011/08/pdf/funding_equity.pdf.

31. Epstein, "Measuring Inequality," 5. Epstein cited "School Finance" as a source of this data (www.edweek.org/media/ew/qc/2011/16sos.h30.finance.pdf).

32. Epstein, "Measuring Inequality," 7. Endnote 8 within the quote references the Education Trust, Washington, DC (2006), "Funding Gaps 2006."

33. We must also recognize that *equal* funding is likely to be inadequate if we are truly interested in outcomes. The poorest, most distressed districts have greater needs, such as for more English as a second language classes, food and health programs, and other things needed to make children ready to learn. Without funding for these programs on top of equal funding for basic education, it is unrealistic to expect teachers to solve bigger problems with less real resources than educators in high-income and high-expenditure districts.

34. Downing, Margaret (2008), "So Much for No Child Left Behind: School Test Scores Rise as More Low-Scoring Students Drop Out," *Houston Press News*, www.houstonpress.com/2008-04-10/news/so-much-for-no-child-left-behind/.

35. McNeil, Linda McSpadden, Eileen Coppola, Judy Radigan, and Julian Vasquez Heilig (2008), "Avoidable Losses: High-Stakes Accountability and the Dropout Crisis," Education Policy Analysis Archives *16*(3):1–48.

36. Of course it is not just in the inner cities where drugs are consumed. Federally sponsored studies have long shown that drug use is pretty evenly distributed across races and social classes in the US. In my own personal history I witnessed far more drug use when I went off to college than I did on The Hill.

37. Anderson (*Code of the Street*) described to America and sociology the split worlds of decent and street people and the codes of the streets thirty years later, but the codes have existed for a very long time and were very much a part of the Homewood street scene.

38. Wideman, *Brothers and Keepers*, 89.

39. Banfield, *The Unheavenly City*.

40. Bourgois, *In Search of Respect*; Pattillo-McCoy, *Black Picket Fences*.

41. Anson, Robert Sam (1987), *Best Intentions: The Education and Killing of Edmund Perry*, New York, Vintage.

42. Raymond, Susan (1993), *I Am a Promise: The Children of Stanton Elementary School*, New York, Docurama Films,.

43. At the end of the school year, the crusading principal featured in *I Am a Promise* leaves the school burned out, frustrated, and crying. I couldn't help but wonder what had become of Nadia as she moved on to middle school.

44. Rymond-Richmond, Wenona (2007), *The Habitus of Habitat: Mapping the History, Redevelopment, and Crime in Public Housing*, PhD dissertation, Northwestern University.

45. Kotlowitz, Alex (1992), *There are No Children Here: The Story of Two Boys Growing up in The Other America*, New York, Anchor Books.
46. Venkatesh, *American Project*.

NOTES TO CHAPTER 6

1. According to the 1970 US census of the population (the census year preceding this period) Pennsylvania had the largest rural population in the nation.
2. Crutchfield et al., *Labor Force Participation*.
3. Crutchfield et al., *Labor Force Participation*.
4. We did find that African Americans living in rural areas were slightly less criminally involved when we did not control for community characteristics, and rural Latinos were slightly more likely to have committed crimes, even after adjusting for selected community characteristics.
5. Lee, Matthew R. and Tim Slack (2008), "Labor Market Conditions and Violent Crime across the Metro-Nonmetro Divide," *Social Science Research* 37(3): 753–68.
6. US District Court for the Western District of Washington, Tacoma Division (1974), 384 F. Supp. 312; 1974 US Dist. LEXIS 1229, www.ccrh.org/comm/river/legal/boldt.htm.
7. And of course as too often happens when conflicts exist between racial or ethnic groups, the dwindling fisheries and consequent economic problems for white communities have been blamed on the Indians and the court decisions that have upheld their treaty rights.
8. In Washington State, tribes have used money generated in casinos to assist local and county governments to mitigate some budget cuts resulting from the Great Recession.
9. Akee, Randall K.O., William E. Copeland, Gordon Keller, Adrian Angold, and E. Jane Costello (2010), "Parent's Incomes and Children's Outcomes: A Quasi-Experiment Using Transfer Payments from Casino Profits," *American Economic Journal: Applied Economics* 2(1):86–115.
10. Akee et al., "Parent's Incomes and Children's Outcomes," 89–90.
11. Recent reports suggests that New Orleans is now more of a middle-class city than it was prior to 2005, but this is because they have had the capacity to rebuild and have jobs in New Orleans to return to. Many low-end workers and the chronically unemployed who resided in places like the Lower Ninth Ward are resettled elsewhere and have not yet returned to the city. Time will tell if New Orleans will move in the direction of redeveloping in the direction of a new vision for the city, or if it will drift back into the patterns of substantial inequality that is more typical of less developed places than are most American cities.
12. De Jong, Gordon F. and Anna B. Madamba (2001), "A Double Disadvantage? Minority Group, Immigrant Status, and Underemployment in the United States," *Social Science Quarterly* 82(1):117–30.

13. Frazier, Franklin (1957), *Black Bourgeoisie: The Rise of a New Middle-class in the United States*, New York, The Free Press.
14. Pattillo-McCoy, *Black Picket Fences*.
15. Wilson, William J. (1978), *The Declining Significance of Race: Blacks and Changing American Institutions*, Chicago, University of Chicago Press.
16. James wasn't technically from Cleveland, but rather Akron, a neighboring formerly industrial city just to Cleveland's south.
17. Anderson, Elijah (1990), *Street Wise: Race, Class and Change in an Urban Community*, Chicago, University of Chicago Press.
18. Durkheim, Emile (1933), *The Division of Labor in Society*, New York, The Free Press.
19. Anderson (*Code of the Street*) or Venkatesh (*American Project*); Jones, Nikki (2010), *Between Good and Ghetto: African American Girls and Inner-city Violence*, New Brunswick, NJ, Rutgers University Press.
20. Buonanno, Paolo (2006), "Crime and Labour Market Opportunities in Italy (1993–2002)," *Labour: Review of Labour Economics & Industrial Relations* 20(4):601–24.
21. Mauro, Luciano, and Carmeci, Gaetano (2007), "A Poverty Trap of Crime and Unemployment," *Review of Development Economics* 11(3): 450–62.
22. Dongil, Kim (2006), "The Effects Of Economic Conditions On Crimes," *Development and Society* 35(2):241–50.
23. Blanco, Lorenzo and Villa, Sandra M. (2008), "Sources of Crime in the State of Veracruz: The Role of Female Labor Force Participation and Wage Inequality," *Feminist Economics* 14(3):51–75.
24. Louw, Antoinette (2007), "Crime and Perceptions after a Decade of Democracy," *Social Indicators Research* 81(2):235–55; Cruz, Jose Miguel (2009), "Democratization Under Assault: Criminal Violence in Post-Transition Central America," Annual meetings of the American Political Science Association Toronto. http://papers.ssrn.com/sol3/papers.cfm?abstract_id=1450237.
25. Black Bottom was an area of Detroit that Great Migration movers lived in early on. Long before deindustrialization it was subsumed by a larger black community, which in the mid-1970s was home to a portion of Detroit's then-thriving black middle class.

NOTES TO CHAPTER 7

1. Though it is not the case in most western nations, even something as fundamental as access to reasonable health care is determined by what is provided by employers for most Americans, and this will remain the case with the health care reforms that are currently being implemented ("Obamacare," or the Affordable Care Act).
2. Crutchfield, Krivo, and Peterson, "Local Labor Markets and Violent Crime."
3. Wilson, *The Truly Disadvantaged*, 58.
4. Wilson, *The Truly Disadvantaged*, 57.

5. Messner, Steven F. and Richard Rosenfeld (2007), *Crime and the American Dream*, Belmont, CA, Thomson Wadsworth.

6. Davey, Monica (2012), "Michigan Labor Fight Cleaves a Union Bulwark," *New York Times*, December 10, 2012. http://topics.nytimes.com/topics/reference/timestopics/subjects/o/organized_labor/index.html; Greenhouse, Steven (2011), "Ohio's Anti-Union Law Is Tougher Than Wisconsin's," *New York Times*, March 31, 2011, www.nytimes.com/2011/04/01/us/01ohio.html?_r=0.

7. Congressional Budget Office (2011), *Trends in The Distribution of Household Income Between 1979 and 2007*, www.cbo.gov/doc.cfm?index=12485.

8. For excellent and accessible discussion of this phenomenon see "Can the Middle Class be Saved," Don Peck, *The Atlantic*, September 2011, www.theatlantic.com/magazine/archive/2011/09/can-the-middle-class-be-saved/8600/2/.

9. See the collection of readings in Lichtenstein, Nelson (ed.) (2006), *Wal-Mart: The Face of Twenty-First-Century Capitalism*, New York, The New Press.

10. Dube, Arindrajit and Ken Jacobs (2004), "Hidden Cost of Wal-Mart Jobs: Use of Safety Net Programs by Wal-Mart Workers in California," UC Berkeley Center for Labor Center, www.dsausa.org/lowwage/walmart/2004/walmart%20study.pdf.

11. Gibson, Rich (2004), "The California Grocery Strike," *Cultural Logic: An Electronic Journal of Marxist Theory and Practice*, http://clogic.eserver.org/2004/gibson.html.

12. National Center For Children in Poverty, "Child Poverty," www.nccp.org/topics/childpoverty.html.

13. Truman, Jennifer (2011), *Criminal Victimization, 2010*, US Department of Justice, Office of Justice Programs, Bureau of Justice Statistics, www.bjs.gov/content/pub/pdf/cv10.pdf.

14. Olivares, Kathleen M., Velmer S. Burton, Jr., and Francis T. Cullen (1996), "The Collateral Consequences of a Felony Conviction: A National Study of State Legal Codes Ten Years Later," *Federal Probation* 60(3):10–17; Kuziemko, Ilyana and Steven D. Levitt (2004), "An Empirical Analysis of Imprisoning Drug Offenders," *Journal of Public Economics* 88(9–10):2043–66.

15. Blumstein, Alfred (1995), "Youth Violence, Guns, and the Illicit-Drug Industry," *Journal of Criminal Law and Criminology* 86(4):10–36; Cook, Philip J. and John H. Laub (1998), "The Unprecedented Epidemic in Youth Violence," *Crime and Justice* 24:27–64; Blumstein, Alfred and Richard Rosenfeld (2009), "Factors Affecting Recent Crime Trends in the United States," in *Understanding Crime Trends*, edited by Arthur Goldberger and Richard Rosenfeld, 13–44, Washington, DC, National Academies Press.

16. Parker, *Unequal Crime Decline*.

17. Parker, *Unequal Crime Decline*, 25–26.

18. Parker, *Unequal Crime Decline*, 108—9.

19. Klofas, John M. (2000), "Metropolitan Development and Policing: The Elephant in the Living Room," *Criminal Justice Review* 25(2):234–45.

20. See Falk, Kathleen (2012), "What We Did in Dane County: How Reform Saved Money and Increased Public Safety," in *To Build a Better Criminal Justice System: 25 Experts Envision the Next 25 Years of Reform*, edited by Marc Mauer and Kate Epstein, 40–41, Washington, DC, The Sentencing Project.

21. Howell, James C. (2012), *Gangs In America's Communities*, Thousand Oaks, CA, Sage.

22. Howell, *Gangs In America's Communities*, 176–79.

23. Howell, *Gangs In America's Communities*, 203.

24. See the special issue of the *Journal of Quantitative Criminology* (2010), "Special Issue: Empirical Evidence on the Relevance of Place in Criminology," guest edited by Anthony A. Braga and David L. Weisburd, 26(1).

25. Weisburd, David, Shawn Busway, Cynthia Lum and Sue-Ming Yang (2004), "Trajectories of Crime at Places: A Longitudinal Study of Street Segment in the City of Seattle," *Criminology* 42(2):283–321.

26. Groff, Elizabeth R., David Weisburd, and Sue-Ming Yang (2010), "Is it Important to Examine Crime Trends at a Local "Micro" Level? A Longitudinal Analysis of Street to Street Variability in Crime Trajectories," *Journal of Quantitative Criminology* 26(1):7–32.

27. Braga, Anthony, Andrew V. Papachristos, and David M. Hureau (2010), "The Concentration and Stability of Gun Violence at Micro Places in Boston, 1980—2008," *Journal of Quantitative Criminology* 26(1):33–53.

28. Kennedy, David (2002), "A Tale of One City: Reflections on the Boston Gun Project," in *Securing Our Children's Future: New Approaches to Juvenile Justice and Youth Violence*, edited by Gary S. Katzmann, 229–61, Washington, DC, Brookings Institution Press; Kennedy, David (2001), *Reducing Gun Violence: The Boston Gun Project's Operation Ceasefire*, National Institute of Justice Research Report, Washington, DC.

29. Klofas, "Metropolitan Development and Policing," 234–45.

30. Bellair, Paul E., and Thomas L. McNulty (2010), "Cognitive Skills, Adolescent Violence, and the Moderating Role of Neighborhood Disadvantage," *Justice Quarterly* 27:538–59.

31. Kirschenman, Joleen and Kathryn M. Neckerman (1991), "We'd Love to Hire Them, But . . .': The Meaning of Race for Employers," in *The Urban Underclass*, edited by Christopher Jencks and Paul E. Peterson, 203–32, Washington, DC, The Brookings Institution.

32. Kozol, *Savage Inequalities*.

33. See Jargowsky, et al., "Is Suburban Sprawl a Juvenile Justice Issue?"; and Jencks, Christopher, and Mary J. Bane (1973), "The Schools of Inequality," *Analyse and Prevision* 16(3):217–32.

34. Readers who want a more in-depth treatment of family disruption, child rearing, and the perpetuation of poverty, family instability, and other social problems should look to the research literature coming out of the Fragile Families Project: McLanahan, Sara (2009), "Fragile Families and the Reproduction

of Poverty," *Annals of the American Academy of Political and Social Science* 621:111–31; McLanahan, Sara (2007), "Single Mothers, Fragile Families," in *Ending Poverty in America: How to Restore the American Dream*, edited by Edwards, Crain, and Kalleberg, 77–87, New York: The New Press. Or they may go to the Future of Children, Princeton University and the Brookings Institution website, at www.princeton.edu/futureofchildren/index.xml.

35. See, for example, Pettit and Hook, *Gendered Tradeoffs*.

36. See, for example, Snedker, Karen A. (2012), "Explaining the Gender Gap in Fear of Crime: Assessments of Risk and Vulnerability Among New York City Residents," *Feminist Criminology* 7(2):75–111; Erez, Edna (2010), "Women, Crime and Social Harm: Towards a Criminology for the Global Age," *Law & Society Review* 44(2):405–07; and Schroeder, Ryan D., Terrence D. Hill, Stacy Hoskins Haynes, and Christopher Bradley (2011), "Physical Health and Crime Among Low-Income Urban Women: An Application of General Strain Theory," *Journal of Criminal Justice* 39(1):21–29.

37. Corcoran, Mary, Sandra Danziger, Ariel Kalil and Kristin S. Seefeldt (2000), "How Welfare Reform is Affecting Women's Work," *Annual Review of Sociology* 26:241–69.

38. Murray, *Losing Ground*.

39. Bane, Mary Jo and David T. Ellwood (1994), *Welfare Realities: From Rhetoric to Reform*, Cambridge, MA, Harvard University Press; Harris, Kathleen Mullen (1993), "Work and Welfare Among Single Mothers in Poverty," *American Journal of Sociology* 99(2):317–52.

40. Hays, Sharon (2003), *Flat Broke with Children: Women in the Age of Welfare Reform*, New York, Oxford University Press.

41. Hays, *Flat Broke with Children*, 8.

42. Hays, *Flat Broke with Children*, 8–9.

43. DeParle (2004), *American Dream: Three Women, Ten Kids, and a Nation's Drive to End Welfare*, New York, Viking.

44. Maher, Lisa (1997), *Sexed Work: Gender, Race and Resistance in a Brooklyn Drug Market*, New York, Oxford University Press.

45. Maher, *Sexed Work*, 54. Cited in the quote is Connell, R.W. 11987). Gender and Power, Stanford, CA, Stanford University Press.

46. Maher, *Sexed Work*, 75.

47. Miller, Jody (2008), *Getting Played: African American Girls, Urban Inequality and Gendered Violence*, New York, NYU Press.

48. Miller, *Getting Played*, 195.

49. Miller, *Getting Played*, 59.

50. Jones, Nikki (2010), *Between Good and Ghetto: African American Girls and Inner-City Violence*, New Brunswick, NJ, Rutgers University Press.

51. Jones, *Between Good and Ghetto*, 10–11.

52. Jones, *Between Good and Ghetto*, 10.

53. Massey and Denton, *American Apartheid*.

54. Peterson and Krivo, *Divergent Social Worlds*.

55. Peterson and Krivo, *Divergent Social Worlds*, 26–27.

56. Peterson and Krivo, *Divergent Social Worlds*, 33.

57. For discussions of urban dynamics see Logan, John R. and Chalres Zhang (2010), "Global Neighborhoods: New Pathways to Diversity and Separation," *American Journal of Sociology* 115(4):1069–1109; Yang, Rebecca and Paul A. Jargowsky (2006), "Suburban Development and Economic Segregation in the 1990s," *Journal of Urban Affairs* 28(3):253–73; Jargowsky, Paul A. (1998), "Urban Poverty, Race and the Inner City: The Bitter Fruit of Thirty Years of Neglect," in *Locked in the Poorhouse*, by Paul A Jawgowsky, 79–94, Lanham, MD, Rowman & Littlefield.

58. Anderson, *Street Wise*.

59. Covington, Jeanette and Ralph B. Taylor (1989), "Gentrification and Crime: Robbery and Larceny Changes in Appreciating Baltimore Neighborhoods during the 1970s," *Urban Affairs Quarterly* 25(1):142–72; Kirk, David S. and John H. Laub (2010), "Neighborhood Change and Crime in the Modern Metropolis," *Crime and Justice* 39:441–502.

60. Papachristos, Andrew V., Chris M. Smith, Mary L Scherer, and Melissa A. Fugiero (2011), "More Coffee, Less Crime: The Relationship between Gentrification and Neighborhood Crime Rates in Chicago, 1991 to 2005," *City & Community* 10(3):215–40.

61. Kirk and Laub, "Neighborhood Change and Crime."

62. See the US Bureau of Justice Statistics for reports on corrections patterns at both the state and federal level (http://bjs.ojp.usdoj.gov/index.cfm).

63. Crutchfield, Robert D., April Fernandes, and Jorge Martinez (2010), "Racial Disparity in the Criminal Justice System: How Much is Too Much?" *Journal of Criminal Law and Criminology* 100(3):903–32.

64. Barlow, David E, and Melissa Hickman Barlow (2002), "Racial Profiling: A Survey of African American Police Officers," *Police Quarterly* 5(3):334–58; Weitzer, Ronald and Steven A. Tuch (2005), "Racially Biased Policing: Determinants of Citizen Perceptions," *Social Forces* 83(3):1009–30; Warren, Patricia Y. and Amy Farell (2009), "The Environmental Context of Racial Profiling," *Annals of the American Academy of Political and Social Science* 623(1):52–63.

65. Western, Bruce (2006), *Punishment and Inequality in America*, New York, Russell Sage Foundation.

66. Pager, Devah (2003), "The Mark of a Criminal Record," *American Journal of Sociology* 108(5):937–75; Pager, Devah (2007), *Marked: Race, Crime, and Finding Work in an Era of Mass Incarceration*, Chicago, University of Chicago Press.

67. Pettit, Becky (2012), *Invisible Men: Mass Incarceration and the Myth of Black Progress*, New York, Russell Sage Foundation.

68. Western, *Punishment and Inequality in America*; Manza, Jeff and Christopher Uggen (2006), *Locked Out: Felon Disenfranchisement and American Democracy*, New York, Oxford University Press.

69. Pettit, *Invisible Men*; Western, Bruce and Becky Pettit (2005), "Black–White Wage Inequality, Employment Rates, and Incarceration," *American Journal of Sociology* 111(2):553–78.

70. Todd R. Clear (2007), *Imprisoning Communities: How Mass Incarceration Makes Disadvantaged Neighborhoods Worse*, New York, Oxford University Press; Dina R. Rose and Todd R. Clear (2004), "Who Doesn't Know Someone in Prison or Jail: The Impact of Exposure to Prison on Attitudes Toward Formal and Informal Social Control," *The Prison Journal* 82(2):208–27; Todd R. Clear, Dina R. Rose, Elin Waring and Kristen Scully (2003), "Coercive Mobility and Crime: a Preliminary Examination of Concentrated Incarceration and Social Disorganization," *Justice Quarterly* 20(1):33–64, reprinted in William T. Lyons Jr. (ed.) (2005), *Crime and Criminal Justice: The International Library of Essays in Law and Society*, London, Aldershot; Dina R. Rose and Todd R. Clear (1998), "Incarceration, Social Capital and Crime: Examining the Unintended Consequences of Incarceration," Criminology 36(3):441–79, reprinted in Suzette Cote (ed.) (2002), *Criminological Theories: Bridging the Past to the Future*, Thousand Oaks, CA, Sage Publications.

71. Drakulich, Kevin M., Robert D. Crutchfield, Ross L. Matsueda, and Kristin Rose (2012), "Instability, Informal Control, and Criminogenic Situations: Community Effects of Returning Prisoners," *Crime, Law, and Social Change* 57:493–519.

72. Ryan, William (1976), *Blaming the Victim*, New York, Vintage.

73. Crutchfield, Robert D. and David Pettinicchio (2009), "Cultures of Inequality: Ethnicity, Immigration, Social Welfare, and Imprisonment," *The Annals of Political and Social Sciences* 623(May):134–47; Crutchfield, Robert D., David Pettinicchio, and Blaine Robbins (2013), "Cultures of Inequality and Threat: National Values and Minority Imprisonment," *Pratiques et Esthétique de la Déviance en Amérique du Nord,* edited by Pascale Antolin and Arnaud Schmitt, 31–52, Bordeaux France, Presses Universitaires de Bordeaux.

74. Crutchfield, Robert D. (1994), "Ethnicity, Labor Markets, and Crime," in *Ethnicity, Race, and Crime*, edited by Darnell F. Hawkins, 194–211, Albany, State University of New York Press.

75. Cook and Zarkin, "Crime and the Business Cycle."

76. Calvin, Allen D. (1981), "Unemployment among Black Youths, Demographics, and Crime," *Crime and Delinquency* 27: 234–44; Moynihan, Daniel Patrick (1990), "Families Falling Apart," *Society* 27:21–22; Patterson, James T. (1995), "Race Relations and the 'Underclass' in Modern America: Some Historical Observations," *Qualitative Sociology* 18(2):237–61.

77. Martin Luther King Jr. Massey Lectures, November 1967, www.prx.org/series/31037-martin-luther-king-jr-massey-lectures.

78. Particular child rearing practices, education inequality, residential segregation and gentrification, and mass imprisonment are all products of or a part of social and economic disadvantage, but they also contribute it its perpetuation.

NOTES TO CHAPTER 8

1. The first usage of this phrase in scholarly writing that my colleagues and I are aware of was in Lewis, Michael (1978), *The Culture of Inequality*, Amherst MA, University of Massachusetts Press.

2. Crutchfield and Pettinicchio, "Cultures of Inequality"; Crutchfield, Pettinicchio, and Robbins, "Cultures of Inequality and Threat."

3. For good descriptions of Pittsburgh and its history see Lorant, Stefan (1999), *Pittsburgh: The Story of an American City*, Pittsburgh, PA, Esselmont Books.

4. Tita, George E. (1999), *An Ecological Study of Violent Urban Street Gangs and Their Crime*, unpublished dissertation, Carnegie Mellon University, Pittsburgh, PA; Cohen, Jacquelyn and George Tita. 1999, "Spatial Diffusion in Homicide: Exploring a General Method of Detecting Spatial Diffusion Processes," *Journal of Quantitative Criminology* 15(4):451–93.

5. See Fagan, Jeffrey (1989), "The Social Organization of Drug Use and Drug Dealing Among Urban Gangs," *Criminology* 27(4):633–69; Esbensen, Finn, and David Huizinga (1993), "Gangs, Drugs, and Delinquency in a Survey Of Urban Youth," *Criminology* 31(4):565–89; Tita, George and Greg Ridgeway (2007), "The Impact of Gang Formation on Local Patterns of Crime," *Journal of Research in Crime and Delinquency* 44(2):208–37.

6. Howell, James C. (2012), *Gangs in America's Communities*, Thousand Oaks, CA, Sage, 205–06.

7. Howell, *Gangs in America's Communities*, 206.

8. For good descriptions of Seattle's history see Murray Morgan (1982), *Skid Road: An Informal Portrait of Seattle*, Seattle, University of Washington Press.

9. For more about Homeboy Industries go to their website at http://homeboyin-dustries.org/.

10. Kalleberg, *Good Jobs, Bad Jobs*, 183 describes flexicurity, writing: "The notion of flexicurity—a portmanteau word combining flexibility and security—has attracted a great deal of attention among European labor market reformers looking for a way to give employers and labor markets greater flexibility while still providing protections for workers from the insecurity that results from this flexibility." See Kalleberg, (2011), chapter 10 for a full discussion.

11. Kalleberg, *Good Jobs, Bad Jobs*, 215.

12. Kozol, *Savage Inequalities*.

13. Population numbers are taken from the Bureau of Justice Statistics, http://bjs.ojp.usdoj.gov/index.cfm?ty=pbdetail&iid=2230.

14. Wideman, *Brothers and Keepers*, 241.

Robert D. Crutchfield is Professor of Sociology at the University of Washington. He is a fellow of the American Society of Criminology and a winner of the University of Washington's Distinguished Teaching Award. Crutchfield served as a juvenile probation officer in Mercer County Pennsylvania and as a parole agent for the Pennsylvania Board of Probation and Parole.